God and Government

The River Academy
P.O. Box 4485
Wenatchee, WA 98807

Other books by Gary DeMar:

God and Government: A Biblical and Historical Study, 1982

God and Government: Issues in Biblical Perspective, 1984

Ruler of the Nations, 1987

Surviving College Successfully, 1988

The Reduction of Christianity: A Biblical Response to Dave Hunt (with Peter Leithart), 1988

Something Greater is Here, 1988

The Debate over Christian Reconstruction, 1988

The Legacy of Hatred Continues (with Peter Leithart), 1989

You've Heard It Said, 1990

America's Christian History: The Untold Story, 1993

Last Days Madness, 1994

War of the Worldviews, 1994

Volume 3

God and Government
The Restoration of the Republic

Gary DeMar

AMERICAN VISION, INC.

Atlanta, Georgia

God and Government: The Restoration of the Republic is produced by American Vision, a Christian educational and communications organization. American Vision publishes a monthly magazine, *Biblical Worldview*, which is edited by Gary DeMar. For more information about American Vision and how to obtain a subscription to *Biblical Worldview* and receive a catalog of materials, write:

American Vision
P.O. Box 220
Powder Springs, Georgia 30127
or call 1–800–628–9460.

E-mail: avpress@mindspring.com
American Vision web site: www.americanvision.org
For prophecy-related books: www.prophecybooks.com

Unless otherwise noted, all Scripture quotations are taken from the *New American Standard Version* of the Bible. Copyright © The Lockman Foundation 1960, 1962, 1963, 1968, 1971, 1972, 1973, 1975, 1977, 1995. Used by permission.

ISBN: 0–915815–14–1 (Volume 3)
ISBN: 0–915815–15–X (3 volume set)

Text and photo acquisition by Gary DeMar

Art Direction by Diane Hosch

Series Design by Erin Sherman

Dedication and Acknowledgments

This book and the entire *God and Government* series is lovingly dedicated to my wife, Carol. She is a remarkable testimony to the principle of self-government outlined in these three volumes: "Strength and dignity are her clothing, and she smiles at the future. She opens her mouth in wisdom, and the teaching of kindness is on her tongue. She looks well to the ways of her household, and does not eat the bread of idleness" (Proverbs 31:25-27).

When I outlined the first volume of *God and Government*, I never conceived that it would grow to three volumes. Neither could I envision the impact it would have around the world, influencing the growing Christian school market, church groups, and Christian activists who believe that this nation and its institutions can be salvaged.

I am personally indebted to the writings of R. J. Rushdoony and Gary North. Their courageous attempts to cover every facet of life have not gone unnoticed by this author and countless others. Douglas Groothuis, Kim Burgess, and Dr. Gary North made many invaluable suggestions. Archie Jones, again, deserves much credit for this work. He encouraged me to write this third volume.

Lastly, Diane Hosch gave special care to the lay-out and agonized with me over the placement of photos, and Charlotte Hale worked wonders with the text.

The Restoration of the Republic should be on the hearts and minds of all Christians. A comprehensive restoration process will take time and commitment. Most of all it will take relying on the sovereign will of our God and the earnest proclamation that Jesus Christ is Lord of heaven and earth. God sent Jesus into the world to save it, not to destroy it or hand it over to the devil. God has called His people to transform the world through the preaching of the gospel and the application of Scripture to every area of life. Through such a process we will win our world back. Your own city, like the *City of Boston* pictured above, can be the starting point.

Contents

Preface

To the earthly politician nothing can seem more absurd than to ascribe to the devotions of private Christians, any power in regard to states and empires. Religion is an element in political changes not recognized by the wisdom of this world.

—James W. Alexander

Civilizations come and go, the kingdom of God goes on forever. This is the point of Nebuchadnezzar's dream of the human colossus (Daniel 2). Kingdoms built on the shaky foundation that man is sovereign cannot last. Pick up any history book and you will read about the demise of every empire-building civilization. They are dust on the cosmic scales of God's justice.

Christians have lost sight of the stone cut without hands that became a mountain that filled the earth (Daniel 2:35). For some reason we just can't believe that Jesus, through His redeemed people, is the fulfillment of that prophecy (cf. 1 Peter 2:5). We have convinced ourselves that defeat is the only option for the church; the only hope is retreat in the face of a creeping secularism. Maybe if things get real bad God will rapture us out of this mess.

It's interesting to note that every time there was any consideration of retreat in the face of opposition, the people of God were rebuked for their unbelief. For example, when the 12 spies were sent out to Canaan, God had promised them that the land would be theirs: "Send out for yourself men so that they may spy out the land of Canaan, *which I am going to give to the sons of Israel*" (Numbers 13:2). You know the story; ten of the spies came back with a report steeped in unbelief. Joshua and Caleb believed God. Sure, there were giants in the land. Joshua and Caleb never denied the presence of giants. So what if there are giants in the land? God is the Lord, even of giants! The promise was made, the land was theirs. Giants are nothing more than a minor and temporary inconvenience.

Forty years were wasted in the wilderness because the people chose to believe the report of the unbelieving spies. The giants turned out to be whimpering dogs. When two spies were sent out to Jericho forty years later, Rahab told the real story: "I know that the LORD has given this land to you and that a great fear of you has fallen on us, so that all who live in this country are melting in fear because of you. We have heard how the LORD dried up the water of the Red Sea for you when you came out of Egypt, and what you did to Sihon and Og, the two kings of the Amorites east of the Jordan, whom you completely destroyed. *When we heard of it, our hearts sank and everyone's courage failed because of you, for the LORD your God is God in heaven above and on the earth beneath*" (Joshua 2:8-11, NIV). There is little difference with the Humanists of our day. They are just as frightened as the residents of Jericho. The answer to our national problems do not reside solely in politics. Public strength comes through private righteousness.

When the righteous, those justified by God's redeeming grace through His Son Jesus Christ, work out their salvation in every sphere of life, we will see the manifestation of evil suppressed. This will mean that individuals, families, and churches must pray and obey.

To the earthly politician nothing can seem more absurd than to ascribe to the devotions of private Christians, any power in regard to states and empires. Religion is an element in political changes not recognised by the wisdom of this world. Yet it cannot be a matter of indifference, even in respect to civil government and national wealth, that hundreds of thousands of families, dispersed abroad in the earth, are daily addressing themselves to God in prayer. And it may turn out to be true, that a nation in which all the families shall be thus employed, will derive from this very peculiarity a character conducive to public strength (James W. Alexander, *Thoughts on Family-Worship*, p. 162).

So then, let us pray and learn and apply what Scripture says about every area of life. Turning to the State for salvation is the greatest of sins; "Salvation is found in no one else, for there is no other name under heaven given to men by which we must be saved" than the name Jesus Christ (Acts 4:12, NIV).

Special Features

The *God and Government* textbook series is designed for individual, church, school, seminar, and group Bible study. The question and answer format requires you to pause and to consider the issues under study in the light of biblical revelation before moving to another question. This educational device is necessary for a faithful application of Scripture to all of life. More often than not books are designed for reading, not reflection and meditation. The following special features are included to make the *God and Government* textbook series a true student's handbook:

1. Each lesson begins with an introduction to provide a frame of reference for the questions that follow.

2. The questions are designed to deal with each topic from a number of vantage points. This is why a number of the questions have a substantial list of Bible passages.

3. Scripture passages are included to encourage you to begin your study from a biblical perspective, always asking the question, "What does God's Word say about this issue?" Keep in mind that the interpretation of any one passage must be interpreted in its larger context. Consider the paragraph, chapter, book, author, Testament (Old or New), period of biblical history, audience, circumstances surrounding the writing, and other interpretive factors when formulating your answer.

4. Each lesson ends with a summary designed to focus your attention on each lesson's main theme. I've chosen quotations from respected Christian authors to summarize each chapter.

5. The unique feature of this textbook series is the answers supplied to each of the questions. The answers are comprehensive in most cases. Try to formulate your own answer before turning to the supplied answers.

6. Volume 3 of *God and Government* describes the competing nature of authority — one Christian and the other Humanistic. These two views of authority are at war with one another, and they work to disestablish one another in history. The Christian view of authority must be revived if America and the world are to survive. In order to enhance your understanding and appreciation of America's rich Christian history, American Vision has produced *America's Christian History: The Untold Story*. This award-winning audio presentation uses original source documents, sound effects, music, and drama to portray the true history of America's founding.

We are entered into covenant with [God] for this work. We have taken out a commission. The Lord has given us leave to draw our own articles; we have promised to base our actions on these ends, and we have asked Him for favor and blessing. Now if the Lord shall please to hear us, and bring us in peace to the place we desire, then He has ratified this covenant and sealed our commission, and will expect strict performance of the articles contained in it. But if we neglect to observe these articles, which are the ends we have propounded, and — dissembling with our God — shall embrace this present world and prosecute our carnal intentions, seeking great things for ourselves and our posterity, the Lord will surely break out in wrath against us and be revenged of such a perjured people, and He will make us know the price of the breach of such a covenant (Written by John Winthrop, 1588-1649, aboard the flagship *Arabella*. This document spells out what happens to a people when they forsake their covenant with God. Our nation needs to heed its warnings.)

How to Use this Textbook

You will gain maximum benefit from this textbook by following these suggestions:

1. Pray for wisdom and insight from the Holy Spirit as you study each lesson. You are dealing with the Word of God when you are searching the Scriptures for answers to the questions, thus, only the Spirit of God can bring out a text's true meaning.

2. Read the introduction to each lesson. They are designed to establish the context for the topic being studied.

3. Answer the questions using the Scripture passages as the foundation for your answer. Do not expect to develop as complete an answer as is found in the textbook. You should, however, be able to summarize an answer in the space provided under each question. An extra lined answer sheet is included in the back of this volume for longer answers. This answer sheet can be copied and passed out to students who are using this textbook as a workbook or supplement to a course in government or history.

4. For group study, each student should answer the questions before the group meets for discussion. This will allow more time for evaluation and informed exchange of ideas. A leader who is familiar with the topics presented in this volume should be chosen for each lesson to guide the discussion.

5. Each lesson is designed for a series of forty-five minute to one-hour sessions to be taught over a period of ten to twelve weeks. The study should not go on for a long period of time. It is best for students to want more than for them to say that they have had enough. The aim is to *introduce* Christians to the topics in such a way that they will want to study on their own.

6. Evaluate current events in the light of the biblical principles under discussion. Daily newspapers, magazines, radio and television news programs, talk shows, and issues that arise during local and national elections are helpful sources of information to help you think through the issues as they arise through your study.

7. Based on your study, construct biblical solutions that can replace humanistic policies and programs. Develop strategies to implement these biblical solutions to correct current problems. This might mean establishing additional study groups so these biblical principles can be shared. As more people learn what the solutions are they will be better equipped to implement them. Pray that we do not hear this lament for our nation: "My people are destroyed for lack of knowledge" (Hosea 4:6).

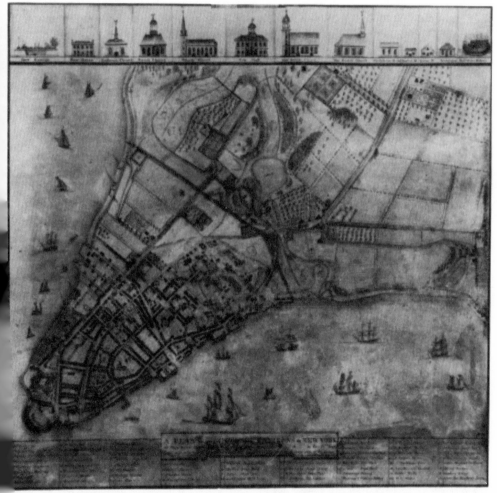

For a nation to survive, the church must nurture the nation. In this *Plan of the City and Environs of New York* we see how important a role churches played in the direction of a city. They are the prominent features in this rare drawing. Our nation must understand how important the church is in the Restoration of the Republic; it should nurture the nation.

Jesse T. Peck, *The History of the Great Republic Considered From a Christian Stand-Point*, 1868.

Personal regeneration must extend until political corruption shall become improbable, unpopular, impossible; until the only way to preferment shall be that of Christian patriotism, and an honest, broad, and noble philanthropy . . .
Do you say this can never be? Never? Then the regeneration which God extends to some men cannot extend to others; then the gospel of Christ is a failure, and "our preaching is vain"; then, in the grand conflict of ages, vice is to prove itself more than a match for virtue; then the word of unchangeable truth, that "righteousness shall cover the earth as the waters cover the sea," shall be demonstrated a failure. This cannot be. Long and terrible indeed will be the conflict; but the triumph is going on before our eyes. Its type is in every man created anew in Christ Jesus. Its progress is in the accumulating numbers of "the sacramental host of God's elect," and in the masterly style in which our national virtues triumph over vile forces and untoward events mighty enough to destroy any government not sustained by Omnipotent Power. Unwavering faith in the ultimate triumph of the right reposes to-day securely on the verities of history as well as upon the unalterable veracity of God. Let us, therefore, confidently expect the gradual but certain development of Christian principles in the Republic, and believe in its future greatness as a Christian power.

—Jesse T. Peck

The authority of Jesus Christ is comprehensive. It includes authority over individuals, families, churches, and the nations. Jesus' authority is exhibited here as a storm rages on the Sea of Galilee: *He arose, and rebuked the winds and the sea; and it became perfectly calm* (Matthew 8:26).

Lesson 1

The Biblical View
of
Authority

God is the ultimate and only independent authority. He is the Sovereign Creator who controls time and history. He establishes authority and deposes those who fight His absolute sovereignty. These truths must be our starting points as we discuss ways to restore the Republic. When a father, mother, elder, or civil official acts "on authority," we know there is an appeal to some *ultimate* authority that is used to legitimize his or her actions. There is always an appeal to that authority for every decision. Such ultimate authority can take various forms (intimidation, power, reason, science, religion, politics, and indoctrination through education); in the end, however, that ultimate entreaty becomes the "God" of the one making the appeal. The first commandment is explicit: "I am the LORD your God. . . . You shall have no other gods before Me" (Exodus 20:2, 3). All authorities must bow in submission before the Lord.

Of course, an appeal to an ultimate authority does not always make that appeal legitimate. For example, a judge might declare that his judicial status establishes him as an ultimate authority, making his rulings law regardless of the source of his authority or the nature of the law. Right and wrong are not the issue, he might argue. What matters to him is the power behind his proposed decree. How are his decrees carried out? What backs up his authority? To him, merely his claim to legitimacy and force makes his ruling "just":

The late greatly admired Chief Justice of the United States Supreme Court and author of the only modern text on the common law in any appreciable use in our law schools, Oliver Wendell Holmes, declared this idea in such a way as to leave no room for doubt as to what was meant. He said in many ways and at many different times that law is whatever the greatest force in the community can make it at any given time. There are no absolutes, he opined (T. Robert Ingram, *What's Wrong With Human Rights?*, p. 13f.)

The issue then is not: Should we have an absolute authority? Rather, we should ask: What is our ultimate authority, and how do lesser or subordinate authorities in relation to God's ultimate governing authority gain legitimacy?

There is no danger in giving up any error, or in embracing any truth. Forsaking truth, and embracing error, angels shrunk into devils. Forsaking error and grasping truth, sinners rise to the dignity of saints, and to the companionship of angels.

—William Plumer

Even force is legitimate when properly sanctioned and exercised. A father who demands that his son or daughter perform certain household duties exercises legitimate authority. The teacher who directs that assignments be turned in on time and in a prescribed manner acts as a legitimate authority in the place of the parents (not the State). The penalties assigned for non-compliance can be backed up by force. A child can receive a lower grade or be made to stay after school to produce the work as assigned, or a spanking might be given.

An ecclesiastical (church) court can excommunicate an unrepentant church member and exclude him or her from partaking of the Lord's Supper, a severe penalty in biblical terms but hardly looked upon as serious in our "modern" age of church hopping. A judge can force a thief to pay restitution to the victim. In each of these examples, legitimate authority is exercised and force applied for cases of non-compliance.

The exercise of authority and use of force are different in each example cited, however. Parents can demand certain things from their children but cannot exercise their legitimate *parental* authority by forcing a thief to pay restitution,

4

unless the thief is their child. The civil sphere, under the jurisdiction of God's law, must exercise its proper authority as a "minister of God" (Romans 13:4). The State can execute a convicted murderer but cannot determine who can be admitted to the Lord's table.

This brings us to an important point. Without an ultimate authority established by an unchanging and sovereign God, all earthly authorities vie for ultimacy and set standards for themselves and ultimately for other people. When the Triune God is rejected as the source and dispenser of authority and power, we can expect cooperation between various authorities to cease and competition, and eventually conflict, to prevail. The most powerful authorities then work to eliminate what they perceive to be their competition. The State is the most powerful authority in terms of temporal punishment; it has the power of the sword. When it sees itself as ultimate and independent of God, all other authorities (e.g., families and churches) are no longer viewed as allies but competitors. Their authority must be eliminated. Children no longer belong to parents and therefore must be educated by the State, to be called in service for the State. Churches can teach "religious" doctrine so long as that teaching does not address issues that are controlled by the State.

The biblical pattern of authority insists that God is our Ultimate authority and He alone establishes subordinate and ministerial authorities. In Romans 13:1 we are instructed to subject ourselves "to the governing *authorities.*" Each is "established by God." The word "authorities" is plural. We owe no single earthly authority our total allegiance. Those hostile to the Christian faith despise such jurisdictional pluralism, a system which maintains there is one Law and Law-giver, but a plurality of jurisdictions or authorities to which we must all submit. No one jurisdiction can claim the right to rule over all other established authorities. All are ultimately responsible to God for legitimacy. No authority can claim independency from the Triune God.

These multiple authorities should not negate the legitimate authority delegated to them by God, nor compete to eliminate one another by force or law. Ideally, family, church, and State cooperate. They exist in the world by God's design. Each exercises real power in its limited sphere of operation. The breakdown of authority comes when the various authorities abdicate legitimacy and responsibility and turn rulership over to what is perceived as a greater human authority, hoping to enjoy security. In Old Testament Israel, family, church, and State were meant to operate under the jurisdiction of the One True King. As sin

5

prevailed and judgment came, the people turned to the State for security. When Gideon won a battle for Israel, the people were ready to make him king: "Rule over us, both you and your son, also your son's son, for you have delivered us from the hand of Mideon" (Judges 8:22). Gideon was quick to remind the people where their loyalty and security should have resided: "I will not rule over you, nor shall my son rule over you; the LORD shall rule over you" (v. 23). Eventually the people abandoned self-, family, and ecclesiastical governments and the legitimate authority delegated to them by God, and turned to the State for salvation. They rejected God as King over them and chose a "king like all the other nations" (1 Samuel 8).

The temptation today is to reject God's ultimate authority and His multiplicity of delegated authorities found in families, churches, and the many civil governments located in city, county, and state governments. The State holds considerable power. Many sinister people would like to use the State to remove God's pattern for order by usurping all other God-ordained authorities and the power they wield and consolidate this authority and power in the State. Such is the wish of those who want to "take counsel together against the LORD and against His Anointed" (Psalm 2:2). Their dream is the dream of Babel and Babylon, destined to failure, to be swept away with the dust of history.

The authority of God's word served to motivate our earliest founders to seek a world where they could build a civilization where Scripture would govern family, church, and State.

Questions for Discussion

1. What is the biblical definition of authority, and how does its comprehensiveness relate to the Three Persons of the Trinity in their governmental activity? (Isaiah 40:13; Genesis 1:1; 2:15-17; 3:14; Matthew 24:36; Luke 12:5; 10:17-20; 1 John 3:8; Mark 2:10-12; Matthew 7:29; John 2:13-22; Luke 8:24f.; Matthew 17:27; John 19:11; Matthew 28:18; Ephesians 5:23; Matthew 16:19; Revelation 1:5; 2:5; 1 Timothy 6:15; Romans 13:1; Genesis 1:2; Numbers 11:26, 29; Isaiah 61:1; Luke 1:35; Matthew 3:16; Acts 2:1-42; 16:6-10; 1 Corinthians 12:4-31; John 3:5)

_____

_____

_____

_____

_____

_____

_____

_____

2. What is the relationship between authority and power? (Luke 9:1; Matthew 12:22-29; 17:14-18; Acts 19:11-20; Daniel 3; 6; Matthew 2:13-18)

_____

_____

_____

_____

_____

3. Where did the battle over authority originate? Explain. (Genesis 2:15, 16; 3:5)

_____

_____

_____

_____

4. Why is it crucial that we understand the importance of authority when discussing what is true or false, right or wrong, good or bad? (Judges 17:6; Ephesians 4:14; Isaiah 6:3; Luke 18:19; John 17:6; 10:35; Romans 7:12; James 1:25)

_____

_____

_____

_____

_____

_____

5. How and why has God established such multiple, delegated authorities as the family, the church, the state, and contractual jurisdictions like employer-employee relationships? (Proverbs 6:20, 21; 15:5; 30:17; Ephesians 6:1-3; Colossians 3:20; Matthew 16:19; 18:15-20; 1 Thessalonians 5:12, 13; 1 Timothy 5:17, 18; Hebrews 13:17; 1 Peter 5:1-3; Matthew 22:21; Romans 13:1-7; 1 Peter 2:13, 14; Leviticus 19:13; Deuteronomy 25:4; 1 Timothy 5:18; cf. Matthew 10:10; Luke 10:7)

_____

_____

_____

_____

_____

_____

_____

6. Explain the limited jurisdiction of biblical authority; i.e., show how family, church, and state exercise their jurisdictional authority without usurping the authority of each other's jurisdiction. (Proverbs 13:24; Matthew 16:19; 1 Corinthians 11:3; Ephesians 5:23)

_____

_____

_____

_____

_____

_____

7. What is the relationship between authority and culture? (Genesis 1:28; 2:10-15; 9:7; Psalm 8; Hebrews 2; 3:17, 18; Romans 8:20-22; Proverbs 21:4; Romans 14:23; Isaiah 64:6)

_____

_____

_____

_____

_____

_____

_____

_____

_____

Summary

"This is a religious viewpoint which affirms that the most important goal for man, group, or species, is the capture and maintenance of power. Power is seen as the chief attribute of God, or if the religion is officially atheistic, then the chief attribute of man. This perspective is a satanic perversion of God's command to man to exercise dominion over all the creation (Gen. 1:26-28). It is the attempt to exercise dominion apart from covenantal subordination to the true Creator God.

"What distinguishes biblical dominion religion from satanic power religion is *ethics*. Is the person who seeks power doing so for the glory of God, and for himself secondarily, and only to the extent that he is God's lawful and covenantally faithful representative? If so, he will act in terms of God's ethical standards and in terms of a profession of faith in the God of the Bible. The church has recognized this two-fold requirement historically, and has established a dual requirement for membership: profession of faith and a godly life" (Gary North, *Moses and Pharaoh: Dominion Religion Versus Power Religion*, p. 2).

Answers to Questions for Discussion

1. Two prominent New Testament words for authority are *dunamis* and *exousia*. The Greek word *dunamis* is best defined as "might," "power," or "ability to perform anything." God is described as the "Mighty One" who "has done great things" (Luke 1:49). Jesus describes His Father as "power" (Mark 14:62). God's work is undeniably carried out because of His power: with God "all things are possible" (Matthew 19:26; Mark 10:27; Luke 18:27). Power, then, is the *ability* to perform.

The basic meaning of the Greek word *exousia* is "rightful, actual, and unimpeded power to act, or to possess, control, use, or dispose of, something or somebody. . . . The uniform biblical conviction is that the only rightful power within creation is, ultimately, the Creator's" (J. I. Packer, "Authority," *The New Bible Dictionary*, rev. ed., 1965, p. 111f.)

God rightly holds absolute authority as Creator and Sovereign of all people, things, and events. The emphasis must be placed on *rightful* authority. When God speaks, saves, deposes, blesses, and judges, He does so with absolute and *rightful* authority. He has no need to confer with anyone for counsel or permission to execute His will: "Who has directed the Spirit of the LORD, or as His counselor has informed Him?" (Isaiah 40:13; cf. Romans 11:34; 1 Corinthians 2:16; Isaiah 29:15, 16). By His own authority He has brought the world into existence (Genesis 1:1), created man (1:26-28; 2:21-25), set the laws for man to live by (2:15-17; Exodus 20:1-17), pronounced judgment upon His enemies (Genesis 3:14), fixed the dates and times of the end of the age without any regard for the wishes of men (Matthew 24:36; Acts 1:7), and He has the authority to consign men to eternal punishment (Luke 12:5).

Further, authority is inherent in the person and work of Christ. Jesus' authority is real because He is Himself God (John 1:1; 20:28). Jesus has deprived the devil of his authority and power by destroying his works (Luke 10:17-20; 1 John 3:8). Jesus used His divine authority to forgive sins (a thing only God can do) (Mark 2:10-12; Matthew 9:1-8). The people marveled at His display of authority and power when compared to the teachers of their day (Mark 1:22, 27; Matthew 7:29; Luke 4:32). He did not teach like the scribes whose instructions were based upon the tradi-

10

tions of men (Matthew 7:29). The cleansing of the Temple set forth Jesus' claim to divine authority. It was *His* Father's house that He would not allow to be turned into a den for robbers (John 2:13-22). Jesus showed His authority over creation by stilling a storm (Luke 8:24) and commanding a fish to do His bidding (Matthew 17:27). Even death is under Jesus' authority (John 10:18; 11:38-44). Jesus reminded Pilate that the authority he possessed was not his own: "You would have no authority over Me, unless it had been granted you from above . . ." (John 19:11). The rebellious nations will be discipled because "all authority has been given" to Him (Matthew 28:18-20).

Jesus holds authority in the church. He gives His church "the keys of the kingdom of heaven" (Matthew 16:19). He is "the head of the church" (Ephesians 5:23) and has authority to remove the "lampstand out of its place" (Revelation 2:5).

Jesus is the head of all political institutions as "the ruler of the kings of the earth" (Revelation 1:5). He remains the "only Sovereign, King of kings and Lord of lords" (1 Timothy 6:15; cf. 1:17; Revelation 17:14; 19:16). The authority given to civil rulers is "established by God" (Romans 13:1).

This Roman centurion understood the nature of Jesus' authority: *For I, too, am a man under authority, with soldiers under me; and I say to this one, "Go!" and he goes, and to another, "Come!" and he comes, and to my slave, "Do this!" and he does it* (Matthew 8:9).

11

Authority and, thus, sovereignty are not self-derived or autonomous. Any government, whether family, church or civil must rule in terms of God's Government or be eliminated. Achan's family was judged when it failed to follow God's specific command not to take what was holy to the Lord (Joshua 7:16-26). Nadab and Abihu, as representatives of the Old Testament church, "died before the LORD when they offered strange fire before the LORD in the wilderness of Sinai" (Numbers 3:4). Belshazzar was slain when he failed to worship the One, True, and Living God and instead "praised the gods of gold and silver, of bronze, iron, wood, and stone" (Daniel 5:4, 30).

The work of God's Spirit also is sovereign and authoritative. He brought order to creation (Genesis 1:2). He equipped the prophets (Numbers 11:26, 29) and instructed the Israelites as a nation (Nehemiah 9:20). The prophet Isaiah was equipped by the Holy Spirit (Isaiah 61:1) and by His authority the prophet Ezekiel was sent to preach to those in captivity (Ezekiel 3:12, 15). In the New Testament, Mary conceived by the "power of the Most High" when "the Holy Spirit" came upon her (Luke 1:35). The Holy Spirit equipped Jesus for ministry (Matthew 3:16) and He came upon the disciples at Pentecost and equipped them for service as well (Acts 2:1-42). The Holy Spirit's authority directed Paul's missionary journeys (Acts 16:6-10). He equips individuals in the church by giving various gifts for the building up of the body (1 Corinthians 12:4-31). The regeneration of the heart of man "dead in trespasses and sins" is accomplished by His sovereign authority and power (John 3:5; Titus 3:5).

The Triune God is Sovereign in both heaven and earth, with individuals, families, churches, and civil governments.

2. God's authority is displayed in *power*. The relationship of both *exousia* (authority) and *dunamis* (power) can be seen in the work of Christ: "And He called the twelve together, and gave them power [*dunamis*] and authority [*exousia*] over all the demons, and to heal diseases" (Luke 9:1). Authority without power is ineffective (Matthew 12:22-29; 17:14-18; Acts 19:11-20). Power without authority is reckless and destructive (Daniel 3; 6; Matthew 2:13-18). A civil government may have power but no real authority to exercise that power. When Nazi Germany, the Soviet Union, and Communist China executed millions of citizens to remove all con-

12

trary opinions, they exercised power without lawful authority. When our nation's Supreme Court legalized abortion in 1973, it exercised power but not legitimate authority. Its claim to authority, and, thus, sovereignty in legalizing abortion on demand was legitimized, as Justice Byron White in his dissenting opinion maintained, through "raw judicial power" (See *Roe v. Wade*, 410 U.S. 113 at 222).

Abandonment of the Christian world view created an ideological vacuum which was filled with displays of power manifested as totalitarian political regimes. Friedrich Nietzsche, whose philosophy spawned theology's "Death of God" movement and the bloody revolutions of Vladimir Lenin (1870-1924) and Adolph Hitler (1889-1945), propagated a religion of power divorced from God-ordained authority. God was replaced with the "Will to Power." Power was all that mattered. Authority was legitimized with power. Paul Johnson observes:

Nietzsche rightly perceived that the most likely candidate [to fill the vacuum left by a retreating Christian world view] would be what he called the "Will to Power". . . .

In the place of religious belief, there would be secular ideology. . . . And, above all, the Will to Power would produce a new kind of messiah, uninhibited by any religious sanctions whatever, and with an unappeasable appetite for controlling mankind. The end of the old order, with an unguided world adrift in a relativistic universe, was a summons to such gangster-statesmen to emerge. They were not slow to make their appearance (*Modern Times: The Modern World from the Twenties to the Eighties*, p. 48).

When political thinking excludes the authority of God's word, the Bible, we can expect religions of power to surface. Because individuals can change only through regeneration, and regeneration comes only through the sovereign action of the Holy Spirit, oppressive political regimes must use external means to obtain "their" citizens' obedience. All repressive ideologies work to eliminate all contrary sentiment which might hinder their "New World Order" based upon the authority and power of man. Remember, authority is ultimately religious, based on our highest concern.

If God's authority is rejected, then God's ways of directing and controlling power also are rejected. Power, however, is never eliminated; it is only

13

transferred from one power-broker to another. Because man is a sinner, his autonomous displays of power too often are despotic and tyrannical. Man's authority and his "Will to Power" find their meaning in the one who can seize and possess the reins of political power. The French Revolution of 1789 and the Russian Revolution of 1917 brought with them displays of power which resulted in the attempted elimination of all competing authorities.

The leaders of both these revolutions not only ignored God but as a matter of deliberate state policy sought with all the means at their disposal to deprive God of any influence upon the lives of millions of citizens and to persecute, imprison and kill his faithful servants. . . . The sovereign God of the Scriptures was dethroned and apostate man enthroned upon the vacant seat. . . . All power and authority on this earth is now proclaimed to proceed from the sovereign will of the state or of the will of the majority or of whoever seizes power (E. L. Hebden Taylor, *The Christian Philosophy of Law, Politics and the State*, p. 6).

The Will to Power can also be found in other "religious" and political systems. Certain "religious" movements like Islam claim the name of God.

Herod was an early *Gangster Statesman* who wielded the sword wilfully to eliminate all those who might be a threat to his throne: *Herod . . . slew all the male children who were in Bethlehem and in all its environs* (Matthew 2:16).

14

Theirs, however, is a false religion, a perversion of Scripture. It is ultimately humanistic because man must save himself through his own deeds of "righteousness." Since regeneration is impossible, church and State are merged and the peoples' lives are controlled by religious-political despots.

While some political systems place all power in the hands of the State, others claim ultimacy for the individual. The humanistic alternative to totalitarianism is "all power to the individual." Anarchy, while not a "system," qualifies as a political ideology because it denies the need for any authority except the inherently good individual. All other ideologies must be eliminated, usually through violence, to make room for the sovereign individual. Modern-day terrorism is a manifestation of anarchy, with elimination of family, church, and civil authorities as the goal. Even civil governments use the desire for individual sovereignty to accomplish their aim of world domination. The Soviet Union exports violence for this purpose, placing authority in the hands of individuals who subvert and eventually destroy the existing order. When this is done, the Marxist regime enters amidst the chaos to establish its totalitarian State, eliminating the revolutionaries in the process. For Communism, anarchy is the political tool that leads to totalitarianism.

Christians must take care not to align themselves with certain "Christian" revolutionary groups that advocate violence as the only hope to change "unjust structures." Christians should be involved in the *restoration* of the republic, not the *razing* of the republic. We have God and time on our side.

Christians need not turn to bloody revolution in this country; they are in the majority. They need to understand God's Word, and to have the courage to apply it in every area of their lives . . . . Did David murder Saul when Saul persecuted him? David was forced to flee Israel and pretend to be crazy in the presence of the Philistines — and not just the Philistines, but the king of Gath, the city of Goliath (I Sam. 21:10-15).

David was God's anointed, yet he did not challenge Saul. He did not surrender, either. He wrote: "I shall not die, but live, and declare the works of the Lord" (Ps. 118:17) (Gary North, "Editor's Introduction," in *Tactics of Christian Resistance*, p. xxxiii).

15

Abuse of authority and power exist within any political system founded on anything less than Scripture. An absolute monarchy can lead to arbitrary and absolute power in one man; elitism places absolute and arbitrary power in the hands of a few men (e.g., scientific experts, social "scientists," the wealthy, the poor, the military, a priestly hierarchy, an intellectual elite, etc); democracy, the political deity of today, locates absolute and arbitrary authority and power in the hands of the majority; even a republic, with its constitutional safeguards, can posit unbridled authority and power in the hands of representatives who use their power to subvert and ignore the parameters of the Constitution to serve the agendas of special interest groups.

Political authority and power do not reside in the hands of the few or the many. At the heart of the Mayflower Compact lay an undisputed conviction that God must be at the center of all law and order and that law without a moral base is really no law at all.

God's law must be over and under all forms of civil government. The word of God must be *over* all governments, to remind citizens and representatives that authority and power are given by God (Romans 13:1). The word of God, the *foundation* upon which civil governments should rest, provides specifics on how to rule. Absolute authority and power belong to God alone; no earthly institution can claim them.

3. The battle over authority began when the serpent questioned God's absolute right to rule and to issue commands, and enticed our first parents to be "like God" (Genesis 3:5). In considering the issue of rightful authority, we first must consider the relationship between independent and dependent authority. God, who created all things, obviously must be the source and dispenser of authority. Therefore, any authority His creatures possess must be due to His grace, and our authority as creatures of God is altogether *delegated, derivative,* and *dependent.*

The Psalmist directs us to remember who we are with these words: "Know that the Lord Himself is God; It is He who has made us, and not we ourselves" (Ps. 100:3). Man is no less dependent on God than is the rest of creation for he himself was created by God and is sustained by Him. Man is the crown of God's creative activity, but he is still a creature and is returning to dust (Gen. 2:7; [3:19]). "In Him we live and move and exist" (Acts 17:28) and apart from God we are nothing. All that man possesses has been given to him by God. As with the rest of creation, if God were to remove His hand from us, we could not even continue to exist. We exist entirely by the will of God (Richard L. Pratt, Jr., *Every Thought Captive,* p. 16).

Authority, therefore, is not creature-generated, but has a transcendent source, God who is above man. The Apostle Paul reminds us that we ought to depend upon God alone for *all* things: "The God who made the world and all things in it, since He is the Lord of heaven and earth, does not dwell in temples made with hands; neither is He served by human hands as though He needed anything, since He Himself gives to all life and breath and all things" (Acts 17:24, 25).

Satan tempted Adam and Eve with a desire for autonomous authority by calling into question God's rightful claim to absolute and independent authority. Since God existed as the absolute, independent, and ultimate authority, Eve immediately should have rebuffed Satan's denial of God's prohibition (Genesis 3:5). Instead, when Satan placed the desire for autonomy in Eve's mind, she succumbed to the devil's lie that God's claim to unlimited and ultimate authority might be tenuous.

In order for Adam and Eve to "be as gods," the relationship between the independent Creator and the dependent creature must have changed radically in one of two ways: (1) God no longer could have been Sovereign Ruler of man and the universe. Creator of all that is, God no longer could maintain ultimate control (Deism); (2) Man, through special knowledge, magic (the power of the forbidden fruit), or an act of his own Will to Power, had achieved a god-like status, dethroning God and replacing Him as Lord of the universe.

If it were *possible* for God to cease being God (the Sovereign Lord of all His creation), and/or man to become God, the principle of evolutionary change must be more ultimate than God Himself. Adam and Eve would have to presuppose evolution, the non-sovereign nature of God, and the changing nature of God. Only if God changed, or man somehow became God's equal, could man escape the wrath of God's judgment as he attempted to usurp God's immutably sovereign position by eating of the fruit of the tree of the knowledge of good and evil. God does not change (Malachi 3:6) and He "upholds all things by the word of His power" (Hebrews 1:3). Man, on the other hand, is "a vapor that appears for a little while and then vanishes away" (James 4:14; cf. Job 7:7; Psalm 39:5; Isaiah 2:22). "For you are dust, and to dust you shall return" (Genesis 3:19).

Moreover, "*knowing* good and evil" (Genesis 3:5) means *determining* good and evil for oneself. Thus Satan tempted man to abandon God's determination or standard of truth, good, and evil and to replace this with his *own* standard of truth, good, and evil. Thus the authority of man's word would have replaced the authority of God's word. Since God's word is a word of power (cf. Genesis 1:3), this would mean *man's* word would become a word of sovereign power. Since man's word could replace God's will and word of power, man's will to power would be able to overcome God's will to power. If one could claim self-authority, that authority could be shared. Man would assume an equal footing with God. The creature could be consulted by the Creator. Scripture is clear, however: "For thus says the LORD, who created the heavens (He is the God who formed the earth and made it, He established it and did not create it a waste place, but formed it to be inhabited), 'I am the LORD, and there is none else' " (Isaiah 45:18).

Satan's question to Eve, "Has God said. . . ?," was the attempt to call into question God's hold on absolute authority. Why should God alone be able to give an absolute mandate? By questioning God's authority, Satan suggested that man could step in as, at least, an equal authority. Then Adam and Eve could be like God, "knowing," that is, determining, for themselves, good and evil.

Notice that Satan did not question the existence of authority as such. Authority could not be denied by the devil. The repudiation of one authority leads to the adoption of another. Authority, therefore, is inescapable. R. J. Rushdoony writes: "Man does not establish authority; he acknowledges it. This is the proper procedure, though seldom observed. Man wants to acknowledge only that authority which he himself establishes or at the least gives consent to. All other authority is offensive to his sense of autonomy and ultimacy" (By What Standard?, p. 145). If God is not acknowledged as the absolute holder of all authority then we will see that attribute claimed by another. In our day the most sinister display of unlimited authority is found in the ultimate State. The State denies God and seeks to harness absolute power for itself and exclude all rival authorities.

4. The question of authority becomes extremely important and practical when we start dealing with life's most basic issues. Everyday living requires that we make a multitude of decisions. How does one choose between two or more ethical opinions?

Without a basis for authority, a standard of authority, the determination of proper ethical decision-making is left up to the shifting opinions of men. In time, however, such an ethic leads to anarchy, everyone doing what is right in his own eyes (Judges 17:6). Such living conditions cannot be long tolerated: coercion usually is exercised to bring rebels (as defined by the new and ultimate authority) under control. Those holding the greatest power become the final arbiters of right and wrong, good and evil, just and unjust, true and false.

The Bible is God's authoritative word to man. Without it he lacks an anchor and must drift in a sea of ethical subjectivism. The Bible secures and stabilizes us and the world in which we live: "[W]e are no longer to be

The Bible is God's authoritative word to man. Without it he lacks an anchor and must drift in a sea of ethical subjectivism. The Bible secures and stabilizes us and the world in which we live. As Christians we are to *examine the Scriptures* (Acts 17:11) so that we will not be *tossed here and there by the waves, and carried about by every wind of doctrine, by the trickery of men, by craftiness in deceitful scheming* (Ephesians 4:14).

children, tossed here and there by waves, and carried about by every wind of doctrine, by the trickery of men, by craftiness in deceitful scheming" (Ephesians 4:14). A dependent and finite creature needs a "touchstone" by which he can test man's various opinionss so he will not be led astray "by every wind of doctrine." George W. Marston in his book *The Voice of Authority* gives us a very helpful example.

> In the days of the gold rush men used a touchstone, a fine grained dark stone, such as jasper, to determine the quality of the gold which they had discovered. Today a Geiger counter is used to locate uranium and other precious metals. In baseball the umpire makes the decisions in the contest between the pitcher and the batter. In the courtroom the judge decides questions of law. In their respective fields the touchstone, the Geiger counter, the umpire and the judge speak with authority (p. xv).

In each case a *standard* of authority must determine truth from error. Man has two choices regarding authority, with the second being no real choice: he chooses either Scripture as his authority for all decision making, or the word of man. Finite, fallible, and fallen creatures need a *benchmark* so they will not stray in decision-making. The term *benchmark* is used by surveyors. Once the *benchmark* is established all other measurements are taken from this single point. If the *benchmark* is wrong then all the measurements will be distorted.

The authority of Scripture is like its Author. The basis of God's authority springs from His very nature and is therefore trustworthy. We can trust God as the ultimate authority because He is holy, righteous, and good (Isaiah 6:3 and Luke 18:19). Jesus maintains that God's word "is truth" (John 17:17) and "the Scripture cannot be broken" (John 10:35). The Apostle Paul declares that "the Law is holy, and the commandment is holy and righteous and good" (Romans 7:12). He goes on to describe Scripture as the very breath of God: "All Scripture is God-breathed. . . " (2 Timothy 3:16, NIV). James describes the word as the "perfect law" (James 1:25). Because God can be trusted, so can His word.

We can also trust God as the ultimate Authority because He is *sovereign, all-powerful,* and *all-knowing.* Because He is sovereign and able to accomplish His every desire, His will can never be thwarted or His word cast down: God's word will not return to Him empty, without accomplish-

21

ing what He desires, and without succeeding in the matter for which He sent it (Isaiah 55:11). Moreover, because He is all-knowing, we can be certain He knows perfectly well what He is doing and saying. Because this is so, we can be sure His infinite power will be used perfectly to accomplish that which He wills.

Scripture is our *benchmark*. If we do not start from it, our view of the world will be distorted and the institutions of authority in which we participate (family, church, and State) will reflect these same distortions. "Nothing but Scripture can claim our obedience, because it is God's Word. Rejection of Scripture amounts to an affront to the divine majesty. He is no disciple of Christ who rejects His doctrine of inspiration. Scripture may not be adulterated (by adding to it by churchly tradition [or pagan ideas]) nor emasculated (by diminishing it according to the supposed dictates of reason [or of 'empirical evidences' or of intuition]). It stands above everything else and judges it" (Clark H. Pinnock, *Biblical Revelation*, p. 96).

Scripture is our *benchmark*. If it is not our starting point, our view of the world will be distorted and the institutions of authority in which we participate (family, church, and State) will reflect these same distortions.

God knows everything. He is not surprised by any event or unaware of any fact. Everything God wants His creatures to know has been given in Scripture as a blueprint for living. God has not revealed everything, but what He has revealed is true and sufficient: "The secret things belong to the LORD our God, but the things revealed belong to us and to our sons forever, that we may observe all the words of this law" (Deuteronomy 29:29; cf. 2 Timothy 3:16, 17). Any doctrine of authority that seeks to put man on an equal footing with God at any point should be rejected. A return to Eve's compromise with Satan is no way to restore the republic.

5. All authority belongs to God alone. Authority which exists in the created realm is there by God's design and permission. The created order, the sun giving heat and light and stars illuminating the sky, operate as inanimate authorities by God's design. God's ordering of the days is an authority structure that must be followed (Genesis 1:14-18; Exodus 20:9, 10). Professors still take their Sabbaticals, and the United States Constitution follows the biblical model for Sunday as a day of worship and rest (Article I, section 7).

God has established numerous authorities for the proper ordering of society. Mothers and fathers have authority over their children (Proverbs 6:20, 21; 15:5; 30:17; Ephesians 6:1-3; Colossians 3:20). Church leaders, elders and deacons, hold authority in the church (Matthew 16:19; 18:15-20; 1 Thessalonians 5:12, 13; 1 Timothy 5:17, 18; Hebrews 13:17; 1 Peter 5:1-3). Civil rulers exercise political authority by God's decree (Matthew 22:21; Romans 13:1-7; 1 Peter 2:13, 14).

In other relationships, contracts can bind individuals and groups subject to the stipulations of the contract. The employer-employee relationship is contractual and carries with it legitimate authority (Leviticus 19:13; Deuteronomy 25:4; 1 Timothy 5:18; cf. Matthew 10:10; Luke 10:7). The courts, the judicial arm of civil authority, enforce the obligations of contracts by punishing the contract-breaker and seeing to it that restitution is paid to the contract-keeper. A contract is based upon God's covenantal design. God sets forth obligations, benefits for obeying the covenant, and reprisals for breaking covenant stipulations.

For any society to function in an orderly fashion, authority must be real and diverse. Parents, elders, employers, and civil servants could not operate in their delegated spheres if their authority were self-derived.

The authority of leaders always could be challenged by the rebellious. Satan, Adam and Eve, Cain, the builders of the Tower of Babel, Abimelech (Judges 9), Saul, Jezebel, Ahab and others supposed they could claim authority autonomously, without regard for the delegated authority of God. In each case the larger society suffered.

While the Bible is the Christian's *sole* authority, God has so created man that various gifts and talents would manifest themselves for the building of a Christian civilization. All society benefits when everyone is free, *within the parameters of God's law*, to exercise his or her gifts and talents.

On the other hand, were authority to be centralized in an earthly institution (e.g., a single family, church, or State) the various gifts and talents attached to the other authority structures in society never could function at an optimum level. The realities of 1 Corinthians 12 could not be realized. Multiple authorities work for liberty, entrepreneurial development, and cultural advancement. All society benefits when everyone is free, *within the parameters of God's law*, to exercise his or her gifts and talents.

Multiple created authority is patterned after the Divine One and Many. There is one God (One) and there are three Persons (Many) in the Godhead, each of whom is God. Each member of the Trinity — Father, Son, and Holy Spirit — has authority (unity of purpose in the exercise of authority) and yet each performs a different task (diversity of function in the use of authority to accomplish the one purpose). "Even within the Triune God there was a certain 'division of labor' *ad extra* — it was preeminently God the Father Who created all things; it was preeminently God the Son Who redeemed all things; and it is preeminently God the Spirit Who is perfecting all things" (Francis Nigel Lee, *Communist Eschatology*, p. 633). The Triune God has impressed His creation with this divine pattern. Thus, He has ordained the family, the church, and civil governments as institutions, lesser authority structures, under His overall sovereignty and government: *many* institutions, but *united* by *one* purpose and duty — obedience to God for His glory.

What, then, should be ultimate in society? The one or the many? Unity or diversity? The individual or the group? Should we have one monolithic authority or should every individual be an authority unto himself? Rushdoony writes:

The *one* and the *many* is perhaps the basic question of philosophy. Is unity or plurality, the one or the many, the basic fact of life, the ultimate truth about being? If unity is the reality, and the basic nature of reality, then oneness and unity must gain priority over individualism, particulars, or the many. If the many, or plurality, best describes ultimate reality, then the unit cannot gain priority over the many; then state, church, or society are subordinate to the will of the citizen, the believer, and of man in particular. If the *one* is ultimate, then individuals are sacrificed to the group. If the *many*, then unity is sacrificed to the will of many, and anarchy prevails (*The One and the Many*, p. 2n.).

There are two extremes to be avoided. First, that the individual is a law unto himself, responsible only to himself. This extreme attempts to counter its opposite, that the *many* are ultimate. If the many were ultimate, anarchy would result. Many individuals could claim authority on their own terms. Second, no one institution, group, nation, or society is ultimate. This opposes the idea that the *one* should be ultimate. If the one becomes ultimate, an institution, group, church, nation, or society can claim to be the final arbiter of truth and power, putting all diversity under its rule. Only God is ultimate; the one and the many are governed by God's Law in all things. Thus, the one and many in society are balanced under the one authority of the Triune God.

Diversification of authority decentralizes the centers of power. Corruption and tyranny are heightened when authority structures, from the individual to civil governments at the local, county, and state levels break down, and all authority rests in one institution, usually the State (i.e., the Central [Federal] Government). Robert A. Nisbet makes the following observation:

> The totalitarian state of the twentieth century is — at least in theory and design — the unlimited extension of political power and the political bond into all areas of human behavior. Nothing is held to be morally or legally exempt from the scope of political government. Religion, family life, labor, industry, profession, and education, as well as music, art, and literature, are deemed to serve their highest function in direct service to the specific ends around which the totalitarian state is formed. Fascism in Italy, Nazism in Germany, and Communism in Soviet Russia, Maoist China, Albania, and Yugoslavia, among other places, all exemplify the totalitarian state in some degree. It is the very nature of the totalitarian state that autonomy or association, freedom of culture, and rights of individual dissent are forbidden, for in them would lie ever-present possibilities of divergence from the aims of the state (*The Social Bond*, p. 132).

Reclamation of multiple authorities comes about when the individual assumes his responsibilities under God and thoroughly transforms his family and, working with other like-minded individuals, transforms his school, church, vocation, local community, state, and national civil government. We cannot expect diverse authority structures to arise on their own, however. Regeneration, the basis of all godly authority, begins with God working on the individual and extends to every facet of life.

A word of caution is needed here. Too often Christians turn to the State for relief because of the failure of individuals, families, businesses, schools, churches, and civil governments at the county and state levels.

26

The State holds limited jurisdiction and competence, and is not man's answer for sin, except in temporal punishment for criminal acts. In fact — as recent history so well attests — the State frequently compounds the ills of society, the economy, education, welfare, etc. when it acts outside of the area of its proper authority and jurisdiction.

6. It has been established that all authority belongs to God and that all earthly authority, whether family, church or State, is delegated and limited. The delegation of authority is diverse. The authority of the State is not the same as that of a father who exercises authority as head of his household. While each government should follow guidelines laid down in Scripture for its particular area of jurisdiction, not all biblical laws apply to each in the same way. For example, the symbol of family authority is the rod (Proverbs 13:24), while the symbol of church authority is the keys (Matthew 16:19), and for the State, the sword (Romans 13:4). Laws found in Scripture give parents the authority to exercise discipline over a child with a rod but not over an erring brother in Christ. This authority belongs to the church. The church can discipline a member but cannot use the rod or wield the sword as punishment. The church has the power of the "keys" to bar unrepentant members from the Lord's table and finally to excommunicate them if they remain unrepentant (Matthew 18:15-20). The State has authority to wield the sword as punishment for capital offenses, but it cannot use its authority to influence the inner workings of the family or church. These "institutions" are outside the State's jurisdiction. If, however, a family member commits a crime (as defined by Scripture) the State may have jurisdiction unless voluntary restitution is made.

These various institutions must often defer judgment to the more legitimate area of jurisdiction. Jesus' words in Luke 20:22-25 establish the authority of the State and also set the boundaries for its civil jurisdiction. John Eidsmoe comments on Jesus' answer to those seeking to impale Him on what they considered an unreconcilable dilemma:

> Christ's words constituted a jurisdictional limit upon the state. He did not say there are things that Caesar would be wise or honorable or generous to leave alone. Rather, He said that some things do not belong to Caesar, but to God. Since things do not belong to Caesar, he has no jurisdiction whatsoever over them. This probably refers, at least in part, to the emperor's demand that all citizens worship

him as though he were a god. No Caesar has the right to make any such demand, and if Caesar does make such a demand, he is to be resisted even unto death (see Exodus 1:17-21; Daniel 3; Daniel 6; Acts 4:13-21; Acts 5:29) (*God and Caesar*, p. 16).

When the church disciplines a local church member over an ecclesiastical matter, the State cannot rightly be approached to use its authority to override what the disciplined member might consider an unfair decision. Even the jurisdictional boundaries of ecclesiastical bodies must be respected, though this is difficult in a multi-denominational context. When one church disciplines a member and excommunicates that member, it is the duty of other ecclesiastical bodies to respect the jurisdiction of the disciplining ecclesiastical court.

Self-government is the foundation upon which all other governments gain their strength and stability. When a nation is filled with self-governed families, we can expect vitality and security in all other governments to flourish, church and State included.

Jurisdictional authority can only be understood when the biblical "chain of authority" is considered. This follows under the theology of "headship": "But I want you to understand that Christ is the head of every man, and the man is the head of a woman, and God is the head of Christ" (1 Corinthians 11:3). In Ephesians 5:23 Jesus is said to be the "head of the church." In the book of Revelation Jesus is designated "the ruler of the kings of the earth" (Revelation 1:5; Psalm 72). In all these cases we find everyone responsible to someone else, and ultimately all are responsible to God. Even Jesus in His humanity, as the Son of God, is under the headship of His Father (Luke 22:42).

7. We begin by defining culture, a word which possesses limited meaning in our day. Culture often offers visions of refinement, of having particular tastes in the fine arts, humanities, and broad aspects of science as distinguished from vocational and technical skills. The biblical definition of culture, however, is as broad as the world. Adam and Eve were commanded to "*cultivate*" the garden and all creation (Genesis 1:28; 2:10-15; 9:7; Psalm 8 and Hebrews 2), i.e., to bring forth the potentialities of the garden (cf. Hebrews 6:7). We can cultivate family, business, church, and social relationships. Henry Van Til provides a comprehensive definition of culture with these words:

It denotes the labor bestowed upon the earth to prepare it for seeding (Gen. 2:15). Man was to belabor the good earth so that under the blessing of God it might bring forth its fruit. This was called *agriculture*. We also speak of the tending of bees as *api-culture*, that of birds as *avi-culture* and of horses *equi-culture*. This list could be extended indefinitely, inasmuch as man has brought the world of created things under cultivation. . . . Today we use the word "culture" of any human labor bestowed on God's creation in its widest sense, including man himself (voice culture, physical culture, etc.), by which it receives historical forms and is refined to a higher level of productivity for the enjoyment of man. Culture, then, is any and all human effort and labor expended upon the cosmos, to unearth its treasures and its riches and bring them into the service of man for the enrichment of human existence unto the glory of God (*The Calvinistic Concept of Culture*, p. 29f.)

Of course all culture, as everything else in the world, has been affected by sin (Genesis 3:17, 18; Romans 8:20-22). "Hence, irrespective of whether [culture] is practiced by dedicated Christians or by absolute infidels, all art, all poetry, all science, all philosophy (and, let us hasten to add, all theology too) displays the disfiguring marks of sin to a greater or lesser extent. Even the very ploughing of the wicked is evil (Prov. 21:4); whatsoever is not of faith, is sin (Rom. 14:23); and even all the righteousness of the people of God are but filthy rags! (Isa. 64:6)" (Francis Nigel Lee, *The Central Significance of Culture*, p. 7).

When the word of God confronts culture in its fallen state, either the traditions that brought about present culture must give way to Scripture or Scripture must be conformed to culture. Of course, all cultural enterprises *must* give way to the absolutes of God's word. Culture, then, is "religion externalized." Religion is not a *part* of culture or just one aspect of culture. Rather, religion gives expression to what we define as culture. Religion — man's fundamental world and life view — *produces* culture. The particulars of cultural expression can be traced back to the religious ideas giving culture its meaning.

[Religion] does not so much consummate culture as give culture its foundation, and serves as the presupposition of every culture. Even when faith and religious root are openly denied, it is nevertheless tacitly operative as in atheistic Communism. A truly secular [non-religious] culture has never been found, and it is doubtful whether American Materialism can be called secular. Even Communism, like Nazism, has its gods and devils, its sin and salvation, its priests and its liturgies, its paradise of the stateless society of the future. For religious faith always transcends culture and is the integrating principle and power of man's cultural striving (Henry R. Van Til, *The Calvinistic Concept of Culture*, p. 39).

The study of any culture will lead to the religion that spawned it. The authoritative word of God must evaluate all that a culture is and if necessary turn it upside down (cf. Acts 17:6); that is, Scripture must empty it of the pagan religious first principles (presuppositions) that brought it into being.

A secularist will make religion a *part* of culture, along with music, art, and literature. The British anthropologist Sir Edward Tylor states that culture is "that complex whole which includes knowledge, belief, art, morals, law, custom, and any other capabilities and habits acquired by man as a member of society" (*Primitive Culture*, p. 1). Belief, or religion, is not a *part* of culture, but, rather, is the basis for knowledge, arts, morals, law, custom, etc. In short, religion is the *basis and source* of culture. Why does a member of society choose the things he chooses to create a culture? What foundational principles are utilized in his evaluation process? Religion is at the root of it all.

When the Bible confronts a non-Christian culture it confronts another religion, another authority. Of course, some cultural traditions do not clash with biblical authority. For example, automotive driving is restricted to the left side of roads in England, while the United States restricts driving to the right side. If a culture left rules for driving to individual motorists, that culture would have to change its system to conform with scriptural principles relating to safety. "Britons may indeed drive to the left and Americans to the right, but what underlies each statute is not whim or happenstance, but the principle of the value of human life and property. There is no love for neighbor or regard for life and property if one drives on all sides of the road or down the middle" (Carl F.H. Henry, *God, Revelation and Authority*, VI:442f.)

The case laws of Exodus 21-23 instruct us to respect the property of others and live in such a way as to insure their safety (e.g., Exodus 21:33-36). The idea that order and consistency must prevail is an absolute found in God's word.

The following statement shows how biblical authority is jettisoned and the prevailing culture is made absolute: "The Scriptures teach respect for the property of others (Exod. 20:15, 17; Mark 10:19; Rom. 2:21; Eph. 4:28) *but do not prescribe what things are or are not to be considered private property. This is left up to each culture*" (Stephen A. Grunlan, "Biblical Authority and Cultural Relativity," in *Christian Perspectives on Sociology*, p. 59. Emphasis mine.). The Bible teaches respect for property and prescribes what constitutes private property. This is why there are laws concerning the theft of oxen, sheep, and the misuse of borrowed property (Exodus 22:1-15). No culture can arbitrarily determine what is or is not property, just as no culture can define what constitutes order. If a culture could arbitrarily determine or redefine what constitutes private property,

While Daniel was in a pagan culture, he did not allow that pagan culture to squeeze him into its mold. *But Daniel made up his mind that he would not defile himself with the king's choice food or with the wine which he drank; so he sought permission from the commander of the officials that he might not defile himself* (Daniel 1:8).

then it could arbitrarily define that which is not private property, and no one's property would be safe; the economic security and freedom of the people would collapse. History is filled with examples of all-powerful central governments arbitrarily determining what constitutes private property. For example, Ahab wanted Naboth's vineyard. The law stated it was Naboth's to do with as the law of God stipulated. According to Stephen A. Grunlan, Ahab and Jezebel had a legitimate case against Naboth. Naboth was stubborn and should have sold his property. In fact, he probably should have given it away, since culture determines what constitutes property. Individuals, families, churches, businesses, and the State should not arbitrarily establish what is real property. The Bible must be our guide.

Adam and Eve took property that belonged to God even though they were given control of the Garden as a stewardship. They were to be the builders of culture on God's terms. God's word, however, is the determiner of what culture *ought* to be. When the Israelites entered the promised land, Scripture was to be their guide, not the Canaanites: "This book of the law shall not depart from your mouth, but you shall meditate on it day and night, so that you may be careful to do according to all that is written in it; for then you will make your way prosperous, and then you will have success" (Joshua 1:8).

This book of the law shall not depart from your mouth, but you shall meditate on it day and night, so that you may be careful to do according to all that is written in it; for then you will make your way prosperous, and then you will have success (Joshua 1:8).

Louis XIV (1643-1715) was an enemy of biblical authority. He consolidated absolute power in himself. He chose the sun as the symbol of his reign and was called the Sun King. His own words — *I am the State* — are ample testimony of his war with God and biblical authority.

Lesson 2

The Enemies of Biblical Authority

Authority is never neutral! Claims to authority rest upon religious presuppositions (presupposed ideas about the fundamental nature of reality). When a clash among competing authorities develops, the battle follows religious lines, because competing authorities "say" contradictory things about the fundamental nature of reality. Those who seek to overthrow existing authority structures do so in the name of morality, goodness, and right. These purveyors of the new order fight their battle with religious zeal and contrast the evil old order with the righteous new. The old order is assumed to be despotic, tyrannical, and repressive, while the new order will bring about liberty, freedom, fairness, and equality. Those rulers who "take counsel together against the LORD and against His anointed" (Psalm 2:2b) want to rid themselves of the old way. They see God's manner of living as being shackled by "fetters" and "cords" (v. 3).

The religious and political rulers of Jesus' day understood the religious character of authority. When Jesus in effect put religious leaders on notice that their authority was suspect, they knew the battle lines were being drawn: "By what authority are You doing these things, and who gave You this authority?" (Matthew 21:23). When Jesus identified His authority with that of His Father, "The Jews took up stones again to stone Him" (John 10:31). Their hostility resulted from Jesus' claims to divine sanction for His actions: "You, being a man, make Yourself out to be God" (John 10:33). Jesus based His authority on His Father's authority, and on Himself as God in human flesh (cf. Mark 2:1-12). The religious and political rulers of His time based their authority on their own man-made traditions. In effect, they had become "gods walking on earth."

Pontius Pilate, a staunch political leader, also understood the religious character of authority. Rome had established itself as the voice of the gods. Pilate, therefore, spoke on behalf of the gods, or so he thought: "Do you not know that I have authority to release You, and I have authority to crucify You?" (John 19:10) Jesus made it clear that Pilate's appeal to authority was groundless as long as it resided in man: "You would have no authority over Me, unless it had been given you from above" (John 19:11). Pilate's appeal to authority was hostile to the rightful authority that Jesus possessed and that God delegates to earthly institutions and rulers. The early church also understood the religious character of authority and put it into practice when Christians obeyed God rather than men (Acts 4:19; 5:29). Neutrality is not an option in the ongoing battles among authorities claiming ultimacy.

There are those, of course, who deny that they need any form of authority. They are the popular atheists and agnostics. Such men say that they must be shown by 'reason' whatever they are to accept as true. But the great thinkers among non-Christian men have taken no such position. They know that they cannot cover the whole area of reality with their knowledge.

—Cornelius Van Til

The religious and political leaders of Jesus' day were in positions of authority because the people wanted what they claimed they could offer. While liberty had been promised in previous times, tyranny was the present effect of those feeble promises. God-ordained authority was rejected for a supposed liberating authority that would free both church and State.

The shift from one authority to another was not an overnight happening. There were degrees of change. For most people these changes were imperceptible. There is, however, always one common denominator when change occurs

— authority always shifts from the absolute of God's word to some standard based upon the fallen character of man. Man himself becomes the final authority. The belief is that by rejecting the absolute authority of God and His word one can be liberated from its demands.

The shift begins when we equate the word of God with some other authority, putting both on an equal footing. For example, throughout church history "Nature" or "Natural Law" has been considered normative for determining how ethical decisions ought to be made without the need for Scripture. We are told, in fact, that Natural Law is almost identical with Scripture. Laws found in the natural realm can be used by Christians and non-Christians to develop, let us say, a just political order. In time, however, we find the appeal to "Natural Law" rather than Biblical law because unbelievers can better identify with a "neutral" law system that does not rest on "religious" presuppositions (so they think). This, we are told, is less offensive to the unconverted.

Scripture was once used to interpret nature because the created order is fallen. While creation speaks of the glory of God (Psalm 19:1-3), it cannot give us the particulars — especially the moral absolutes and laws — necessary for law, business, politics, education, art, medicine, and technology. Again, we are told, it is much easier to address the unbeliever through reason than through special revelation, the Bible. These two major shifts, (1) Nature is equal to Scripture and (2) the mind can replace Scripture as an interpretive standard, set the scene for a multiplicity of competing authorities to arise, all vying for ultimacy. With multiple authorities competing with one another, public opinion, history, elite opinion, feelings generated by personal desires and/or guilt, tradition, and circumstances require an ultimate single standard of authority to clear up the confusion. Rarely is Scripture appealed to at this point. As public opinion shifts, and the confusion of competing authorities increases, there is an appeal for some central power to settle the authority question. Those able to convince the masses that they hold the expertise and wield the greatest power will determine what authority will once again be ultimate.

We trust those who claim to be "in the know." History shows us that many political leaders sought the advice of an elitist class to establish authority for their revolutionary ideas. If the people can be convinced that the "experts" have the answers and the power to implement their "solutions," they will give up nearly everything to be saved from authority confusion. For example, Lenin's entire life was spent among the members of his own sub-class, the

37

bourgeois intelligentsia, which he saw as a uniquely privileged priesthood, endowed with a special gnosis [knowledge] and chosen by History for a decisive role. Socialism, he wrote quoting Karl Kautsky, was the product of "profound scientific knowledge . . . . The vehicle of [this] science is not the proletariat but the bourgeois intelligentsia: contemporary socialism was born in the heads of individual members of this class" (Paul Johnson, *Modern Times: The World from the Twenties to the Eighties*, p. 52).

In time, Lenin was able to capture the nation by concentrating authority in himself and convincing the masses that the "new" authority was "better." He was so sure of his position that he named those who followed his authoritative expertise, the "majority" (*Bolsheviks*). He did this in 1903 when they were clearly in the minority of even revolutionary Communists. The old regime was overthrown. The new authority, based on "a special knowledge," would bring in a new era. How can the uninformed expect to compete with such specialized knowledge? The impression one gets is that if you are not part of the "guild," then your ability to add anything relevant is questioned or denied.

Prior to the Reformation of the 16th century, the ability to know was reserved by an elitist religious class. The church was the reservoir of knowledge and thus the final authority and dispenser of truth. The people were dependent upon the church for specialized theological wisdom. Even the Bible was reserved for the church and was not translated into the language of the people. It remained in Latin until some dared to translate it. Some lost their lives in the attempt.

Educational advances brought about by the printing press changed all of that. Books became a Protestant tool to change western Europe and eventually the New World. The ideas of the early reformers were propagated by pamphleteers who carried the truths of the Bible far and wide. No longer was knowledge held by the few. Even anti-biblical revolutionary movements understand the necessity of transmitting their views to the masses. "Lenin, as purposeful as ever, had two major objectives: first, to unify the Russian Socialists under his leadership, and, second, to get a newspaper of his own, an essential component of any communications network in the era before radio and television" (John P. Roche, "The History and Impact of Marxist-Leninist Organizational Theory," *Foreign Policy Report*, April 1984, p. 14).

Of course, there are experts in a number of fields to whom we should look for expertise, but only when their views square with biblical absolutes. But, theirs is

38

not the final word. Too often the elitist despises the majority, believing only the privileged few are gifted enough to determine the way we should go. The majority is to follow blindly.

The danger in warning about elitism is to go too far in the other direction, to raise the majority to the position of ethical decision-making as opposed to the arbitrary decisions of the elite. The egalitarian wishes to level authority to the group. To him all opinions are equal. Rushdoony writes:

> Now Scripture gives no justification for an equalitarian order, and it also gives no ground whatsoever for an elitist order. Only a godly order, established in terms of Biblical law, is tenable in terms of Scripture. Elitism and equalitarianism are alike humanistic; they move in terms of man and man's hopes. The Bible is heedless of either philosophy. Scripture requires a God-centered society, one in which God's law militates against equalitarian and elitist goals. Both equalitarianism and elitism are in essence contemptuous of man in the name of man. The elitist despises the majority of man, and the equalitarian despises all able and independent men, but, in essence, both despise all men as men and love rather their *idea* of men, not man himself in the singular (*Institutes of Biblical Law*, p. 179).

Neither the opinions of the majority nor those of the elite few can rightly replace the word of God. There are some, however, who look to experts as the final authority on various ethical issues. Such thinking places the finite character of man, no matter how skilled, on the same level as the word of God.

> They are like the Pharisees who taught that God gave Moses not only a written law but also an oral one, handed down through the generations to only the privileged few. This was the key to the power of the Pharisees: they had the knowledge to unlock the meaning of the Pentateuch, to be recipients of wisdom had by no others. Not possessing esoteric knowledge, the masses have no choice but to turn their lives over to the elite to be managed (Herbert Schlossberg, *Idols for Destruction*, p. 195).

The will of the individual, the group, a skilled elite or a political body must submit to the unchanging authority of Scripture. Where the individual claims ultimate authority, a nation heads toward anarchy. When the group clamors for ultimacy statism results. Neither the individual nor the group can claim sole authority.

A number of authorities compete for our allegiance. In each case, we move away from the *benchmark* of Scripture. The problem in identifying counterfeit ultimate authorities is that they often *seem* reliable. If we fail to identify the only true ultimate and unchanging authority, we open ourselves to the persuasiveness of other seemingly viable authorities. The topic of authority unquestionably is religious in nature; it deals with ultimate values and claims total allegiance; it is the god of that system claiming ultimacy; it is the law-giver.

Martin Luther holds the Bible for all to see: the artists and artisans; philosophers and musicians; debators and explorers; scholars and scientists. Scripture is the standard for all that a man thinks or does. For a civilization to continue, all of life must be centered around the word of God.

Questions for Discussion

1. What relationship exists between *reason* and authority? (Romans 10:2; 1:18-32; 1 Peter 1:13; Ephesians 2:1; 2 Corinthians 4:4; Romans 3:11; 8:7; 1 Corinthians 2:14; Psalm 32:9; 73:21, 22; Romans 12:1, 2; Ephesians 4:17, 18; Colossians 2:8; Isaiah 1:18)

_____

_____

_____

_____

_____

_____

_____

2. In what way can *conscience* be an enemy of biblical authority? (1 Samuel 24:5; 2 Samuel 24:10; Job 27:6; Jeremiah 17:9; 1 Corinthians 4:4; Romans 2:14, 15; Acts 23:1; 1 Timothy 1:5, 19; 3:9; Hebrews 13:18; 1 Peter 3:16, 21; John 8:9; Romans 2:15; Titus 1:15; Hebrews 10:22; 1 Timothy 4:2; Matthew 23:4)

_____

_____

_____

_____

_____

_____

_____

3. In what way can *emotions* or *feelings* be an enemy of biblical authority? (John 10:35; Ephesians 4:30; Exodus 20:5; 32:19; Ephesians 4:26; Numbers 20:8-11)

_____

_____

_____

_____

_____

4. In what way can *natural law* or *natural theology* be an enemy of biblical authority? (Genesis 3:15ff; Romans 8:20-23; 1 Corinthians 1:22; 2:14; Romans 1:18; Acts 17:32; Colossians 2:8)

_____

_____

_____

_____

_____

_____

5. In what way can *circumstances* or *experience* be enemies of biblical authority? (Luke 24:11; John 20:24-29; Numbers 13 and Joshua 2:8-11; John 9:2-12; Romans 8:28; Acts 28:1-6)

_____

_____

_____

_____

_____

_____

6. In what way can *tradition* be an enemy of biblical authority? (1 Corinthians 11:2; 2 Thessalonians 2:15; Mark 7:3-9)

_____

_____

_____

_____

_____

7. In what way can *public opinion* or the *will of the people* be an enemy of biblical authority? (Exodus 23:2; Numbers 14; Isaiah 30:9-11)

_____

_____

_____

_____

_____

_____

Summary

"The teachings of Scripture are the final court of appeal for ethics. Human reason, church tradition, and the natural and social sciences may aid moral reflection, but divine revelation, found in the canonical Scriptures of the Old and New Testaments, constitutes the 'bottom line' of the decision making process. Informed ethical reflection will carefully weigh the various words of men, both past and present, but the Word of God must cast the deciding vote. Evangelicals believe that the canonical Scriptures are the very Word of God, the only infallible and inerrant rule of faith and practice, and consequently are the highest authority for both doctrine and morals" (John Jefferson Davis, *Evangelical Ethics: Issues Facing the Church Today*, p. 9).

The Israelites were corrupted by Egyptian ways. For them, ethics was not based on the will of God but on the desires of men. *And [Aaron]. . . fashioned it with a graving tool, and made it a molten calf; and they said, "This is your god, O Israel, who brought you up from the land of Egypt"* (Exodus 32:4).

Answers to Questions for Discussion

1. Man's ability to reason independently often is considered to be a trustworthy standard of ultimate authority. For many, the touchstone of authority rests with, "Is it reasonable?" But who defines what is reasonable? If a decision does not agree with *one's* way of thinking, with *one's* view of right and wrong, it cannot be reasonable and, therefore, is not true. Who is to decide what is reasonable when two "reasonable" people fail to agree on an issue?

The history of non-Christian philosophical thought — with many conflicting philosophies and schools of thought — offers perfect proof that reason alone is hardly an adequate starting point in making ethical decisions. This becomes even more obvious when we consider that the inevitable course or "development" of man-centered philosophical thought (or religious philosophy) moves from man's claim to knowledge on his own to skepticism and doubt regarding man's ability to know *anything* for certain. Such conflict occurred in ancient and medieval times and is reoccurring in our day. When a self-styled, independent thinker investigates the insolvable problems which are involved in attempting to know anything on his own in a Godless world, man *always* arrives at skepticism, or at outright denial of his ability to know anything by his unaided reason. Only the acceptance of God's own revealed word (Scripture) can break this self-destructive philosophical cycle and allow man to know that he truly *can* know.

On the other hand, the Christian-based authority, Scripture, prevents an individual from developing an unhealthy irrationalism where thinking is abandoned in favor of mysticism or intuition, or one's whims or feelings. The mind certainly is the *vehicle* God uses to transmit His revelation to us, but the mind never is the *standard* by which we determine the reliability of that revelation.

Too often, however, we believe without thinking or distort the thinking process by denying God as the reference point for right thinking. The Apostle Paul warns that even our zeal for God can be unfounded when true knowledge is ignored or suppressed: "For I bear them witness that they have a zeal for God, but not in accordance with knowledge" (Romans

44

10:2; 1:18-23). There are many who believe in "God," but it is a god of their own imagination (Romans 1:24-32). Their minds are "depraved" (Romans 1:28).

Peter tells us to gird our minds for action (1 Peter 1:13). Scripture informs us that the mind is necessary for proving what the will of God is, but that vehicle of determination, the mind, is in a state of disrepair and is in need of renewal (Romans 12:2). R. J. Rushdoony rightly observes: "The Christian is not hostile to reason as reason, but to Reason as god. The Christian does not believe in reason; he believes in God and uses reason under God" (*The Word of Flux*, p. 36). The unregenerate man is spiritually dead in "trespasses and sins" (Ephesians 2:1); the "god of this world has blinded the minds of the unbelieving" (2 Corinthians 4:4); the rebellious has his mind "set on the flesh" and therefore is "hostile toward God" (Romans 8:7); he does not understand (Romans 3:11) and in reality, "cannot understand" the things of God (1 Corinthians 2:14).

Martin Luther (c.1483-1546) wrote: *If I profess with the loudest voice and clearest exposition every portion of the truth except precisely that little point which the world and the devil are at that moment attacking, I am not confessing Christ, however boldly I may be professing Christ.*

Of course, there is danger in depreciating the mind, and embracing a "mindless" Christianity. Some believe "because it is impossible" (attributed to Tertullian, c. 160-240). One attribute that separates man from animals is man's ability to reason: "Do not be as the horse or as the mule which have no understanding, whose trappings include bit and bridle to hold them in check. . ." (Psalm 32:9). The ethically rebellious are compared to non-rational animals: "When my heart was embittered, and I was pierced within, then I was senseless and ignorant; I was like a beast before Thee" (Psalm 73:21, 22; cf. Daniel 4:28-33). The mind must be brought into proper focus; it is fallen but not eradicated. The mind is indispensable. God has revealed His redemptive message through words to our minds. We need ears to hear, eyes to see, and a mind to understand.

But some will say: But I have "the mind of Christ" (1 Corinthians 2:16) so I do not need to concern myself with reason, logic, and right thinking. Having "the mind of Christ" means having an ethical standard by which we judge all things. The mind of Christ is *imputed* to us like righteousness is *imputed*. We are not *made* righteous when we come to Christ; we are *declared* righteous. Being declared righteous is not the end of our new life in Christ. We are to work out what it means to be righteous. This is called sanctification. Sanctification should effect you as an individual, how you deal with other people, your family, business associates, the church, and civil government. The same is true in having "the mind of Christ." Working out what it means to have the mind of Christ is essential to the Christian who must battle contrary ideologies on a daily basis.

Christians are instructed, therefore, to "renew" their minds (Romans 12:2) and to "walk no longer just as the Gentiles also walk, in the futility of their mind, being darkened in their understanding, excluded from the life of God, because of the ignorance that is in them, because of the hardness of their heart" (Ephesians 4:17, 18). Renewal comes by "the washing of regeneration and renewing by the Holy Spirit" (Titus 3:5). The Holy Spirit regenerates and makes the heart and mind new. We were once dead in trespasses and sins, but now we are alive unto God (Ephesians 2:1). The newness of life, however, does not make us independent thinkers. As Christians, we still are subject to the final authority of God's word.

Renewal of the mind never should be seen as a means of freeing

Christians from reliance on God as our unswerving and certain standard of authority. The Apostle Paul, who was able to debate the philosophers of his day (Acts 17), warned us about the deceitfulness of reasoning independently of God: "See to it that no one takes you captive through philosophy and empty deception, according to the tradition of men, according to the elementary principles of the world, rather than according to Christ" (Colossians 2:8). For the Christian, therefore, "human reason is neither an autonomous master nor a useless appendage, but a servant of the resurrected Christ in the work of the extension of his kingdom. According to the biblical story human reason, like man himself, is the good creation of God, now subject to the power and bondage of sin, and yet renewable through the work of Christ and the Holy Spirit" (John Jefferson Davis, *Foundations of Evangelical Theology*, p. 130).

God calls us to "reason together" (Isaiah 1:18), not as equal partners but as Independent and all-knowing Creator and dependent and ignorant creatures.

2. In addition to reason, a number of authorities are proposed as viable ways of determining the rightness or wrongness of a particular issue independently of Scripture. Each of these proposed authorities offers some elements of truth. A conscience governed by the word of God is trustworthy. Public opinion, when expressed in accord with *biblical* opinion, can be a worthwhile force against statist oppression. But when men propose these and other authorities as ultimate and independent of the word of God, the Christian must be ready and able to subordinate them to his only reliable rule of faith and practice, the written word of God.

We often hear, "Let your conscience be your guide" because our conscience often convicts us of wrong doing and helps us discern proper moral behavior.

Conscience is an inner self-knowledge which is moral in character. By it man knows instinctively and constitutionally that there are at the same time a distinction between right and wrong and an obligation to choose what is right and refuse what is wrong. That is why a person who conducts his life in accordance with what he knows to be just and honorable is called conscientious. The conscience is a line connecting man to his Creator: it is one aspect of

King Solomon knew that he could not depend on his conscience as a reliable guide to make decisions that would affect Israel and surrounding nations. Scripture is the guide for kings and kingdoms.

the image of God in which man was created (Philip Edgcumbe Hughes, *Christian Ethics in Secular Society*, p. 27).

The Old Testament does not have a word for "conscience," but expresses the idea of conscience as a "troubled heart": "And it came about afterward that David's conscience bothered [Lit., *heart struck*] him because he had cut off the edge of Saul's robe" (1 Samuel 24:5), and "Now David's heart troubled [Lit., *smote*] him after he had numbered the people" (2 Samuel 24:10). Job

As with the mind, the conscience never can be a completely trustworthy guide if it operates outside the realm of biblical authority. How do you know when conscience gives proper direction? Scripture tells us "the heart is more deceitful than all else and is desperately sick; who can understand it?" (Jeremiah 17:9). The desire to detach the conscience from biblical authority leads to deification of the creature. "*Conscience* means responsibility with reference to right and wrong; conscience implies creaturehood and subjection. Conscience must be under authority, or it ceases to be conscience and becomes a god. The humanistic desire to live beyond good and evil is actually a desire to live beyond responsibility and beyond conscience. Under the facade of conscience, an assault is launched against conscience and authority" (Rousas J. Rushdoony, *Institutes of Biblical Law*, p. 122).

The following example shows the danger of allowing conscience to become the final voice of authority in decision- making. "In Utica (N.Y.) Msgr. John R. Madden, an official of the diocese of Syracuse, voted, as a member of a regional health commission, to allocate Federal funds to Planned Parenthood for the performance of abortions. When challenged, Msgr. Madden said that he had voted according to his *conscience*" (James Hitchcock, "The Dissenting Church," in *Bad News for Modern Man* by Franky Schaeffer, p. 179). He set his conscience over the clear statements of biblical revelation. The murder of the unborn is condoned because his conscience was his guide.

The biblical concept of conscience is related to the authority of God's perfect judgment. Paul emphatically declares that no man's conscience, nor any human court is qualified to judge the things of God: "I am conscious [*synoida*, the Greek verb form of the noun *syneidesis*, "conscience"] of nothing against myself, yet I am not by this acquitted; but the one who examines me is the Lord" (1 Corinthians 4:4). Paul makes it clear that even his conscience should be evaluated in the light of Scripture, for the Lord is his final judge.

Man's conscience, however, certainly was not obliterated because of the fall. Unbelievers, because they are created in the image of God, still must contend with their consciences: "For when Gentiles who do not have the Law do instinctively the things of the Law, these, not having the Law, are a law to themselves, in that they show the work of the Law written in their hearts, their conscience bearing witness, and their thoughts alternately accusing or defending them" (Romans 2:14, 15). The "work of the Law written" on the heart testifies that those without Special Revelation (the Bible) are guilty before God and cannot avoid the implications of God's law. The conscience gives *joint* witness to the "things of the law." John Murray writes: "Conscience may approve or disapprove. When it approves we have a good or pure conscience (*cf.* Acts 23:1; I Tim. 1:5, 19; 3:9; Heb. 13:18; I Pet. 3:16, 21). When conscience disapproves and convicts of sin then we have a bad or guilty conscience (*cf.* John 8:9; Rom. 2:15; Tit. 1:15; Heb. 10:22)" (*The Epistle to the Romans*, II:2).

But we must keep in mind that the conscience often is an unreliable witness, because of sin. Though the mind operates, despite sin having entered the world, the conscience also operates, with the same sinful effect. The conscience can be mistaken, even "seared" (1 Timothy 4:2). As unbelieving men and women rebel against God their consciences lose much ethical sensitivity: "To the pure, all things are pure; but to those who are defiled and unbelieving, nothing is pure, but both their mind and their conscience are defiled. They profess to know God, but by their deeds they deny Him, being detestable and disobedient, and worthless for any good deed" (Titus 1:15, 16; cf. Romans 1:18-32). In the final analysis only Scripture, God's objective standard of authority, can determine infallibly what is right and wrong.

The individual with a "seared" conscience seeks to remove God's divine image by suppressing the truth in unrighteousness (Romans 1:18). The more one denies God, the more the conscience hardens. The Christian with a "weak conscience" has not jettisoned the traditions of men as his standard of righteousness. Because of the shed blood of Jesus Christ, the conscience is purified "from dead works to serve the living

God" (Hebrews 9:14). When an individual becomes a Christian he recognizes he no longer can be his own standard of authority as he once desired. He must submit his entire being to Christ's lordship.

The conscience should be "listened to" when it convicts us of sin. But, we must not assume our "speaking" conscience is correct in its assessment of every action we might take or every idea we might want to implement. Do we feel guilty (is our conscience "smitten" or "pricked") because of actual sin, or have we been made to "feel" guilty because of an arbitrary ethical standard imposed on us? Is our conscience manipulated because we do not know biblical truth on a particular issue? Many times people who claim to know what is right place unreasonable (unbiblical) demands on others. When these demands cannot be met, guilt ensues. Jesus condemned the Scribes and Pharisees because "they tie up heavy loads, and lay them on men's shoulders; but they themselves are unwilling to move them with so much as a finger" (Matthew 23:4). The only remedy for these "guilt-manipulators" is a conscience firmly grounded in Scripture. The conscience never should be ignored, but neither should it be manipulated by self-professed purveyors of morality. "A godly conscience, informed by the word of God, leads men into a productive life and into a freedom before God. Conscience having its origin in God's creative act, can only thrive under God's law" (Rousas J. Rushdoony, *Revolt Against Maturity*, p. 272).

3. As with the mind and conscience, our emotions are distorted because of mankind's fall into sin. This does not mean we deny our emotions a proper role in the way we live; doctrine and life are interrelated. We are whole human beings, made up of mind, emotions, and body. No aspect of our being should be depreciated. But since we are fallen creatures, we cannot elevate one aspect of our nature above another as a standard of ultimate authority.

One problem with following our "feelings" is that it "tends to put the emotional cart before the intellectual horse. That is the problem of subjectivity — making decisions on the basis of one's interpretation of inward impulses (feelings) and other 'road signs' that cannot be objectively verified. While the emotional element is real, it is misinterpreted because the process has been turned inside out. . . . One's own feelings

51

are not an authoritative source of direction for making decisions. But because they are mistakenly taken as divine guidance, they are often regarded as being authoritative" (Gary Friesen, *Decision Making and the Will of God*, p. 248).

The family is a government that must rest on the sure foundation of Scripture if it is to survive. All decisions must be taken to the benchmark of Scripture for what ought to be done.

When we abandon the Bible as our ultimate authority, feelings and emotions can take over (the same could be said about the intellect). Many of us are moved emotionally by situations that should be evaluated from a biblical perspective. The young, unmarried woman who becomes pregnant often appeals to our emotions, hoping we will abandon a "hard line" on the abortion issue in favor of her "special" set of circumstances. We must ignore this initial tug at the heart strings in favor of an absolute and reliable ethic. Our initial emotional response may be either right or wrong. Only a thorough biblical treatment of the issue of abortion (or any issue) should determine what *ought* to be done.

The Bible tells us not to "pity" the guilty (Deuteronomy 13:8; 19:13, 21). Pity, however, is appropriate in other instances (Joel 2:18). Paul tells us that we are to be angry and yet not sin (Ephesians 4:26), but he warns us to put away "all bitterness and wrath and *anger* and clamor and slander" (v. 31). What is the difference? Anger motivated by the word of God is right; anger prompted by our own feelings of right and wrong must be put away. John R. W. Stott directs us to Scripture and the proper role emotions play. Here he discusses anger:

I go further and say that there is a great need in the contemporary world for more Christian anger. We human beings compromise with sin in a way in which God never does. In the face of blatant evil we should be indignant not tolerant, angry not apathetic. If God hates sin, his people should hate it too. If evil arouses his anger, it should arouse ours also. "Hot indignation seizes me because of the wicked, who forsake thy law" [Psalm 119:53]. What other reaction can wickedness be expected to provoke in those who love God? (*God's New Society: The Message of Ephesians*, p. 186).

Jesus was angry on a number of occasions (e.g., Mark 3:5; John 2:13-17); but His anger never led to sin, because Scripture governed His emotions.

Scripture deals with a number of concepts usually defined as emotions: grief, joy, sorrow, awe, fear, anxiety, woe, happiness, love, anger, etc. These "emotions" do not exist in an ethical vacuum but in response to an event, idea or circumstance: "Jesus wept" when He learned of Lazarus' death (John 11:35). The "Holy Spirit of God" can be grieved because of our sin (Ephesians 4:30). God is said to be "jealous" for His own character (Exodus 20:5). Any "emotional" response can lead an individual astray unless a biblical reference point is first established. Grief can become despair; righteous indignation, contemptuous hate; and awe can become terror unless Scripture guides our every thought.

Unanchored emotions lead to moralism. *Moralism* is based on the false doctrine that man can justify his own worth before God by performing acts he believes ("feels") are moral. The following example of a woman deciding to abort her unborn baby typifies the results of emotions placed above biblical authority:

"What would have happened if I had not had the abortion? My husband maintains that I would have miscarried from the sheer weight of emotional stress. I maintain that the two of us would no longer be together, that our relationship would have cracked under the strain. Of course, only God knows what might have been. But I like to think that our decision was one in favor of dominion, a decision based on responsibility and discipleship" (*theOtherSide* [June 1980], p. 48, quoted by David Chilton in *Productive Christians in an Age of Guilt-Manipulators*, p. 140).

When we base our decision-making on feelings, we open ourselves to those who know how to manipulate people through appealing to a twisted conscience that has been prompted by emotions gone astray. Herbert Schlossberg here assesses emotionalism gone wild:

> The crowning irony of this thoroughly immoral age is that more than perhaps any other it is incessantly and unapologetically moralistic. There is nothing so brutal that it cannot be defended with the joyous trumpeting of self-righteous satisfaction. An invasion is called an act of love; destroying a village is an act of salvation; reducing a poor man to perpetual dependence or killing an infant an act of compassion. There are a few miserable little despots who do not use this language. No matter how vicious the action, the justification will be the promotion of equality, the helping of the poor, the protection against unfair competition, the extension of compassion, the defense against wicked imperialism or communism (*Idols for Destruction*, p. 267).

Our emotions, whatever they are and however great their intensity, must be brought captive to Christ. They must become Christian emotions. We must learn to take delight in things that God delights in and to repudiate what He hates.

4. There are two Natural Law traditions. The first tradition is Greek in origin and is usually credited to both Plato (428-347 B.C.) and Aristotle (384-322 B.C.). The Greeks, in particular Plato and Aristotle, reasoned that order and unity exist through the universe "naturally." Plato spoke of a creation and Aristotle postulated a Prime Mover. The Greeks based Natural Law entirely on reason. But, ultimately, who determines what is "reasonable"? In Plato's *Republic*, the State would be the arbiter of right and wrong and the protector of the common good. Children would be bred and reared by the State — or killed by the State — for State purposes. Aristotle believed there is a "higher law" in nature, but man had to use his reasoning abilities to discover it.

Natural Law is Greek and pagan in origin. Plato (428-347 B.C.) spoke of a natural order but did not envision a personal God who directed man through a transcendant law. For Plato, the State determines right and wrong.

There are two false assumptions here. First, nature is viewed as normative, not subjected to an ethical fall (Genesis 3:15ff.; Romans 8:20-23). But, nature is fallen; there is death, decay, and cruelty. Should we view this as normal and allow such cruelty to be part of our judicial system? For example, the animal creation fights for territory and kills other animals for food. Is this "natural"? What standard does one use to determine what is natural and what is not? Should such behavior be implemented into law?

Cursed nature is not normative, any more than fallen man is. We cannot look to nature and discover absolute standards of thought, absolute standards of law, or absolute standards of judgment. Even if cursed nature were normative, perverse men would

55

misinterpret nature. If Adam rebelled against the verbal revelation of God Himself, before he fell into sin, what should we expect from the sons of Adam, now that nature is cursed and no longer the same kind of revelation of God that it was in the garden?

It still testifies of God, as we read in Romans 1:18; man holds back the truth in active unrighteousness. But cursed nature is not the same open revelation of God that it once was, and we dare not use nature as an ethical, political, or any other kind of guidepost for building human institutions. We have to abandon "natural law" as a source of reliable information. Nature is cursed, and we are ethical rebels, spoiling for a fight or a misinterpretation. That's why we need the revelation of God in His word, the Bible, and through His Word, Jesus Christ (Gary North, *Unconditional Surrender*, p. 38).

The second fallacy is man's assumption that his reasoning abilities are intact and, therefore, that his mind is able to judge nature unhindered by rational distortion. Scripture tells us unbelievers suppress the truth in unrighteousness (Romans 1:18). The Apostle Paul also informs us that the "natural man does not accept the things of the Spirit of God; for they are

The god of Aristotle (384-322 B.C.) was impotent. While his god was the *first cause* (Prime Mover), law was left to man and his abilities to determine right from wrong.

56

foolishness to him, and he cannot understand them, because they are spiritually appraised" (1 Corinthians 2:14). Paul had the Greeks in mind when he stated that they "search for wisdom" (i.e., rational arguments independent of fixed absolutes) and reject God in the process (1 Corinthians 1:22). The Greeks mocked Paul when he spoke of the resurrection because it did not fit their world view (Acts 17:32). A Natural Law ethical or political theory holds no more than "empty deception" for those who adopt it: "See to it that no one takes you captive through philosophy and empty deception, according to the tradition of men, according to the elementary principles of the world, rather than according to Christ" (Colossians 2:8).

The second Natural Law tradition emerges from a synthesis of the Christian theory of law and Greek philosophy. Thomas Aquinas (1225-1274) assumed that man's mind was not radically affected by the fall and that Natural Law is nothing more than the rule of reason. The Natural Law theory presented by Aquinas was certainly more attractive than that of Aristotle since Aquinas equated Natural Law with Biblical Law. Aquinas' God was more than Aristotle's "Prime Mover"; He was the Creator and Savior of the world. Though this made the Natural Law theology of Aquinas much easier to accept, still it was only Aristotle and pagan Greece in disguise. Christians could discern a Natural Law because they viewed nature through the corrective lens of Scripture. Later, however, Natural Law was accepted as an independent law system, not subject to the evaluation of biblical law. Thus two ethical systems developed: one for the Christian (Biblical Law) and one for the non-Christian (Natural Law), leaving the State to operate with Natural Law while the church operates with Biblical Law. Of course, even Biblical Law was reduced to New Testament ethics, summarized as an abstract principle, "love." Archie Jones writes:

> Christian Natural Law. . . loses the specificity, concreteness, and applicability of Biblical Law, and becomes vague, abstract, and uncertain, and hence increasingly removed from the ken of the common man and increasingly useless as a guide to or restraint on Government. When combined with natural men freed to proclaim their naturally ungodly hearts' desires as law, this spells trouble. . . . Lacking clear, concrete, and detailed universals, those placed

in the ministry of government (Rom. 13:1-5) lack specific rules by which to rule ("Natural Law and Christian Resistance to Tyranny," in *Christianity and Civilization: The Theology of Christian Resistance*, pp. 111 and 112).

In effect, the Bible is excluded from all political consideration since there is a supposedly reliable "natural" law from which the State can build a just society. Reason coupled with the "natural order of things" supposedly supplies a reliable system by which a nation can be run. For example, Nazism rejected special revelation because it was unmovable and thus outside the power of the State to control. The philosophers of the day replaced special revelation with a natural revelation that could be controlled by the State. "A classic example of the claim that knowledge of God and His will is gained from general revelation is found in the ideology of Nazi Germany. Hitler's National Socialist propagandists appealed to the revelation of God in reason, conscience, and the orders of Creation as justification for the Nazi state theology or cultural religion. Biblical revelation in Old and New Testaments was regarded by the Third Reich as a 'Jewish Swindle' and thus was set aside in favor of Nazi natural theology" (Bruce A. Demarest, *General Revelation*, p. 15).

It is unfortunate that when the world is crying for absolute standards to help in decision-making, many Christians still appeal to Natural Law, knowing full well that its origins are pagan. Here is what passes for a "good system of ethics":

Natural law ethics are adequate to the task. The philosophy of natural law has been time honored since the *ancient Greeks*. Though intellectual fashions change, the objective moral order, *knowable* by man and within the reach of mankind, can be *reasonably* seen as the most stable basis of personal, national and international order and happiness (Connaught Marshner, "Right and Wrong and America's Survival," in *Future 21*, p. 129. Emphasis mine).

The author of this article admits that Natural Law comes from ancient Greece, where the philosophies of Plato and Aristotle placed man at the center of the universe. She goes on to say that they are "knowable by man" and "can be reasonably seen." Why then is there so much disagreement around the world as to what constitutes a just society if reason is so

58

"natural"? Reason certainly does not work in the Soviet Union or on a pro-abortionist. The murder of nearly 60 million people by Joseph Stalin (1879-1953), and the death of nearly two million unborn babies every year is the result of the repudiation of biblical law in favor of Natural Law. Natural Law is rooted in nature and nature is evolving to bring about the inevitable. What ever is, is right.

Those who advocate Natural Law see it as equal to biblical law. We are told that we need "both" standards. Mrs. Marshner continues:

If order is to be restored to society, and the underpinnings of freedom preserved, America must return to non-consequential ethics. What would be the basis for such ethics? Some say the sole possible basis is revealed religion. *This is a mistake. First of all, the Bible and other revealed documents do not answer explicitly all the ethical questions that arise.* . . (p. 128. Emphasis mine).

If revealed religion (the Bible) is not the "sole possible basis" for decision making, then what is? The Bible says "no one can serve two masters" (Matthew 6:24). The Apostle Paul writes that Christians are not to be unequally yoked with unbelievers (2 Corinthians 6:14). How then can Christians be unequally yoked with unbelieving ethical systems? "For what partnership have righteousness and lawlessness, or what fellowship has light with darkness? Or what harmony has Christ with Belial, or what has a believer in common with an unbeliever?" (vv. 14, 15)

Natural Law is flawed from its inception because it assumes that "nature" (creation) is not fallen, man's reasoning abilities are not distorted due to the fall, and ethics is based on "philosophy" and not "religious precepts." Again, Mrs. Marshner has little use for the Bible: "Citizens must defend their rights, and they must defend them intellectually, by employing and invoking an objective system of right and wrong. This new traditional system of ethics is based on *philosophical precepts, not on religious precepts, and can be understood and accepted by anyone willing to master the intellectual rigors of it*" (p. 132. Emphasis mine). Who will determine what an "objective system of right and wrong" will be? What if the precepts of the Bible are rejected by those "willing to master the intellectual rigors" of these "philosophical precepts"? If history is any indicator, the Bible will be rejected in favor of self-serving, humanistic Natural Law. Religion is an enemy to Natural Law. Stalin's words should

silence all who appeal to the supposed inherent reasonableness of Natural
Law:

> We guarantee the right of every citizen to combat by argument,
> propaganda and agitation, any and all religion. The Communist
> Party cannot be neutral toward religion. It stands for science, and
> all religion is opposed to science ("Declaration to American Labor
> Delegation," Moscow, September 7, 1927).

So much for objectivity, "non-consequential ethics," and "philosophical
precepts."

One last nail needs to be driven into the coffin of Natural Law. If
Natural Law is adequate as a basis for ethical standards, why were the
Israelites required to hear the *revealed* law read at least once every seven
years? Gary North writes:

> Human reason, unaided by God's revelation — untwisted by God's
> grace — cannot be expected to devise a universal law code based on
> any presumed universal human logic. What mankind's universal
> reason *can* be expected to do is to *rebel* against God and His law.
> Ethical rebels are not logically faithful to God.
>
> Biblical law had to be read to everyone in Israel at least once
> every seven years (Deut. 31:10-13). God presumed that men would
> not understand His law unless they heard it (Deut. 31:13). Every
> resident of the land had to listen to this law. If the whole of biblical
> law had been ingrained into the consciences of all men from the
> beginning of time, or if the terms of the law, including the laws'
> explicit penalties, were always available to all men through the
> exercise of man's universal reason, then the law would not have
> required the priests to read the Mosaic law before the congregation
> of Israel every seventh year (*Moses and Pharaoh: Dominion Religion
> Versus Power Religion*, p. 236).

5. Each day confronts us with numerous circumstances that need interpretation. We often are tempted to use circumstances or experience as
legitimate authorities in decision-making. Circumstances and experiences must be interpreted before any sense can be gained from them. For
example, when Jesus was crucified, circumstances seemed to indicate that
His life was over and His mission unrealized. Because the apostles failed to

Circumstances are not a stable authority in determining right from wrong. The circumstances of Jesus' death and burial sent the apostles back to their fishing boats.

interpret the circumstances in terms of biblical revelation, they would not believe Jesus rose from the dead; they thought the story was "nonsense" (Luke 24:11). The circumstances of Jesus' death so convinced Thomas that Jesus was still dead that he would not believe that Jesus rose from the dead until he saw Jesus' scarred hands and side (John 20:24-29).

When twelve spies were sent into the land of Canaan God promised the land would be theirs. God told Moses, "Send out for yourself men so that they may spy out the land of Canaan, *which I am going to give to the sons of Israel. . .*" (Numbers 13:2). For ten of the spies the *circumstances* lead to one conclusion. There were giants in the land. Circumstances seemed to overrule God's promise that He would give the land to His people. Joshua and Caleb, two of the twelve spies, never denied there were giants in the land, but believed God's promise in spite of the circumstances (14:30). All twelve spies were confronted by the same circumstances. Because ten spies evaluated the situation independent of God's word, an entire generation was denied access to the promised land with 40 years spent in the wilderness until that entire generation died (those over 20 years of age).

Job's miserable comforters were the classic misinterpreters of circumstances. They were convinced that Job's condition was the result of some gross sin: "Remember now, who ever perished being innocent? Or where were the upright destroyed?" (Job 4:7). Of course, they were wrong. Even Job was sure there was some discernable reason for God's actions. God does not have to give a reason to satisfy the curiosity of man, the creature (cf. Romans 9:14-29). Job was reconciled to God's sovereignty in spite of the circumstances that gave no answers: "I know that Thou canst do all things, and that no purpose of Thine can be thwarted. 'Who is this that hides counsel without knowledge?' Therefore I have declared that which I did not understand, things too wonderful for me, which I did not know. 'Hear, now, and I will speak; I will ask Thee, and do Thou instruct me.' I have heard of Thee by the hearing of the ear; but now my eye sees Thee; therefore I retract, and I repent in dust and ashes" (Job 42:2-6).

Circumstances do not always add up to what we imagine. Those who sought to evaluate the circumstances responsible for the condition of the man born blind produced wrong conclusions. By looking at current circumstances according to their view of the world, they produced two options, both incorrect: "Rabbi, who sinned, this man or his parents, that he should be born blind?" (John 9:2). The circumstances, coupled with Jesus' understanding of the world, made sense. The circumstances alone did not. In some cases, we may never be able to evaluate circumstances correctly but only trust that "God causes all things to work together for good to those who love God, to those who are called according to His purpose" (Romans 8:28).

After the Apostle Paul's shipwreck on the island Malta, some of the natives attempted to piece together varied circumstances in order to know this stranger's character. In both cases they erred. When he was bitten by a viper that came out of the bundle of sticks heated by the fire, some thought he was a criminal who escaped the judgment of the sea but was finally caught by the forces of justice; and when he did not swell up or die, they assumed he was a god (Acts 28:1-6; cf. 14:8-18).

After the Apostle Paul shipwrecked on the island Malta, some of the natives attempted to piece together varied circumstances in order to know this stranger's character. On the evaluation of the circumstances alone, they were wrong.

Today, the circumstances of "bad news" reported in newspapers and television broadcasts lead many Christians to give up in despair of ever seeing the reality of the Kingdom of God. We put more faith in the military might of political powers than we do in God and the power of His word. Circumstances, no matter how sinister, should not shape our world view. Greg L. Bahnsen offers this counsel: "The newspaper has no prerogative to challenge God's word of truth. Nor do those who read the newspapers. As faithful disciples of Christ, we are to trust God as the sovereign controller over human history, 'who works all things after the counsel of His own will' (Eph. 1:11), 'declaring the end from the beginning and from ancient times things not yet done, saying, "My counsel shall stand, and I will accomplish all my purpose" ' (Isa. 46:10), so that 'none can stay his hand' (Dan. 4:35). With the Psalmist we should declare, 'Whatever the Lord pleases, he does, in heaven and on earth' (115:3). If God says something is to happen, then it shall happen; it is to our discredit if we are men of little faith with respect to his promises" ("The Prima Facie Acceptability of Postmillennialism," *The Journal of Christian Reconstruction*, Symposium on the Millennium, Vol. III, No. 2, p. 54).

6. There are two types of tradition. The first type brings to mind family and national customs. Families pass traditions from one generation to another, usually centering around such holidays as Thanksgiving and Christmas. Such national traditions as our Fourth of July and Memorial Day celebrations are part of our American heritage. These types of traditions rarely take on any ethical demands — unless the family or the nation is elevated to a position of undue or ultimate authority.

A second type of tradition is an ethical tradition that becomes authoritative for all people. There is *biblical* tradition which is special revelation. Basically, when the Bible speaks of such tradition it becomes synonymous with revelation. Paul praises the Corinthians because they remember him in everything, "and hold firmly to the traditions," just as Paul delivered them (1 Corinthians 11:2). He encourages the Thessalonian Christians to "stand firm and hold to the traditions which you were taught, whether by word of mouth or by letter from us" (2 Thessalonians 2:15; cf. 3:6). These traditions were manufactured neither by Paul or the nation. They find their heritage in revelation: "For I delivered to you as of first importance what I also received . . ." (1 Corinthians 15:3-8).

Human ethical tradition which demands our obedience usually conflicts with biblical tradition, i.e., special revelation. In time, human tradition *replaces* biblical tradition.

The traditions of men involve distance from God, futile worship, abandonment of the divine commandments in favor of the human (Mark 7:3-9). They involve a philosophic speculation which can capture the mind because [they are] not rooted in Christ (Col. 2:8). In fact the supreme tradition is sin, the ancestral conduct handed down from generation to generation (1 Peter 1:18) (Ronald A. Ward, *Commentary on 1 and 2 Thessalonians*, p. 165).

This is most clearly seen in Mark 7. Jesus is confronted by the Pharisees because He does not follow *their* traditions. In fact, their traditions were so used to nullify the validity of God's unchanging law: "Neglecting the commandment of God, you hold to the tradition of men. . . . You nicely set aside the commandment of God in order to keep your tradition" (Mark 7:8, 9). Jesus had strong words for those who rejected the word of God and in doing so put their own parents in a life threatening situation. They so twisted Scripture that their parents were being left without financial assistance. Jesus pronounced the death sentence on them: "For Moses said, 'Honor your father and your mother': and, 'He who speaks evil of father or mother, let him be put to death'" (Mark 7:10, cf. Exodus 20:12; Deuteronomy 5:16; Exodus 21:17; Leviticus 20:9).

All of this is not to say that non-revelational tradition is not important. Tradition is history. There is value in the study of creeds and councils. While they are not the final word, they are helpful in understanding how the early church reacted to heretical doctrines. In the final analysis, however, Scripture is our final authority:

Sola Scriptura meant the primacy of scripture as a theological norm over all tradition rather than a total rejection of tradition. Creeds, confessions, and councils were to be received insofar as they were consistent with scripture. The *sola scriptura* principle also presupposed the essential clarity of scripture. The central message of the Bible was plain enough to be understood by all and needed no priestly hierarchy to explain it (John Jefferson Davis, *Foundations of Evangelical Theology*, p. 227).

These early councils and creedal formulations have worked through the cardinal doctrines of the faith: Council of Nicaea (325) — Jesus is God; Council of Constantinople (381) — The Holy Spirit is God; Council of Ephesus (431) — Fallen man is totally depraved; and, Council of Chalcedon (451) — Jesus is both God and Man. Without these historic councils and creeds each generation of Christians would have to work through the essentials of the faith. Tradition, then, is important to the church and, yet, still subservient to Scripture.

7. There are many who hold to the ideal of a majority of the people making decisions and using the collective will of the people to enact such opinion into law. The voice of the people, therefore, becomes a nation's standard of authority; political leaders often take the "pulse of public opinion" to determine their vote on an issue. The assumption is, by allowing the majority to rule, we will have a just society. Such an idea leads to totalitarianism. When one group of citizens (51% of the voting population) votes for certain laws to favor themselves, what happens to the 49% of the population who find themselves in the minority? Our civil representatives are tied to a written constitution. They swear to "uphold the Constitution," not the latest Gallup poll.

One of the biggest national problems today is that of reducing the level of power concentrated in our national political government. Many people complain about the civil government's size and inefficiency but few want their favorite programs cut. The citizenry believes governmental power should be used to secure special favors since they are in the majority. The people reject God's law and appoint for themselves "leaders" who will fulfill their wishes. Isaiah writes: "For this is a rebellious people, false sons, sons who refuse to listen to the instruction of the LORD; who say to the seers, 'You must not see visions'; and to the prophets, 'You must not prophesy to us what is right, speak to us pleasant words, prophesy illusions. Get out of the way, turn aside from the path, let us hear no more about the Holy One of Israel'" (Isaiah 30:9-11; cf. 2 Timothy 4:3f.).

Instead of seeking absolutes outside the collective will of man, political leaders often cater to the wishes of the majority to secure for themselves the favors that come from governmental position. As long as the majority can be satisfied (or at least those claiming the majority position), power is assured.

66

The idea that God's will is always found in the will of the people is a false one. Modern day political theorists assume that totalitarian regimes could be converted to just societies with a healthy dose of democracy (power resides in the people). But won't the people put into law their beliefs? Won't their views of law, ethics, economics, war, peace, politics, business, and art find their way into the governmental system of the nation? Suppose their views are contrary to Scripture. Does a majority opinion overrule Scripture? This is why "a democracy cannot exist as a permanent form of government. It can exist only until the voters discover that they can vote themselves largess [a generous bestowal of gifts] out of the public treasury. From that moment on, the majority always votes for the candidate promising the most benefits from the public treasury — with the result that democracy always collapses over a loose fiscal policy, always to be followed by dictatorship" (Alexander Tyler). Would it be right to grant a cannibalistic tribe a "democratic" approach to politics? God forbid!

The devil tempted Jesus to repudiate the authority of His Father and live life independent of His Father's will. Jesus' obedience to His Father's will restored the relationship broken by Adam.

When Samuel saw Saul, the LORD said to him, "Behold, the man whom I spoke to you! This one shall rule over My people" (1 Samuel 9:17).

Lesson 3

God's Sovereignty Over the Nations

God, the Creator of heaven and earth, established boundaries for the nations according to His most wise counsel and ordained His law as the standard of righteousness for all peoples. When nations refuse to acknowledge God's rule and government, He promises sure judgment: "Now therefore, O kings, show discernment; take warning, O judges of the earth. Worship the LORD with reverence, and rejoice with trembling. Do homage to the Son, lest He become angry, and you perish in the way, for His wrath may soon be kindled. How blessed are all who take refuge in Him" (Psalm 2:10-12). "Homage to the Son" has reference to the Lord Jesus Christ and to His word. Jesus instructed His disciples to "make disciples of all the nations" (Matthew 28:19). Jesus' commission will result in the nations paying homage to Him, the Son, by observing all He commanded (v. 20).

God did not reserve His commandments for just the nation Israel and the church. Scripture makes it clear that all kings in Israel should copy the law in the presence of the Levitical priests so the rulers would be careful to observe every word of the law (Deuteronomy 17:18, 19). Even nations outside Israel were required to follow the law as it was given to the nation Israel. Sodom and Gomorrah were destroyed because they broke the law of God (Genesis 13:13). God commanded the prophet Jonah to preach to the Ninevites (Assyrians) because their wickedness had come up before God (Jonah 1:2). The reason is clear: "There shall be one standard for you; it shall be for the stranger as well as the native, for I am the LORD your God" (Leviticus 24:22). The prophet Amos set forth the coming judgment of God to Damascus, Gaza, Tyre, Edom, Ammon, and Moab. These non-Israelite nations stood accountable for their transgressions: "For three transgressions...and for four I will not revoke its punishment" (Amos 1:3, 6, 9, 13; 2:1). Non-Israelite nations were to be judged along with Judah and Israel (2:4, 6). There is one law and one Lawgiver.

Wherever [Christianity] has gone it has rebuked oppression, repressed violence, and compelled vice, abashed, to skulk in darkness. It has given to us, as a nation, the free institutions which command the admiration and excite the hopes of the down-trodden in all lands. It has given to Christendom the power which it now exercises over the destiny of the whole world.

—Moses Hoge

The New Testament shows similar emphasis, as we should expect. The God of the New Testament is the same God of the Old Testament. God does not change (Malachi 3:6), therefore His law does not change (Matthew 5:17-20). Though Christians do not make blood sacrifices as remission for sins, we do keep this Old Testament law in Christ. The Bible states that "all things are cleansed with blood, and without shedding of blood there is no forgiveness" (Hebrews 9:22; cf. Leviticus 17:11). Shed blood still is required, but Jesus became our perfect and final sacrifice for sins: "[B]ut now once at the consummation of the ages He has been manifested to put away sin by the sacrifice of Himself" (Hebrews 9:26). All ceremonial laws, laws applied to the redemptive work of Christ, are fulfilled when an individual repents of his sin and unconditionally surrenders himself to Jesus.

The redemptive work of Jesus does not free us from an obligation to keep the moral and civil laws laid down in the Bible, however. Scripture shows no instance of an individual, Christian or pagan, who is no longer

70

required to keep these laws. We are freed from the "curse of the law" (Galatians 3:13), but not from the demands of the law: "Do we then nullify the Law through faith? May it never be! On the contrary, we establish the Law" (Romans 3:31). Of course, the non-Christian is neither free from the curse of the law nor from the demands of the law: "He who believes in Him is not judged; he who does not believe has been judged already, because he has not believed in the name of the only begotten Son of God" (John 3:18).

Turmoil that reaches our newspaper headlines can be traced to repudiating the saving work of Jesus Christ and denying His law as a standard for the nations. Man first sinned by rejecting the absolute government of God. Adam and Eve attempted to interpret life by their own standards. What is true for individuals is multiplied for the nations. Daniel's prophetic dream depicted the character of nations which opposed the ordinances of God and their eventual destruction. The kingdoms were humanistic, anthropocentric (man-centered), kingdoms: "You, O king, were looking and behold, there was a single great statue" of a man (Daniel 2:31). God brought an end to man's attempt to rule without His saving work and law structure by crushing the colossus: "Then the iron, the clay, the bronze, the silver and the gold were crushed all at the same time, and became like chaff from the summer threshing floors; and the wind carried them away so that not a trace of them was found" (v. 35).

The Roman empire presents a classic example of the Messianic man-centered State, of the denial of God's Law, and of the implementation of humanistic law. Caesar declared himself god and his decrees were to be acknowledged as the laws of the gods. The Roman rulers understood that their claim to divine rule was threatened by God's unlimited and universal reign. Peter declared confidently "that there is salvation in no one else; for there is no other name under heaven that has been given among men, by which we must be saved" (Acts 4:12). The gospel of Jesus Christ, with its claim of divine prescriptions, threatened the very nature of the Roman State. Rome had to submit itself to the position of "minister" *under* God or be crushed by the power *of* God. Rome did not submit.

The modern State claims divine honors similar to Rome. While our coins still retain the motto "In God We Trust," our federal government often acts as if it were the final voice of authority. "When a state claims divine honors, there will always be warfare between Christ and Caesar, for two rival gods claim the same jurisdiction over man. It is a conflict between two kingdoms, between two kings, each of whom claim ultimate and divine powers" (John W. Whitehead, *The Second American Revolution*, p. 18). The loss of religious freedom in the United States is a manifestation of the long-standing assault on the Christian religion. This assault was first waged on *theological* grounds (witness the theological liberalism of the late 1800s; the Unitarianism of the early 19th century; the Transcendentalism of the 1830s; the "Social Gospel" of the 1880s-1920s; the theological modernism or liberalism of the 1920s; and the "Neo-Orthodoxy" of the 1940s and 1950s, etc.).

Then an assault was waged on *philosophical* grounds (take note of the rationalism of the 1800s; the empiricism of the mid 19th century; the Positivism and Pragmatism of the 1800s-1980s, etc.). The theological and philosophical subversion now accomplished, the assault was fought on the grounds of *legal philosophy*: Legal Positivism and Pragmatism (1800s-1980s). From this position the battle shifted to a political and legal assault (though a veiled one): through electing politicians who would abandon the Constitution and Christian principles; and through appointing judges who would reinterpret the Constitution so as to abandon its Christian principles and substitute left-wing humanist principles.

Christianity threatens all totalitarian regimes because the Christian citizen's ultimate allegiance belongs to God, who rules all earthly kingdoms and calls those who rule to rule according to laws set forth in Scripture, rather than the whims of men.

Early Christians were accused of "acting contrary to the decrees of Caesar, saying that there is another king, Jesus" (Acts 17:7). There is no evidence that the early church advocated that people act contrary to the prevailing law-system, except when State laws conflicted with those of the Bible. However, those who heard the disciples preach understood the implications of Jesus Christ's demands. If Jesus is truly the Messiah, then even the State must submit to His authority and rule: no middle or neutral ground exists. Jesus' words make it clear that only one master can claim absolute authority: "No one can serve two masters; for either he will hate the one and love the other, or he will hold to one and despise the other" (Matthew 6:24). The State *and* God cannot claim absolute sovereignty. One must submit to the other. Obviously, the State must submit to the Lordship of Jesus Christ or perish in its attempt to overthrow His

72

rule. Any attempt by the nations to oppose the rule of God is an act of futility. God laughs at and scorns their attempts to overthrow the advancing kingdom of Christ (cf. Psalm 2).

Jonah arose and went to Nineveh according to the word of the LORD. Now Nineveh was an exceedingly great city, a three ·y's walk. Then Jonah began to go through the city one day's walk; and he cried out and said, "Yet forty days and Nineveh ·ll be overthrown" (Jonah 3:3, 4).

Questions for Discussion

1. What is God's position among and His evaluation of the nations? (Psalm 2; 93:1; 96:10-13; 97:1-9; 99:1; Isaiah 9:6, 7; 40:15)

_____

_____

_____

_____

_____

_____

_____

2. What is the kingship of Jesus Christ and what does it mean to acknowledge Him as King?(Psalm 2; John 3:5-7; Romans 3:31; 2 Corinthians 10:5; Revelation 17:14)

_____

_____

_____

_____

_____

_____

3. What titles were given to the rulers of Israel? What do these titles tell us about the function (jurisdiction) of those who rule?(1 Samuel 10:1; 15:17ff.; 16:12, 13; 24:1-7; 2 Samuel 8:18 and 1 Chronicles 18:17; 2 Samuel 20:26 and 2 Samuel 23:38; 1 Kings 4:2-6; Romans 13:4, 6)

_____

_____

_____

_____

_____

_____

4. What titles were given to rulers of the nations surrounding Israel? What do these titles tell us about the function of these rulers? (Isaiah 44:28; 45:1; Jeremiah 25:9; 27:6)

_____

_____

_____

_____

_____

_____

_____

_____

5. What was to be the standard of the king's rule?(Deuteronomy 17:18-20; 1 Kings 3:9; Psalm 72:1, 2)

_____

_____

_____

_____

_____

_____

_____

6. Does God have two standards of justice, one for Christian and one for pagan rulers?(Leviticus 24:22; Numbers 15:16; Deuteronomy 1:16-17; 4:4-8; Psalm 2:10; Proverbs 16:12)

_____

_____

_____

_____

_____

_____

_____

7. Should Christians be involved in instructing rulers and civil representatives in the demands of God's law? Explain. (Psalm 119:46; Matthew 10-18; 14:4; Mark 6:18; Luke 3:13-14; 19:1-10)

_____

_____

_____

_____

_____

_____

_____

_____

8. What happens to nations that fail to follow God's law as a standard for righteousness? (Deuteronomy 28:15-63; Psalm 82 [especially v. 7]; Nehemiah 9:34-37; Isaiah 1:4-31; Daniel 2:31-45; Acts 12:20-23)

_____

_____

_____

_____

_____

_____

_____

9. Who ultimately appoints rulers? (Psalm 75:6-7; Daniel 2:21; 4:17, 25, 32; 5 [especially verses 18-28])

_____

_____

_____

_____

_____

_____

_____

Summary

"It is the duty of nations, as the subjects of Christ, to take his law as their rule. They are apt to think enough that they take, as their standard of legislation and administration, human reason, natural conscience, public opinion or political expediency. None of these, however nor indeed all of them together, can supply a sufficient guide in affairs of state.... The truth is, that revelation is given to man to supply the imperfections of the law of nature; and to restrict ourselves to the latter, and renounce the former, in any case in which it is competent to guide us, is at once to condemn God's gift and to defeat the end for which it was given. We contend, then, that the Bible is to be our rule, not only in matters of a purely religious nature, in matters connected with conscience and the worship of God, but in matters of a civil or political nature. To say that in such matters we have nothing to do with the Bible, is to maintain what is manifestly untenable. To require nations, who possess the sacred volume, to confine themselves, in their political affairs, to the dim light of nature, is not more absurd than it would be to require men, when the sun is in the heavens, to shut out its full blaze and go about their ordinary duties by the feeble rays of a taper [a slender candle] " (William Symington, *Messiah the Prince, or, The Mediatorial Dominion of Jesus Christ*, pp. 234-235).

Righteousness exalts a nation, but sin is a disgrace to any people (Proverbs 14:34).

Answers to Questions for Discussion

1. "The LORD reigns," declares Scripture. Notice that the reign of God is comprehensive; it knows no geographical limitation: "Say among the *nations*, 'The LORD reigns' " (Psalm 96:10). God's reign is not limited to the nation Israel. Every nation is responsible to acknowledge the reign of God. Any attempt to deny God's reign will be met with judgment: "Why are the nations in an uproar, and the peoples devising a vain thing? The kings of the earth take their stand, and the rulers take counsel together against the LORD and against His Anointed (*Messiah*): 'Let us tear their fetters apart, and cast away their cords from us!' He who sits in the heavens laughs, the LORD scoffs at them. Then He will speak to them in His anger and terrify them in His fury" (Psalm 2:1-5).

The fact of God's reign terrifies those who seek to free themselves from His rightful position as the reigning monarch of all creation: "Now therefore, O kings show discernment; take warnings, O judges of the earth. Worship the LORD with reverence, and rejoice with trembling" (vv.10-11). No nation can claim the exclusive title reserved for the Messiah of God. All civil governments are subordinate to God and are *under* His jurisdiction. The Bible makes it clear that *the* government, the absolute *reign* of God, rests upon the shoulders of Jesus Christ (Isaiah 9:6, 7). This is not simply a future reign, but a present reality. The promise of government by the Messiah is realized at His birth: "For a child will be born to us, a son will be given to us; and the government will rest on His shoulders" (Isaiah 9:6a). Notice that "there will be no end to the incease of His government or of peace" (v.7a). God then removes any nation standing in the way of the increase of the Messiah's government.

The nations do not influence God's decision on how He will evaluate all their actions. The nations are in God's hands, and He controls them. Their conspiratorial desires to manipulate other nations are vain. Even Israel, God's chosen nation, is not favored when evaluated in terms of His holy character. Because of Israel's disobedience, Jesus states that the kingdom will be taken from Israel and will be given to the Gentiles, that is, the true Israel, those who unconditionally surrender their wills before Jesus Christ (Matthew 21:33-46; cf. Romans 9:6-8).

Isaiah describes the perspective we need when considering the actions of the nations: They are nothing more than a drop in the bucket and dust on the scales compared to the grandeur, glory, and holiness of God (Isaiah 40:15).

2. Jesus Christ is King because of Who He is. "Not by usurpation, but legally. He holds his crown by immediate tenure from heaven. God the Father has decreed him to be king. 'I have set my king upon my holy hill: I will declare the decree.' Psa ii 6, 7. God has anointed and sealed him to his regal office. 'Him hath God the Father sealed.' John vi 27. God has set the crown upon his head" (Thomas Watson, *A Body of Divinity*, p.187).

Jesus has a kingly title: "He is Lord of lords and King of kings" (Revelation 17:14; 19:16). He bears the ensigns of royalty: a crown (Hebrews 2:9), a sword (Revelation 1:16; 2:16), a scepter (Hebrews 1:8), and a coat of arms (Revelation 5:5). He is called "the ruler of the kings of the earth" (Revelation 1:5). It is by Him that "kings reign" (Proverbs 8:15). His throne is everlasting (Hebrews 1:8). Even the angels worship Him: "And let all the angels of God worship Him" (Hebrews 1:6). He is the center of all a person, family, church, group, organization, or nation does. He is God, the Creator and Preserver of the Universe (John 1:1; Colossians 1:17). He "upholds all things by the word of His power" (Hebrews 1:2).

Republican institutions in the hands of a virtuous and God-fearing nation are the very best, but in the hands of a corrupt and irreligious people they are the very worst and the most effective weapons of destruction (Philip Schaff, 1819-1893).

Because all actions originate in the heart (Mark 7:20-23), acknowledging Jesus Christ as king also must begin in the heart. In this sense, "His kingdom is spiritual. He rules in the hearts of men. He sets up his throne where no other king does; he rules the will and affections, his power binds the conscience; he subdues men's lusts, 'He will subdue our iniquities.'Mic vii 19" (Thomas Watson, *A Body of Divinity*, p.187f.). His sword, the word of God, "is able to judge the thoughts and intentions of the heart" (Hebrew 4:12). No nation can survive unless Jesus Christ is acknowledged as King and its citizens embrace Him as such personally.

The Bible emphasizes this idea in a variety of ways: *First*, Jesus speaks to Nicodemus about the necessity of a "new birth," a comprehensive transformation of the entire individual (John 3:5-7). Man is not considered sick. Rather, the unregenerate sinner is "dead in trespasses and sins" (Ephesians 2:1). Only the regenerating power of the Holy Spirit can make a dead man live. *Second*, the written word of God is acknowledged as the only rule of faith and *practice*. Law is not found in the vote of the people, the decree of the courts or the pronouncement of rulers. The law of God is Christ the King's law; therefore, it must be obeyed. Moreover, being set free in Jesus Christ liberates neither citizen nor ruler from the *obligations* of the law (Romans 3:31) only from the final *curse* of the law (Galatians 3:13). The consequences of broken law are well established (Deuteronomy 28:15-68). *Third*, the mind is renewed (Romans 12:2). Every individual operates from a particular "world view" and evaluates all life from his perspective of established religious presuppositions. Prior to acknowledging Christ as Savior, Lord, and King, all life is seen from man's perspective: "For as [a man] thinks within himself, so he is" (Proverbs 23:7). The new creature in Christ should evaluate life from the perspective of the word of God, thinking God's thoughts after Him, "taking every thought captive to the obedience of Christ" (2 Corinthians 10:5). *Fourth*, those who do not want Jesus as King "will wage war against the Lamb, and the Lamb will overcome them, because He is Lord of lords and King of kings, and those who are with Him are the called and chosen and faithful" (Revelation 17:14).

3. The Bible reveals that the jurisdiction of the State and the jurisdiction of the church are to be separate, though the separation is not absolute.

The word of God is the element which breaks down any absolute wall of separation some may seek to erect. For this reason, civil servants often are given religious titles. The king in Israel was the LORD'S anointed set apart for a *civil* task in the same way the priest was set apart and anointed for his *ecclesiastical* (religious) task (Numbers 3:3). David, who was to replace Saul as the LORD'S anointed, respected the special office of the king: "Far be it from me because of the LORD that I should do this thing to my lord [Saul], the LORD'S anointed, to stretch out my hand against him, since he is the LORD'S anointed" (1 Samuel 24:6).

Those subordinates who served with David also enjoyed religious titles. "In 2 Samuel 8:18, at the end of a list of David's chief officers, David's officers are designated 'priests' (using the common Hebrew word, [*cohen*], for that cultic [ecclesiastical] office). Not being from the tribe of Levi, but Judah, these sons could not be cultic [ecclesiastical] functionaries"(Greg L. Bahnsen, *Theonomy in Christian Ethics*, p. 323). In 1 Chroniles 18:17, the parallel passage, they are designated as "chiefs at the king's side." "The same phenomenon is found in 2 Samuel 20:26. There Ira the Jairite (possibly one of David's mighty warriors; cf. 2 Samuel 23:38) is named in a late list of David's officers (in the same position of 'David's sons' from the earlier list) as 'priest unto David.' Again, Ira could not qualify for cultic [ecclesiastical] service since he descended from Manasseh (cf. Numbers 32:41; Deuteronomy 3:14; 1 Kings 4:13) and thus was not a member of one of the Levitical families" (Bahnsen, p. 324). The reason for the title "priest" is not immediately evident until we understand that these "priests," in their governmental role, were to give *counsel* to the king. Only the title of "priest" was significant enough to give these counselors' role the importance it deserved: they were to counsel the civil minister in godly law and actions. The New Testament emphasizes a similar title for all rulers by designating them as "ministers of God" (Romans 13:4, 6).

4. Even outside Israel, rulers were given religious titles for civil functions. Cyrus is given the title of "shepherd." This title is usually reserved for God Himself (Isaiah 40:11; cf. John 10) and the rulers of Israel (Jeremiah 23:4), but God calls a non-Israelite "My shepherd" (Isaiah 44:28): "It is I who says of Cyrus, 'he is My shepherd! And he will perform all My desire.'" Cyrus is given an even more significant title: "Thus says the LORD to

Cyrus His *anointed*, whom I have taken by the right hand, to subdue nations before him, and to loose the loins of kings; to open doors before him so that gates will not be shut" (45:1). "Such is the designation for the High Priest in Israel and for the King over the people; especially is it known as the title for the coming deliverer, the righteous 'Messiah.'

"If ye forsake God he will forsake you." — If, forgetful of your dependence on Jehovah, ye violate his laws and condemn his ordinances, his protection and favour will be taken from you, and then cometh confusion and every evil work. *Left to yourselves, you will speedily become the prey of your enemies or work your own destruction. Vain will be all your devices, feeble all your powers and unavailing all your exertions.* Ashbel Green (1762-1848). Taken from "Obedience to the Laws of God the Sure and Indispensable Defence of Nations" (May 9, 1798).

Hence the rulers of the nations are given titles which clearly indicate that they are considered by God's word to be *ministers of God*" (cf. Romans 13:4, 6) (Greg L. Bahnsen, *Theonomy in Christian Ethics*, p. 348f.). Such special designations of "shepherd" and "anointed" tell us that even those rulers who do not seek to govern according to the law of God still are obligated to function in that capacity. Moreover, they will be held responsible for their actions.

5. The written word of God is to be the standard for the king's rule: "Now it shall come about when he sits on the throne of his kingdom, he shall write for himself a copy of this law on a scroll in the presence of the Levitical priests. And it shall be with him, and he shall read it all the days of his life that he may learn to fear the LORD his God, by carefully observing all the words of this law and these statutes" (Deuteronomy 17:18, 19). The king, as well as his people, come under God's law.

82

No "divine right of kings," in which the king was a law unto himself, existed in Israel. The idea of the "divine right of kings" has been challenged with great force by Samuel Rutherford, a Presbyterian minister who served as a commissioner at Westminster Abbey in London and rector of St. Andrew's Church in Scotland. His book *Lex, Rex* caused enough controversy to have him placed under house arrest and possible execution. Summoned to appear before Parliament at Edinburgh, he died before he could comply with the order. John Whitehead, in *The Second American Revolution*, says of Rutherford's thesis:

> *Lex, Rex* challenged the fundamental principle of seventeenth-century political government in Europe: the divine right of kings. This doctrine held that the king or state ruled as God's appointed regent. Therefore, the king's word was law. (Although Scripture was seen as normative, it was the king alone who interpreted and embodied that norm.) Counter-balanced against this position was Rutherford's assertion that the basic premise of government and, therefore, of law must be the Bible, the Word of God rather than the word of man. All men, even the king, Rutherford argued, were *under* law and not above it. This religious concept was considered both heresy and treason and punishable as such" (p. 28).

The purpose of the law was so the king's "heart may not be lifted above his countrymen" (v. 20). Citizens and king are to serve the same law. King Solomon prayed for "an understanding heart to judge Thy people to discern between good and evil" (1 Kings 3:9). Solomon's standard of right and wrong was the Bible. Only when he ignored Scripture, did judgment come to his kingdom. This is no less true in the New Testament, where Jesus is one with the Lord who gave Moses the law (John 10:30); and that we are to keep His commandments (John 14:15; 15:14). By keeping Jesus' commandments, we keep the commandments of God, for Jesus is God (John 1:1).

6. God's standard of justice is the same for all His creatures. This includes nations which consider themselves non-Christian. Some believe that because they do not acknowledge God as Lord and King they somehow are exempt from following the law of God. Sodom and Gomorrah enjoyed no such exemption: "Now the men of Sodom were wicked exceedingly and sinners against God" (Genesis 13:13). This wicked city was destroyed for

breaking God's law: in particular, the sin of homosexuality (Genesis 19:4-5; Leviticus 18:22; 20:13). Jonah went to preach to the non-Israelite city of Nineveh because of their sins. If the Ninevites were not obligated to keep the law of God, then how could they be expected to repent (Jonah 3)? The stranger, an individual *outside* the covenant community, must obey the law of God: "There shall be one standard for you; it shall be for the stranger as well as the native, for I am the LORD your God" (Leviticus 24:22; cf. Numbers 15:16; Deuteronomy 1:16-17).

Mary Queen of Scots said of John Knox, *I fear the prayers of John Knox more than an army of ten thousand men!* John Knox (c.1514-1572) opposed a number of the Queen's policies, especially her plans to unify Scotland with Catholic Spain by marrying Don Carlos, the son of Philip II, king of Spain. In Knox's eyes, such a union would destroy the Reformation in Scotland.

The law as given to Israel was a standard for nations surrounding Israel. When other nations hear of the righteous judgments within Israel, these nations will remark with wonder: "Surely this great nation is a wise and understanding people" (Deuteronomy 4:6). The psalmist proclaims to the kings and judges of the earth "to take warning...and worship the LORD with reverence..."and "do homage to the Son" (Psalm 2:10-11). "It is striking how frequently the other nations are called upon in the Psalms to recognize and to honor God, and how complete is the witness of the prophets against the nations surrounding Israel. God does not exempt other nations from the claim of his righteousness; he requires their obedience and holds them responsible for their apostasy and degeneration [e.g., Amos 1:3-2:5] " (J.H.Bavinck, *An Introduction to the Science of Missions*, pp.12-13).

Henry VIII, king of England from 1509-1547, opposed much of the Reformation, especially Martin Luther's doctrines. The king used every means to continue Tudor rule.

The New Testament presupposes the moral order laid down in what we call the "Old Testament." John the Baptist used the law of God to confront Herod in his adulterous affair: "Herod...had John arrested and bound in prison on account of Herodias, the wife of his brother Philip, because he had married her. For John had been saying to Herod, 'It is not lawful for you to have your brother's wife' " (Mark 6:17, 18; cf. Leviticus 20:10; Deuteronomy 22:22). This was not mere advice. John lost his own head in the exchange.

In Romans 13 the civil magistrate is termed a "minister of God" who has the responsibility and authority to punish evildoers. As God's servants these rulers must rule God's way. Just as a minister in the church is obligated to implement the law of God as it touches on ecclesiastical matters, a civil servant must implement the law of God in civil affairs. The determination of good and evil must derive from some objective standard. In Hebrews 5:14 the Christian is instructed to train his senses "to discern good and evil." In Romans 13:4 the civil authorities are to wield the sword punishing evil doers and promoting the good.

God certainly does not intend the standard of good and evil to be simply whatever a ruler autonomously desires or thinks it to be. The standard of good and evil is nothing less than that which the Creator, Sustainer, Ruler, and Judge of heaven and earth ordains, decrees, and declares it to be: the revealed word and law of God.

7. The psalmist declares he "will speak of Thy testimonies before kings, and shall not be ashamed" (Psalm 119:46). These testimonies are the "commandments" which he loves (v. 47). Jesus informs His disciples that persecution will give them opportunity to speak "before governors and kings...as a testimony to them and to the Gentiles" (Matthew 10:18). John the Baptist confronted Herod the tetrarch with the abiding validity of God's law in the area of marriage. Herod had an adulterous affair with his brother's wife: "Herod had seized John, and bound him, and put him in prison on account of Herodias, the wife of his brother Philip. For John had been saying to him, 'It is not lawful for you to have her' " (Matthew 14:3-4; cf. Mark 6:18).

Prior to this, civil servants approached John the Baptist regarding their obligations to the law of God: "Some tax-gatherers also came to be baptized, and they said to him, 'Teacher, what shall we do?'And he said to them, 'Collect no more than what you have been ordered to.' And some soldiers were questioning him, saying, 'And what about us, what shall we do?' And he said to them, 'Do not take money from anyone by force, or accuse anyone falsely, and be content with your wages' " (Luke 3:13-14). John was not appealing to them on the basis of some "neutral" law, but referred to the sixth, ninth, and tenth commandments of the Decalogue (Exodus 20).

Zaccheus, an unscrupulous tax collector, followed the laws of restitution by promising to pay back those he defrauded: "If I have defrauded anyone of anything, I will give back four times as much" (Luke 19:8; cf.Exodus 22:1; Leviticus 6:5). Christians are obligated to inform those who rule in the civil sphere of the demands of the law and the consequences of disobedience.

8. Because God's laws are a standard for all nations, consequences of disobedience follow pagan nations as well as covenant nations. External blessings accrue to societies that conform to the laws of God, and there are curses for those societies that fail to conform externally to these laws (Deuteronomy 28:1-68). The laws of God which relate to blessings and curses are operative for all peoples. The prophet Amos made this clear when he denounced the nations surrounding Israel. Damascus, Gaza, Tyre, Edom, Ammon, and Moab incurred the curses of Deuteronomy 28:15-63 (Amos 1:3; 2:5). Those judges who fail to render verdicts according to the absolute standard of the law of God "will die like men, and fall like any one of the princes" (Psalm 82:7).

The Levites stood before the people to remind them of their sins and the reason for God's judgment on their nation: "For our kings, our leaders, our priests, and our fathers have not kept the law or paid attention to Thy commandments and Thine admonitions with which Thou hast admonished them. . . . Behold, we are slaves today, and as to the land which Thou didst give to our fathers to eat of its fruit and its bounty, behold, we are slaves on it" (Nehemiah 9:34, 36). Slavery, where even our bodies are ruled by despotic leaders (v. 37), is the result of a nation's failure to keep the commandments of God. Breaking God's commandments means "transgressors and sinners will be crushed together, and those who forsake

87

Esther accused Haman of treachery before King Ahasuerus: *A foe and an enemy, is this wicked Haman!* (Esther 7:8). Haman met his just end: *So they hanged Haman on the gallows which he had prepared for Mordecai, and the king's anger subsided* (v. 10).

the LORD shall come to an end (Isaiah 1:28). Harlotry, injustice, murder, theft, the taking of bribes, and afflicting the helpless are the result of a nation repudiating the laws of God for the laws of men (humanism). Even the greatest kingdoms of the world will be reduced to dust if they fail to honor God's law (Daniel 2:31-35). One of the most sobering judgments of God is the one that falls on Herod for his humanistic government: "On an appointed day Herod, having put on his royal apparel, took his seat on the rostrum and began delivering an address to them. And the people kept crying out, 'The voice of a god and not of a man!' And immediately an angel of the Lord struck him because he did not give God the glory, and he was eaten by worms and died" (Acts 12:21-23).

9. God as Savior and Judge appoints all rulers and deposes all rebels and tyrants. He, therefore, never is surprised about the development of the nations because the heads of foreign powers are His servants. For example, Pharaoh (Romans 9:17), Herod, and Pilate (Acts 4:25) were raised up by God to do God's will. The psalmist says that God "puts down one, and exalts another" (Psalm 75:7). God's dealings with Nebuchadnezzar surely are the most revealing actions of sovereignty brought upon an earthly ruler. Daniel acknowledges the sovereignty of God in the appointment and removal of kings by stating that God "changes the times and the epochs; He removes kings and establishes kings" (Daniel 2:21a). The rule and authority that men in power enjoy come from the gracious hand of God: "The Most High is ruler over the realm of mankind, and bestows it on whom He wishes, and sets over it the lowliest of men" (4:17).

Nebuchadnezzar was reminded of his rightful position as a ruler *under* God (4:25, 32). When the king comes to his senses, God returns the kingdom to Nebuchadnezzar: "So I was reestablished in my sovereignty, and surpassing greatness was added to me" (4:36).

Saul's kingship was removed because of his failure to keep the commandments of God. Saul went to the extreme of consulting the dead on behalf of the living, *a medium at En-dor* (1 Samuel 28:7).

All those who rule derive their authority from God, whether they acknowledge it or not. Mary Queen of Scotland was reminded of this on numerous occasions by John Knox.

Lesson 4

Establishing Christian Leadership

All discussion of the duties of the citizenry and those called to minister in the civil sphere must begin with the Sovereign God of Scripture. Civil government as a work of nature cannot be supported by a faithful reading of the Bible. There is no neutral "social contract" whereby men and nations agree and, therefore, legitimize civil government. The "social contract" theory of the origin of civil govrnment is the religion of Babel (Genesis 11).

Family, church, and civil governments are not contractual. For example, marriage is a divine government, instituted by God at creation (Genesis 2:22-25). The covenant that men and women make in marriage is modeled after the divine model of relationships, the duties of which are set forth in Scripture. The husband, therefore, is to model the love for his wife after the love Jesus has for the church in giving Himself up for her (Ephesians 5:25).

Ecclesiastical government (church government) results from Christ's institution. Jesus declares that it is His church that is to be built (Matthew 16:18). When Christians establish local churches, the divine blueprint must be followed. There are earthly rulers in the church (Acts 20:28; Hebrews 13:17), but Jesus is the head (Ephesians 5:23). There are many locales where churches operate, but the living Christ is their authority (Matthew 28:18; Revelation 2:12-17).

As in family and ecclesiastical governments, civil government is an extension of God's rule over nations: "For the kingdom is the LORD'S, and He rules over the nations" (Psalm 22:28). Man, on the other hand, copies or images the government of God in the civil sphere: "Thou dost

91

make him to rule over the works of Thy hands; Thou hast put all things under his feet" (Psalm 8:6); "Let every person be in subjection to the governing authorities. *For there is no authority except from God, and those which exist are established by God*" (Romans 13:1). The specifics of civil government, like that of marriage and ecclesiastical governments, are set forth in Scripture. Governmental principles do not flow "naturally"; they, too, are ordained by God.

Everywhere there arises before our eyes the spectre of a society where security, if it is attained at all, will be attained at the expense of freedom, where the security that is attained will be security of fed beasts in a stable, and where all the high aspirations of humanity will have been crushed by an all-powerful State.

—J. Gresham Machen

Four primary duties proceed from the biblical model established for civil government. First, the people must understand their obligations as citizens. Because governmental power is God-ordained, certain obligations are part of the governmental process. There can be no autonomy among the citizenry. Anarchy — power invested in the individual to do what he or she feels is right — is not tolerated by God. The Zealots of the New Testament sought the overthrow of tyrannical civil government through the power of the sword placed in the hands of the "chosen" few. Gamaliel recounts the history of such attempts: "For some time ago Theudas rose up, claiming to be somebody; and a group of about four hundred men joined up with him. And he was slain; and all who followed him were dispersed and came to nothing. After this man Judas of Galilee rose up in the days of the census, and drew away some people after him, he too perished, and all those who followed him were scattered" (Acts 5:36, 37).

Second, those who minister in the civil arena must understand that they derive their authority from God Himself. Civil government is not an independent government outside the jurisdiction of God's sovereign rule. But rulers are not directly chosen by God as were Moses and Joshua (Numbers 12:1-8; Deuteronomy 34:9-12). God made provision for the ratification of leaders through a godly citizenry.

Third, in a Christian society, the people endorse those who rule by voting them into office and they confirm the laws they enact by keeping them in office. This is why Jethro instructed Moses to "teach [the people] the statutes and the laws, and make known to them the way in which they are to walk, and the work they are to do" (Exodus 18:20).

Fourth, there is no legitimate claim to a "divine right" whereby rulers can enact any law. All rule must be in terms of God's revealed law. It is important to note that citizens, especially Christian citizens, have an obligation to question unbridled and autonomous political power. This is why at the death of Solomon that "Jeroboam and all the assembly of Israel came and spoke to Reheboam" about the tyrannical rule of the king (1 Kings 12:3). A Christian society, as a "holy" and "royal priesthood" (1 Peter 2:5, 9; cf. Exodus 19:6), has a duty to confront the unrighteous in civil government.

One of the problems with respect to obedience is that too many commentators are still under the influence of a medieval and reformation perspective which at this point is very faulty. This influence is *the divine right doctrine*, which assumes that divinely ordained authority is beyond questioning. The divine right of kings gave way, for many, to the divine right of husbands, an equally pernicious idea. Indeed, all legitimate authority is established by God, but this does not entitle authorities to the unquestioning obedience God alone is entitled to. *All* human authorities are to be obeyed *in the Lord*, i.e., in terms of a questioning and devout attention to the word of God as superior to man (R.J. Rushdoony, *Salvation and Godly Rule*, p. 390f.)

Christians are obligated to obey those in authority, leaders are required to rule in terms of God's word, but no earthly authority must be obeyed in *all* cases. There are times when "we must obey God rather than men" (Acts 5:29). Again, the Bible is our guide. Human government, therefore,

93

resides under the control of God. Justice reflects the righteousness of God, while the need for retribution reflects the sinfulness of man. The temporal powers, when exercising authority as a ministry of justice, must know and enforce the parameters of justice. This makes for the working of a just society (not a perfect society). There is to be no bias judgment; no favorable treatment under the law; no partiality in judgment. Righteousness is the standard.

Just as God, the supreme Judge, is no respecter of persons (Acts 10:34; Rom. 2:11; Eph. 6:9; Col. 3:25) and is Himself absolutely righteous, so too those who exercise governmental authority on earth are required to display impartiality towards all without exception — otherwise they show themselves to be betrayers of the power entrusted to them and despisers of the law they administer. Thus the judges of Moses' time were solemnly charged, "You shall not be partial in judgment; you shall hear the small and the great alike; you shall not be afraid of the face of man, *for the judgment is God's*" (Deut. 1:7) (Philip E. Hughes, *Christian Ethics in Secular Society*, p. 185).

In this way citizens and civil representatives know the extent of jurisdiction. Freedom and security prevail under such a system when the people realize rulers "do not judge for man but for the LORD" (2 Chronicles 19:6). The fear of the Lord should guide the heart of all who rule. Citizens have a duty to remind rulers that "the LORD our God will have no part in unrighteousness, or partiality, or the taking of a bribe" (v. 7).

The Bible gives many examples of Christians involving themselves in the political process. Many Christians consider politics a dirty business, an area where Chrst has no business. If politics is "dirty," it becomes necessary for Christians to involve themselves. Here are a few examples of political involvement from the Bible. Noah, as an agent of the civil magistrate, is given authority to execute murderers (Genesis 9:1-7); Joseph is made ruler in Egypt (Genesis (41:38ff.); Israel is kept in bondage by a political ruler who sets himself up in opposition to the kingdom of God (Exodus 1:815:1-21); God gives instructions to both priests and kings (Deuteronomy 17:14-20); the book of Judges shows the interrelationship between religion and rule; 1 Samuel 8 shows how the rejection of God as Israel's true King leads the people to choose an earthly king as a substitute (an attempt to equate the State with the kingdom of God); the books of

Samuel, Kings, and Chronicles tell the story of the rise and fall of kings and kingdoms; and individual kings are singled out for special counsel (Jeremiah 38:17-28). The list could go on.

That God is vitally concerned with political affairs is quite easy to demonstrate: it is God who ordained governments in the first place (Rom. 13:1; Rom. 2:21). He is the One who establishes particular kings (Prov. 16:12; Psa. 119:46, 47; 82:1, 2). Therefore, He commands our obedience to rulers (Rom. 13:1-3). Rulers are commanded to rule on His terms (Psa. 2:10ff.). Even in the New Testament activity of political import is discoverable. Jesus urged payment of taxes to *de facto* governments (Matt. 22:15-22). In response to reminders of King Herod's political threats against Him, Jesus publicly rebuked the king by calling him a vixen (Luke 12:32). He taught that a judge is unjust if he does not fear God (Luke 18:2, 6). John the Baptist openly criticized King Herod (Luke 3:19, 20). Peter refused to obey authorities who commanded him to cease preaching (Acts 5:29). The Apostle John referred to the Roman Empire as "the beast" (Rev. 13) (Kenneth Gentry, "The Greatness of the Great Commission," in *The Journal of Christian Reconstruction*, Symposium on Evangelism, ed. Gary North, Vol. VII, No. 2 [Winter, 1981], p. 45).

The denial of political involvement is the denial of most of the Bible. Christians are responsible to act righteously as citizens and, if God so calls, to participate in politics in a ministerial capacity. Every regenerate man is a priest, a minister of God (Isaiah 61:6; 66:21; 1 Peter 2:5, 9; Revelation 1:6). Citizenship is closely tied to righteousness. Jesus Christ is King of the church *and* "Lord of lords and King of kings" (Revelation 17:14).

Questions for Discussion

1. What duties do citizens have in relation to those who rule over them?
   a. Exodus 22:28; 1 Peter 2:13-17; Ephesians 6:1; Proverbs 13:24; Matthew 18:15-18; 1 Corinthians 6:1-11; Romans 13:4

   _____

   _____

   _____

   _____

   _____

   b. Ezra 6:10; 1 Timothy 2:1-2; Exodus 18:13, 17; Deuteronomy 17:16; 1 Kings 10:26-29; 2 Samuel 11; 1 Kings 11:1; Proverbs 21:1; 1 Kings 3

   _____

   _____

   _____

   _____

   c. Matthew 10:18; Acts 24-26; 1 Corinthians 9:16

   _____

   _____

   _____

   _____

   d. Jeremiah 29:7; John 14:27; Romans 5:1; compare Nehemiah 4:7-18; Ecclesiastes 3:8; Joel 3:10; Matthew 24:6, 7; Luke 11:21, 22; Exodus 22:2; Romans 13:4; Matthew 28:18-20

   _____

   _____

   _____

   _____

e. Matthew 22:17-21; Romans 13:7

_____
_____
_____
_____
_____
_____
_____
_____
_____

f. Exodus 18:17-27; Deuteronomy 1:13-17; 1 Samuel 8; 1 Kings 12; Proverbs 11:11; 29:2

_____
_____
_____
_____
_____
_____
_____
_____
_____

2. What duties does the State have in relation to the citizenry? (Acts 23:12-31; Romans 13:4; 1 Timothy 2:1-2)

_____
_____
_____
_____
_____
_____
_____
_____
_____

3. What qualifications does the Bible set forth for those who operate in positions of leadership, whether ecclesiastical or civil? (Exodus 18; Judges 9; Romans 13; 1 Timothy 3:1-7; 4:12)

_____

_____

_____

_____

_____

_____

_____

4. Are there Biblical examples of men and women resisting the State when the State enacts laws that put Christians in the position of disobeying a command of God? (Exodus 1:15-22; 2:1-10; Joshua 2:1-14; Judges 6:11ff.; Daniel 3; Acts 4:13-31; 5:17-32; 12:1-11)

_____

_____

_____

_____

_____

_____

_____

5. Should Christian churches and schools seek licensing from the State for religious affairs? (Matthew 22:21; Philippians 2:11; Acts 5:29; compare Deuteronomy 6; Proverbs, _passim._; Ephesians 5:21-6:4)

_____

_____

_____

_____

_____

_____

_____

Summary

" 'The powers that be are ordained of God.' So writes the Apostle Paul in Romans 13. The state is not god as the humanists teach. It is ordained of God. The civil government is not divine, but it is divinely sanctioned. The Christian realizes immediately that civil government as such is not the enemy. Civil governments have been established by God. As such they are an important part of God's plan for the governing of His creatures and the advancement of His kingdom.

"Three times in Romans 13 Paul refers to civil rulers as ministers of God. When the term 'minister' is used, Christians immediately think of the pastor of a church. It is a common name for a clergyman. The word refers to service. Jesus said that He came not to be ministered unto but to minister and to give His life a ransom for many. In countries such as Great Britain the term minister is regularly used. The top cabinet leaders are called ministers. The head of the civil government is the Prime Minister. This retains a good biblical word even if the content has been lost.

"A minister is to be a servant. That is still used of persons in civil government in the United States. They are called 'public servants'. . ." (Robert L. Thoburn, *The Christian and Politics*, p. 48f.)

John Wycliffe wrote of his English translation of the Bible that *This Bible is for the government of the people, by the people, and for the people.*

Answers to Questions for Discussion

1. a. Submission to Earthly Authority (Exodus 22:8; Romans 13:1; 1 Peter 2:13-17): The Bible directs us to submit "to every human institution" (1 Peter 2:13). While Peter has *civil* authority in mind here ("whether to a *king* as the one in authority, or to *governors* as sent by him for the punishment of evildoers and the praise of those who do right"), this text is inclusive of all God-ordained authorities. As Bible-believing Christians we must always remember that authority means much more than *civil* authority. The family exercises real authority over its members: "Children, obey your parents in the Lord, for this is right" (Ephesians 6:1). The symbol of authority for the family is the rod of correction: "He who spares his rod hates his son, but he who loves him disciplines him diligently" (Proverbs 13:24).

The church, through its leaders, has real authority to discipline members: "And if your brother sins, go and reprove him in private; if he listens to you, you have won your brother. But if he does not listen to you, take one or two more with you, so that BY THE MOUTH OF TWO OR THREE WITNESSES EVERY FACT MAY BE CONFIRMED. And if he refuses to listen to them, tell it to the church; and if he refuses to listen even to the church, let him be to you as a Gentile and a tax-gatherer. Truly I say to you, whatever you shall bind on earth shall have been bound in heaven; and whatever you loose on earth shall have been loosed in heaven" (Matthew 18:15-18). The Apostle Paul goes so far as to place ecclesiastical authority on a par with the civil courts: "Does any one of you, when he has a case against his neighbor, dare to go to law before the unrighteous, and not before the saints? Or do you not know that the saints will judge the world? And if the world is judged by you, are you not competent to constitute the smallest law courts?" (1 Corinthians 6:1-11). The symbol of the church's authority is the "keys of the kingdom of heaven" (Matthew 16:19).

As citizens Christians must submit to those who rule because God has established them in their positions of authority by His own sovereign will (Romans 13:1). Civil rulers, as well as family and ecclesiastical rulers, are "ministers of God." This is why rulers should not be cursed by the people:

"You shall not curse God, nor curse a ruler of your people [because he represents God]" (Exodus 22:28; cf. Romans 13:1). This does not mean, however, that sinful practices and policies of rulers are what God demands. Unlawful practices of rulers should not go unnoticed or unchallenged (cf. Mark 6:18). Moreover, Christian citizens are obliged to disobey laws that prescribe something contrary to the laws of God (cf. Exodus 1:15-22; Daniel 3; Acts 4:18; 5:29): "We read of Peter, 'They called the apostles in and had them flogged. Then they ordered them not to speak in the name of Jesus and let them go.' But notice what Peter and John did. With their backs still painfully tender, the blood scarcely dry from the flogging they had received, *they went straight out and disobeyed the state and courts of their day*. And day after day, in the temple and courts from house to house, they never stopped teaching and proclaiming the good news that Jesus is the Christ'" (Franky Schaeffer, A *Time for Anger*, p. 54). Jesus made it clear that evil rulers must be exposed (cf. Luke 13:32).

The Bible directs us to submit to those who are in authority over us, *to every human institution* (1 Peter 2:13). Peter has in mind civil authorities: *whether to a king as the one in authority, or to governors as sent by him for the punishment of evildoers and the praise of those who do right*. The early settlers understood this principle well. The *First Meeting of the Assembly in Virginia* attests to this fact.

Anarchists espouse no authority greater than the individual. With anarchy the State and civil governments at all levels would be abolished. They would be replaced by free association and voluntary cooperation of individuals and groups. The idealism of such a view is immediately dashed to pieces when one considers the fallen nature of man. Of course, non-Christian anarchists do not believe that man has a sinful nature.

Some Christian groups (e.g., the Anabaptists) taught that our freedom in Christ liberated us from the necessity of civil rulers. Even a cursory reading of Scripture will show how false this view is. How will Christians be protected against those determined to destroy the church if civil government and obedience to civil authority are not legitimate? Christians suffer when civil officials do not perform their duty under God. For example, Sosthenes, "the leader of the synagogue," was beaten by "the Jews" in "front of the judgment seat" of the "proconsul of Achaia," while Gallio looked on doing nothing (Acts 18:1-22). When the civil magistrate performs his duty, the church flourishes. When Paul was "dragged out of the temple," he was rescued "by the soldiers because of the violence of the mob" (Acts 21:27-36). When there was a conspiracy to kill Paul, the Roman civil authorities stepped in to foil the plot (Acts 23:12-24). John Calvin writes:

Those who desire to usher in anarchy object that, although in antiquity kings and judges ruled over ignorant folk, yet that servile kind of governing is wholly incompatible today with the perfection which Christ brought with his gospel. . . . But whatever kind of men they may be, the refutation is easy. For where David urges all kings and rulers to kiss the Son of God [Ps. 2:12], he does not bid them lay aside their authority and retire to private life, but submit to Christ the power with which they have been invested, that he alone may tower over all. . . . But most notable of all is the passage of Paul where, admonishing Timothy that prayers be offered for kings in public assembly, he immediately adds the reason: "That we may lead a peaceful life under them with all godliness and honesty" [I Tim. 2:2] (*Institutes of the Christian Religion*, Book IV, Chapter XX, section 5).

Such a view of civil authority should not leave us with totalitarianism as the only alternative. Personal liberty is not to be forsaken for false security

102

under tyranny. While we are commanded to "submit" to those in authority over us, we are not commanded blindly to worship those in authority over us. The biblical view of authority avoids the extremes of Anabaptists and Machiavellians.

b. Praying for Civil Authorities (Ezra 6:10; 1 Timothy 2:1-2): Our rulers need the prayers of Christians. "Paul asks for such prayers on behalf of all men, but especially for leaders in government: 'for kings, and for all that are in authority' [1 Timothy 2:1]. This is not limited to kings or presidents; it includes congressmen, state representatives, judges, city councilmen, school board members, and policemen. They all hold positions of authority, they all are ministers of God, they all face difficult decisions, and they all need our prayers" (John Eidsmoe, *God and Caesar: Christian Faith and Political Action*, p. 27).

Christians are commanded to pray for all men, especially for leaders in civil government. They are ministers of God, and as such, are given tremendous responsibilities to which God will hold them responsible.

103

The reasons are as follows: *First*, to offer them support for the difficult tasks that often burden them. The burden of office is great (Exodus 18:13, 17, 18). Fathers and mothers certainly understand what it means to be loaded with family responsibilities. Civil authorities also have families and some are employed in business. These combined obligations produce great stress, as do the temptations political power brings. Many are tempted with power (Deuteronomy 17:16), wealth (1 Kings 10:26-29), and pleasure (2 Samuel 11; 1 Kings 11:1).

Second, to pray that God would change their minds if they stray from the biblical blueprint or remove them from office if they continue to rebel against God's law and make war against God's church. I remember talking with a congressman on a particular piece of legislation. He told me that he would not change his mind, no matter what argument might be raised against his position. His stand was certainly presumptuous and arrogant. This was Pharaoh's argument: ten times in a row. In the end, God wins out. The Christian is assured that God controls the king's heart: "The king's heart is like channels of water in the hand of the LORD; He turns it wherever He wishes" (Proverbs 21:1). Many of the imprecatory Psalms are directed against tyrannical rulers and were to be prayed by the congregation of Israel: "Contend, O LORD, with those who contend with me. Fight against those who fight against me" (Psalm 35:1). "May their table before them become a snare; and when they are in peace, may it become a trap" (Psalm 69:22).

Third, to give them wisdom in applying the absolutes of God's word to civil situations. This was Solomon's prayer: "And now, O LORD my God, Thou hast made Thy servant king in place of my father David, yet I am but a little child; I do not know how to go out or come in. And Thy servant is in the midst of Thy people which Thou hast chosen, a great people who cannot be numbered or counted for multitude. So give Thy servant an understanding heart to judge Thy people to discern between good and evil. For who is able to judge this great people of Thine?" (1 Kings 3:7-9). Knowing all the facts in a given situation is not enough. Rulers must apply wisdom, a gift from God, to align the facts with the biblical model for government outlined in Scripture.

c. Proclaiming the Word of God to Civil Authorities: (Matthew 10:18; Acts 24-26): In the Old Testament, Samuel confronted King Saul on numerous occasions because of the king's unfaithfulness. When Saul assumed the priestly office contrary to the law (1 Samuel 13:8-10), Samuel proclaimed this word to him: "You have acted foolishly; you have not kept the commandment of the LORD your God, which He commanded you, for now the LORD would have established your kingdom over Israel forever. But now your kingdom shall not endure" (1 Samuel 13:13, 14; cf. 10:1-8; 15:10-35). David was confronted by Nathan the prophet for the sins of murder and adultery: "Then the LORD sent Nathan to David" (2 Samuel 12:1). King Uzziah was confronted by Azariah and "eighty priests of the LORD" because he was burning incense to the LORD, a task reserved "for the priests, the sons of Aaron" (2 Chronicles 26:16-23).

Jesus told His disciples that they would be "brought before governors and kings" for His sake (Matthew 10:18). The Apostle Paul declared, "Woe is me if I do not preach the gospel" (1 Corinthians 9:16). When Paul was brought before the civil officials of Rome He was obligated, for he was under compulsion by God, to preach the gospel. King Agrippa was confronted with the claims of Jesus Christ and responded by saying, "In a short time you will persuade me to become a Christian" (Acts 26:28). Paul responds by saying, "I would to God [lit., *I pray to God*], that whether in a short or long time, not only you, but also all who hear me this day, might become such as I am, except for these chains" (v. 29).

It is not enough to have "conservative" rulers who merely follow after the traditions of men and in many cases despise Jesus Christ and His law. Christians should be working for distinctively and consistently *Christian* leaders whose lives are conformed to the image of Jesus Christ and who seek to make the word of God the law of the land as it relates to civil affairs. Moreover, Christians must preach the whole counsel of God to all men — especially to rulers, to whom much has been given and of whom much will be required.

This gives the State a very high and important function. It also makes more clear the importance of civil officials obeying the law of God, just as preachers are to preach the whole counsel of God. In addition, it makes clearer the limits of the citizen's duty to honor and obey those in power in civil government. We would not honor or believe or obey a minister in a church who teaches false doctrine or exhorts us to do evil. Similarly, we should not honor or obey a minister of civil government who demands that we do evil. In fact, our duties would include working to vote out of office such a civil "servant."

d. Pursuing Peace (Jeremiah 29:7; John 14:27; Romans 5:1): Peace only can be realized through the life-transforming gospel of Jesus Christ. Genuine and lasting peace will not come through law, force, political promises or compromises, the elimination of poverty, worldwide "public education," the establishment of a one-world humanistic government, and other proposed utopian dreams. To pray for peace, as we are instructed to do, is no substitute for preaching the gospel so the nations are discipled according to the word of Jesus Christ (Matthew 28:18-20). Wars do not come because of environmental factors. Rather, they are the result of man's inherent sinfulness: "What is the source of quarrels and conflicts among you? Is not the source your pleasures that wage war in your members? You lust and do not have; so you commit murder. And you are envious and cannot obtain; so you fight and quarrel. . ." (James 4:1-2).

A very misunderstood and misapplied verse of Scripture is: "And let the peace of Christ rule in your hearts, to which indeed you were called in one body; and be thankful" (Colossians 3:15). Christians often say: Well, I have peace about this matter; therefore, I know God wants me to do this or that. The context of this verse has nothing to do with a peaceful feeling that can be used for guidance to determine the will of God. Paul is talking about the "new self" that should be putting "aside anger, wrath, malice, slander, and abusive speech" (v. 8), all sources of conflict. Within the Christian community "there is no distinction between Greek and Jew, circumcised and uncircumcised, barbarian, Scythian, slave and freeman, but Christ is all, and in all" (v. 11). The Christian is to "put on a heart of compassion, kindness, humility, gentleness and patience; bearing with one another, and forgiving each other, whoever has a complaint against any one; just as the Lord forgave you, so also should you" (vv. 12, 13). Paul then goes on to say "let the peace of God," the absence of conflict, "rule," act as an arbiter to resolve conflicts, "in your hearts," where you have been "renewed to a true knowledge according to the image of the One who created" you (v. 10).

Humanist institutions deny the reality of sin; therefore, they believe man can save himself. There is no way to resolve conflicts except through

106

the consolidation of power and force. The following is an excerpt from The Preamble to the Charter of the United Nations. It is an example of man's attempt at peace without Christ: "We the peoples of the United Nations, determined to save succeeding generations from the scourge of war, ...to unite our strength to maintain international peace and security, and to ensure, by the acceptance of principles and the institution of methods, that armed force shall not be used, save in the common interest. . . have resolved to combine our efforts to accomplish these aims."

While we are exhorted to pray for peace, the Bible takes evil and the reality of war seriously. It recognizes that if men will war with God they will most certainly war with other men.

Peace, according to the drafters of the United Nations Charter, comes by and through the efforts of man. Do you see the remnants of Babel? "Come, let us build for ourselves a city, and a tower whose top will reach into heaven, and let us make for ourselves a name" (Genesis 11:4). Man as a rebel against God believes that by uniting other men and nations, peace will prevail. But it is peace with a price. The united strength will result in tyranny. We will have "peace," but it will be defined in man's terms. All dissenting opinions are silenced. The peace that the Lord wants us to pray for and promote is His peace, not peace as men define it. War between individuals and nations is the result of man's war with God. Only the gospel can make "peace with God" and, thus, peace with men and nations (Romans 5:1). William Symington of Glasgow, Scotland, wrote that the Christian

> religion directly tends to promote blessings of peace. Securing peace with God, it inculcates peace between man and man; it puts a check to those ambitious designs and wicked passions which will be found, on the one side or on the other, or perhaps on both, to originate those wars which prove a scourge and a curse to mankind; while it teaches all to aim at bringing about that happy predicted state of things, when men *shall beat their swords into ploughshares, and their spears into pruning-hooks; nation shall not lift up nation against nation, neither shall they learn war any more* [Isaiah 2:4] (*Messiah the Prince*, p. 282).

Does this mean that a nation should not defend itself against the sinful military advancements of aggressive nations? The Bible takes evil and the reality of war seriously (Nehemiah 4:7-18; Ecclesiastes 3:8; Joel 3:10; Matthew 24:6, 7; Luke 11:21, 22; 14:31, 32); it recognizes that if men will war with God they certainly will war with other men.

Under certain circumstances the individual is given the authority to defend himself, and if need be, kill an intruder (Exodus 22:2). If an individual, who is not given the authority to wield the sword in a civil capacity, can protect himself, then we must conclude that the civil magistrate who does have authority to wield the sword can defend the nation. The civil magistrate is God's "avenger who brings wrath upon the one who practices evil" (Romans 13:4). The civil magistrate's symbol of authority is the "sword," an instrument of judgment (Romans 13:4). Israel was commanded to have an army of armed men (Deuteronomy 20). The Old and New Testaments are filled with instances of nations at war with Israel and Israel's defense of its borders.

While peace is what we all desire, war often is a reality we must face and prepare for. We are told that King Uzziah "went out and warred against the Philistines, and broke down the wall of Gath and the wall of Jabneh and the wall of Ashdod; and he built cities in the area of Ashdod and among the Philistines" (2 Chronicles 26:6). The king was a military strategist. The cities he built were probably military outposts, similar to our army and air bases overseas, to give him better access to the plans of the Philistines. The king prepared for war to avert war.

Moreover, Uzziah had an army ready for battle, which entered combat by divisions, according to the number of their muster, prepared by Jeiel the scribe and Maaseiah the official, under the direction of Hananiah, one of the king's officers. The total number of the heads of the households, of valiant warriors, was 2,600. And under their direction was an elite army of 307,500, who could wage war with great power, to help the king against the enemy. Moreover, Uzziah prepared for all the army shields, bows and sling stones. And in Jerusalem he made engines of war invented by skillful men to be on the towers and on the corners, for the purpose of shooting arrows and great stones (2 Chronicles 26:11-15).

But our nation has ignored the Bible and the wisdom granted to King Uzziah. We have been told that war will not come if we eliminate our defenses and seek military equality with our enemies. If peace can only rule in the hearts of Christians, then good intentions will not avert war. The Soviet Union has no such peace-making heart. Given the opportunity, they would destroy us. History gives us ample evidence that their intentions are less than noble: the captive nations of Eastern Europe, the brutal assault on Afghanistan, the exporting of weapons and men to fuel the flames of conflict in Central America, Asia, and Africa, and the shooting down of a Korean commercial airliner filled with 269 innocent men (one of whom was United States Congressman Lawrence P. McDonald), women, and children on August 31, 1983.

e. Paying Taxes (Matthew 22:17-21; Romans 13:7): Because civil governments are ordained by God and act as *service* institutions, for they are ministers of God (Romans 13:4), they are in need of tax money to pay for the rendered services. Jesus states that Caesar is due tax money because he performs tasks that benefit them: "Render to Caesar the things that are Caesar's; and to God the things that are God's" (Matthew 22:21). The strength of the Roman army kept Israel safe from foreign enemies. This was a benefit to Israel. A tax therefore was due. Jesus did not endorse the way Caesar governed, but He upheld the biblical institution of civil government and its authority to exact limited taxation. While there were unscrupulous tax collectors, the collection of taxes is not evil in itself. The converted tax-gatherer Zaccheus repaid those he defrauded four times (Luke 19:8; cf. Exodus 22:1; Leviticus 6:5; Numbers 5:7; 2 Samuel 12:6). He sinned because he defrauded, not because he collected.

Jesus drew a distinction between God and His things (*all* things), and Caesar and *his* things (only those things that God, who is Lord of all things, allots to Caesar). Jesus certainly did not want to equate Caesar with God, nor the rightful claim of God to all that we have to any claim of Caesar to all that we have. The distinction Jesus drew requires us to obey Caesar, but only within the *limited* jurisdiction or scope of Caesar's authority. Because Caesar is not God, Caesar's authority is not absolute, nor is his claim on our obedience. Because Caesar is not God, and so does not own all things, his claim on us in regard to taxation is not absolute.

High taxes result from the majority of the citizens turning to the State for security. The civil magistrate's power is used to create a tax system which takes money from the so-called wealthy and distributes confiscated revenues to the less fortunate. The result is slavery. The State often has used man's desire for security to subvert freedom. William Shirer, author of *The Rise and Fall of the Third Reich*, wrote:

> To combat socialism [Otto von] Bismark put through between 1883 and 1889 a program for social security far beyond anything known in other countries. It included compulsory insurance for workers against old age, sickness, accident and incapacity, and though organized by the State it was financed by employers and employees. It . . . [had] a profound influence on the working class in that it *gradually made them value security over political freedom and caused them to see in the State, however conservative, a benefactor and a protector* (p. 96n).

Bismark did this as a conservative, anti-socialist measure. Conservative Party leader Joseph Chamberlain (1836-1914) followed suit in Britain and President Theodore Roosevelt (1858-1919) did it here, as did William Taft (1857-1930).

110

Adolph Hitler remarked in *Mein Kampf*: "I studied Bismark's socialist legislation in its intention, struggle and success" (p. 155). Hitler knew the people would trade freedom for security. These socialist programs were paid for by taxes. Our own nation's taxing policy fits in with the desires of the people. Power-hungry politicians pick up on this dependency and use it for great political gain: "The idol state uses the language of compassion because its intention is a messianic one. It finds the masses harassed and helpless, like sheep without a shepherd, needing a savior" (Herbert Schlossberg, *Idols For Destruction*, p. 185). All too often the people trust their lives to these political saviors and eventually find the promise of security has become the first step toward slavery.

f. Supporting Christian Leadership (Exodus 18: 17-27; Deuteronomy 1:13-17; 1 Samuel 8; 1 Kings 12): The people are responsible for supporting godly leadership. Moses chose leaders who had come through the tested ranks of family, business, and community leadership: "Choose wise and discerning and experienced men from your tribes, and I will appoint them as heads" (Deuteronomy 1:13). Responsibility for choosing godly leaders rested with the people. Moses then chose from those presented to him as worthy leaders: "So I took the heads of your tribes, wise and experienced men, and appointed them heads over you, leaders of thousands, and of hundreds, of fifties and of tens, and officers for your tribes" (1:15). Judges were chosen with the same ethical and experiential considerations (Deuteronomy 1:16, 17). King Saul was rejected as king because he did not keep "the commandment of the LORD" (1 Samuel 13:13). "Has the LORD as much delight in burnt offerings and sacrifices as in obeying the voice of the LORD? Behold, to obey is better than sacrifice, and to heed than the fat of rams. For rebellion is as the sin of divination, and insubordination is as iniquity and idolatry" (1 Samuel 15:22, 23).

Today, Christians have the freedom and duty to vote for responsible leadership, using the standard of God's Law as the measure for their political choices: "By the blessing of the upright a city is exalted, but by the mouth of the wicked it is torn down" (Proverbs 11:11). There is a direct relationship between those who rule and the condition of the nation: "When the righteous increase, the people rejoice, but when a wicked man rules, people groan" (Proverbs 29:2).

The church has a role in civil government, since the church holds the power of the "keys" and thus should discipline all the members, including those members who hold political office. Puritan New England understood the obligations of both church and state.

Puritan law treated all men equally. Church members were dealt with the same way as anyone else. On the other hand, a church had the right to discipline any of its members even if they were officers of the government. However, the only punishments the Church could impose were religious ones such as excommunication, restriction from the sacraments, etc. A man could not be removed from public office by the Church (James T. Draper and Forrest E. Watson, *If the Foundations Be Destroyed*, p. 53).

The Church has a real obligation to discipline those members who claim neutrality in the civil realm. When a church member who holds political office votes for a certain policy (e.g., a woman's "right" to abortion), and all the while maintains that he cannot impose his morality upon society as a whole, the church leadership must call the civil ruler to account. If the law is a *civil* law, as is protecting the life of the unborn, the church member has a duty to work for the prohibition of abortion. If the church nurtures its members through instruction, worship, and discipline, the citizenry will be directly affected. The ungodly will not get elected and those already in office will be voted out. We will not see the restoration of civil government until we see the restoration of the church.

Those who rule in the political realm are responsible to enact laws that are biblical in nature as they relate to civil affairs. Notice the minister present as Col. Henderson calls to order the first legislature of Kentucky.

2. Civil governments have responsibility to punish evil-doers and promote the good. Civil government at every level is to exercise its authority in its stated jurisdiction and to settle disputes between conflicting jurisdictions. When disputes occur or crimes are committed, the State must act swiftly and justly to settle them. The standard of judgment is the word of God, "for it [the God-ordained authority] is a minister of God to you for good" (Romans 13:4). Notice that Paul states the civil magistrate is a minister to *you* for good. Paul has a biblical moral order in mind when he speaks about the operation of the State as a minister. Good and evil can only be defined in terms of a standard: God's standard (cf. Hebrews 5:14).

The State must protect the *Christian* religion. Any obstacle that would jeopardize the preaching of the word of God in carrying out the Great Commission must be removed by civil government. Civil rulers should have the interests of "godliness" and "dignity" in mind as they administer justice. This is why Paul instructed Christians to pray for their rulers, so "that we [Christians] may lead a tranquil and quiet life in all godliness and dignity" (1 Timothy 2:2). Many wish to maintain that the State must be religiously and morally neutral. The Bible makes no such suggestion. Even our Constitution assumes the protection of the *Christian* religion. The First Amendment had the specific purpose of excluding all rivalry among *Christian* denominations. Other competing religions were not protected by the First Amendment. Chief Justice Joseph Story wrote:

> [T]he real object of the [F]irst Amendment was not to countenance, much less to advance [Islam], or Judaism, or infidelity, by prostrating Christianity, but to exclude all rivalry among *Christian* sects [denominations], and to prevent any *national* ecclesiastical establishment which would give to an hierarchy the exclusive patronage of the *national* government (*Commentaries on the Constitution*, 1833).

Paul expected even the Roman civil government to protect him from those who threatened the Christian religion (Acts 23:12-31; cf. 25:11). This means civil government cannot be religiously neutral. If the Christian religion is not supported, then some other religion will be, usually a State religion that degenerates into secularism. The State cannot be neutral toward all religions because all religious views or philosophies necessarily entail moral systems, and conflict with those of other religious systems. If the State were truly "neutral," it would enact no laws, for each law would penalize someone's religion or religious view or religious practice. Anarchy would reign.

The Apostle Paul writes that God the Father "put all things in subjection under [Jesus'] feet, and gave Him as head over all things to the church" (Ephesians 1:22). "It is for the sake of the Church that he is invested with universal regal authority: in other words, the *end* of Christ's universal Mediatorial dominion is *the good of the Church*. Thus far, all is clear and undeniable. But *the nations* are among the 'all things,' over which Christ is appointed 'Head.' It follows, then, that Christ is appointed *Head over the nations for the good of the Church*" (William Symington, *Messiah the Prince*, p. 266).

3. The qualifications for leadership are moral in nature. Rulers must be "men of truth, those who hate dishonest gain" (Exodus 18:21). The standard by which they are to rule is not to be their own and no amount of monetary and political gain will move them from their allegiance to God and His word. They are to "fear God." Jethro's counsel to Moses was to "choose wise and discerning and experienced men from" the tribes of Israel (Deuteronomy 1:13). Notice the connection between ethics and experience. Symington writes:

It is not every individual who is qualified to hold office in a nation. Good natural talents, a cultivated mind, and a due share of acquaintance with the principles of government and with the constitution and laws of the country, seem indispensable. Scripture, not less than common sense, discountenances the practice of setting persons of feeble intellect to bear rule. 'Wo unto thee, O land, when thy king is a *child* [Ecclesiastes 10:16]! Thou shalt provide out of all the people *able* men [Exodus 18:21]. Take ye *wise* men and *understanding*, and I will make them rulers over you' (Deuteronomy 1:13]. Not less essential are *moral* qualifications. High and incorruptible integrity, well regulated mercy, strict veracity, and exemplary temperance, all specified with approbation in the Word of God (*Messiah the Prince*, p. 243).

It is a sign of judgment when God puts the immature and inexperienced in positions of leadership: "And I will make mere lads their princes and

114

capricious children will rule over them, and the people will be oppressed, each one by another, and each one by his neighbor; the youth will storm against the elder, and the inferior against the honorable. . . . O My people! Their oppressors are children, and women rule over them" (Isaiah 3:4, 5, 12).

When choosing men for leadership roles, ethical and moral considerations should abound. Choosing someone because of party affiliation is no reason to vote them into office.

The Apostle Paul builds on these principles when he sets forth the qualifications of leadership in the church. Ethical considerations abound. Leaders must be able to control their own appetites (1 Timothy 3:1-7). "It is significant that St. Paul's counsel concerning the qualifications of an elder are written to Timothy, who was half-Greek, and who was laboring in a Gentile city. For Jewish Christians, such counsel (1 Tim. 3:1-13) was not necessary; they already were thoroughly familiar with the meaning of eldership and its qualifications. Moreover, there is no reason to restrict Paul's counsel concerning the election of elders (or bishops) to the institution of worship. . . . His counsel sets forth the requirements for eldership [leadership] in every realm, church, state, school, etc." (R. J. Rushdoony, *Law and Society*, p. 368f.)

The ethical leads to the practical. For example, how does a voter know whether a political candidate reflects biblical moral behavior? "You will know them by their fruits" (Matthew 7:16). We should see their ethics worked out in everyday situations. Ethics, then, must be made visible. A voter should not simply trust a politician's position on an issue. His voting record and his lifestyle should be open for all to see. The individual who is scrupulous in personal, family, and business affairs will gain positions of leadership if the citizenry respects such behavior. Unfortunately, the immorality in civil government is a reflection of immorality in self-, family, and church governments.

Those who are faithful in small things (an ethical evaluation) will be entrusted with greater responsibilities (Matthew 25:23). Jethro's advice to Moses was that "able men" must rule (Exodus 18:21). Ability is cultivated through time as the word of God is applied to life's situations and is evaluated by the citizenry. Timothy is told, "Let no one look down on your youthfulness. . ." (1 Timothy 4:12). While Timothy was young, he was no "mere lad." Apparently, he conducted himself in a way that reflected his faith in ethical terms. His life (ethical behavior) was an example (observable behavior) for others to evaluate and imitate.

Civil leadership, like ecclesiastical leadership, is designed to be ministerial. Those in authority must follow the pattern of God as *ministers* rather than attempt to define the role of governmental ledership in terms of how others rule (Luke 22:24-30; cf. 1 Samuel 8:5). In Romans 13:4, in describing the role of the civil magistrate, the Greek word *diakonos* is used. It is translated "deacon" (1 Timothy 3:8), "servant" (Mark 10:43; 1 Corinthians 3:5) or "minister" (Romans 13:4). "This term and its cognates are used in the New Testament, with one possible exception [Phil. 2:25; cf. also Phil. 2:30], with reference to the service of God and sometimes of the highest forms of ministry in the worship of God (cf. Luke 1:23; Acts 13:2; Rom. 15:6, 27; II Cor. 9:12; Phil. 2:17; Heb. 1:7, 14; 8:2; 10:11). Hence, if anything, this designation enhances the dignity attaching to the ministry of rulers" (John Murray, *The New International Commentary on the New Testament: Epistle to the Romans*, Vol. 2, p. 154f.) It also underscores the ruler's duty to *serve*, rather than to "lord it over" those

116

under his authority.

Outside the New Testament, the term *diakonos* is used in the title, "deacon (*minister*) of the city." Within the New Testament, the term clearly is filled with religious meaning and often is translated "service" or "serve." It is applied to the "ministry" of Christ (Matthew 20:28), of Paul (1 Timothy 1:12), and those within the church (Acts 6:1-6). Jesus came not to be ministered unto, but to minister. The tyrant wants others to minister unto him as God, to serve his ungodly ideas and desires. The godly ruler, however, is to be Christ-like, and so is to serve the people, under God, by protecting those who are good according to God's standards and restraining and punishing those who do evil, again, as evaluated by God's standards.

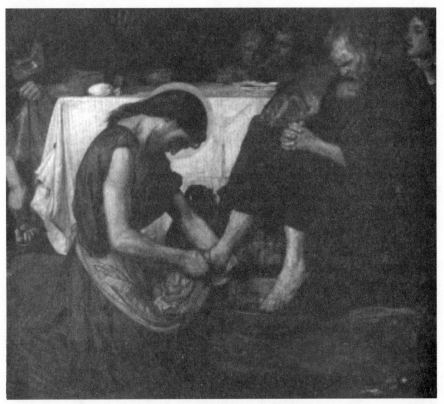

If I then, the Lord and the Teacher, washed your feet, you also ought to wash one another's feet. For I gave you an example that you also should do as I did to you. Truly, truly, I say to you, a slave is not greater than his master; neither one who is sent greater than the one who sent him (John 13:14-16).

In Romans 13:6, the Greek word *leitourgos* is used. John Murray again writes: "The title here accorded the civil ruler shows he is invested with all the dignity and sanction belonging to God's servant within the sphere of [civil] government. This is borne out sill further by the purpose for which he is God's servant; he is the minister of God for that which is *good*" (*Romans*, Vol. 2, p. 152). It should be underscored here that the standard of goodness spoken of in Scripture is none other than God's standard of goodness: God's law-word. The civil ruler, like the ecclesiastical minister, and no less than the ecclesiastical minister, is to minister according to the perfect and immutable standard of God's law. No more than the ecclesiastical minister should preach or teach the false doctrines of sinful men, should the civil minister rule according to fallen men's vain imaginings or philosophical deceit about what is good and what is evil.

4. The Bible shows resistance to tyranny was legitimate and often commanded. There are cases where divine assistance released outspoken Christians from the hands of the State. The Hebrew midwives were commanded by "the king of Egypt" to put to death all the male children being born to the Hebrew women (Exodus 1:15-16). The Hebrew midwives disobeyed the edict of the king: "But the midwives feared God, and did not do as the king of Egypt had commanded them, but let the boys live" (v. 17). God shows His approval of their actions: "So God was good to the midwives, and the people multiplied, and became very mighty. And it came about because the midwives feared God, that He established households for them" (vv. 20-21). Jochebed, Moses' mother, also disobeyed the edict of the king by hiding her child and later creating a way of escape for the child so he would not be murdered by the king's army: "But when she could hide him no longer, she got him a wicker basket and covered it over with tar and pitch. Then she put the child into it, and set it among the reeds by the bank of the Nile" (v. 3). Jochebed even deceived Pharaoh's daughter into believing that she was in no way related to the child (vv. 7-9).

Rahab hid the spies of Israel and lied about their whereabouts. When a route for escape became available, she led them out another way from that of the pursuing soldiers. She is praised by two New Testament writers for her actions: "By faith Rahab the harlot did not perish along with those who were disobedient, after she had welcomed the spies in peace" (Hebrews 11:31). Rahab is listed with Abraham as one whose faith was reflected in her works: "And in the same way [as Abraham] was not Rahab the harlot also justified by works, when she received the messengers and sent the out by another way?" (James 2:25) By sending the spies out by another way, she subverted the king's desire to capture the spies.

Shadrach, Meshach, and Abed-nego refused to follow the command of the king to worship the golden statue: "These men, O king, have disregarded you; they do not serve your gods or worship the golden image you have set up" (Daniel 3:12). When the three were thrown into the furnace, the angel of the Lord came to their aid (v. 25). King Darius signed a document that prohibited anyone from making "a petition to any god or man besides" himself (Daniel 6:7). Anyone refusing to obey the order "shall be cast into the lion's den" (v. 7). Daniel refused the edict. The Bible states that Daniel went out of his way to disobey the order: "Now when Daniel knew that the document was signed, he entered his house (now in his roof chamber he had windows open toward Jerusalem); and he continued kneeling on his knees three times a day, praying and giving thanks before his God, as he had been doing previously" (v. 10).

The New Testament has similar accounts of resistance to tyranny. When Peter and John were ordered by the rulers and elders of the people to stop preaching in the name of Jesus (Acts 4:18), the two apostles refused to follow their injunction: "Whether it is right in the sight of God to give heed to you rather than to God, you be the judge; for we cannot stop speaking what we have seen and heard" (vv. 19-20). Peter and John could not stop speaking what they had seen and heard because they had been commanded by Jesus to preach in His name (cf. Matthew 28:18-20; Acts 1:8; 1 Corinthians 9:16). On another occasion, some of the apostles were arrested for preaching and healing in the name of Jesus. Again, they were put in a "public jail" (Acts 5:18). During the night "an angel of the Lord. . . opened the gates of the prison" and commanded them to disobey the rulers rulers of Israel: "Go your way, stand and speak to the people in the temple the whole message of life" (v. 20). When the apostles again were confronted with the command not to preach and teach, their response was quick and sure: "We must obey God rather than men" (v. 29).

The apostles' obedience to God conflicted with the desires of the State.

This resulted in the first apostolic death: "Now about that time Herod the king [Agrippa I] laid hands on some who belonged to the church, in order to mistreat them. And he had James the brother of John put to death" (Acts 12:1-2). Peter was later arrested for similar "crimes" against the State (v. 3). God, at least, does not show His disapproval of rebellion against tyrants in these specific cases. He even sent one of His angels to release Peter from prison (vv. 6-8).

And behold, an angel of the Lord suddenly appeared, and a light shone in the cell; and he struck Peter's side and roused him, saying, "Get up quickly." And his chains fell of his hands (Acts 12:7).

5. Civil government is only one government among many; therefore, its governing authority is only one among many. Biblically speaking, civil governments have no jurisdiction in family, ecclesiastical (church) or educational affairs, except when crimes are committed as outlined by Scripture. Education comes under parental authority.

> Children are born into an already existing hierarchy (Ephesians 5:21-6:4): a hierarchy created and established as a functioning team to subdue and take dominion over the creation (Genesis 1:26-28; 9:1-17). . . . The family is an educational institution. It is a training institution for leadership in fulfilling the Creator's mandates. For example, one basic requirement for holding the office of elder or deacon in the church is for married men to rule over their households effectively (1 Timothy 3:2, 12). Implicit here is the concept that leadership in the church is first established in the family and then transmitted to the other institutions of society (John W. Whitehead, *The New Tyranny*, pp. 20-21).

The State seeks to license educational and ecclesiastical (church) establishments in order to control the children and, thus, the future direction of society and the world. Whoever controls society controls *all* institutions. This is why Humanists want direct control over families, churches, schools, businesses, the judiciary, congress, foreign affairs, and every influential institution. It is God or the State. Control of any one aspect or institution does *not* lead to control of others. This is why Humanists want control of them all.

One area where control is most prevalent is the control of children by the State through education. The Christian Schools of Ohio (CSO) understood this very well. They contended that the Ohio Minimum Standards were "unlivable for Christian schools." A court case ensued. The Minimum Standards had the following purpose: "[The State Board of Education] shall formulate and prescribe minimum standards to be applied to all elementary and high schools in this state *for the purpose of requiring a general education of high quality.*" When the defense attorney attempted to enter into evidence the Standford Achievement Test scores, which showed that 90 percent of the children of the Tabernacle Christian School had made between one-and two-years' academic progress in an eight-month period, it was said to be "irrelevant and immaterial" (Blair

121

The abuses of State authority can be seen in the arrest, trial, and execution of Jesus: *Judas then, having received the Roman cohort, and officers from the chief priests and the Pharisees, came there with lanterns and torches and weapons* (John 18:3).

Adams and Joel Stein, *Who Owns the Children?*, p. 14). In this case, the State's interest was not in the *quality* of education, only the *control* of education.

Christians must avoid State control of education at all costs. Education must remain in the hands of the parents and those to whom they delegate the responsibility (Christians who are ecclesiastically responsible). The question of State control becomes a question of lordship. The Bible is unreserved in its answer: "Jesus Christ is Lord" (Philippians 2:11). God owns all things and has authority over all things. The civil government has authority only over a few things — which do not include the education of our God-given children.

The early church made it clear that the State has authority, but its authority does not extend beyond what God ordains. When the civil authorities demanded that the apostles stop their "teaching," the apostles refused: "We must obey God rather than men" was their answer (Acts 5:29). "The Sanhedrin was, in effect, attempting to license or assume approval authority over the apostles' educational program — the education being in terms of the Gospel. The apostles stoutly resisted. They were persecuted. They were beaten for conducting unlicensed teaching" (John W. Whitehead, *The New Tyranny*, pp. 49).

The Bible makes it clear that the State has authority, but its authority does not extend beyond what God ordains. Even an all-powerful civil government cannot claim a divine right and rule in terms of autonomous power.

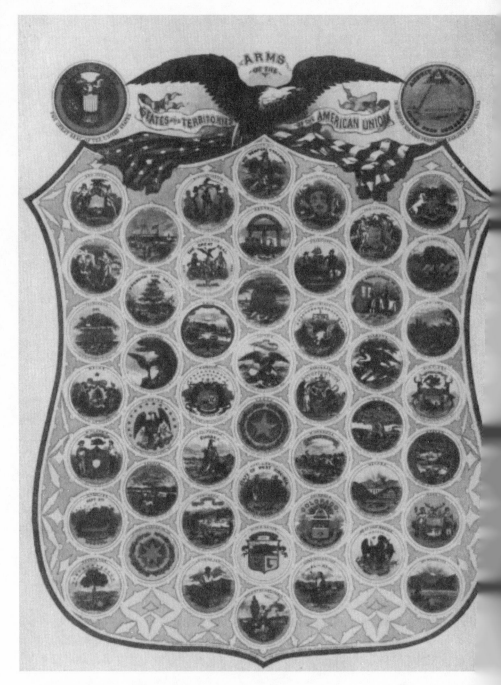

The Restoration of the Republic will not take place until we see the restoration of individuals. Individual restoration brought about by the regenerating work of the Holy Spirit. The larger society benefits from the transformation of individuals, families, and churches.

Lesson 5

The Restoration
of the Republic

Restoration of the Republic begins with the individual. Only the conversion of many can result in long-term societal restoration. I assume that you already are a Christian; that you have repented of your sins and have turned to Jesus Christ as your only hope for salvation, and are in no way depending on your own so-called "good works" to make you acceptable with God. You must recognize God as a God of love and justice — two inseparable attributes. Because God loves His people He sent Jesus, His only Son, to die for their sins. Justice necessitated the death of Jesus. Divine justice had to be satisfied. Peace with God (not the devil) had to be made (Romans 5:1). This message must be preached world-wide. No nation can experience the restoration process without repentance of sin and unconditional surrender to God through Jesus Christ.

Regeneration is only the first step, however. Born again, we, in fact, are spiritual infants, babes in Christ: "Like newborn babes, long for the pure milk of the word, that by it you may grow in respect to salvation, if you have tasted the kindness of the Lord" (1 Peter 2:2, 3). Peter tells us there is a growth process. We must not remain "babes." Many Christians never leave infancy, however, but resemble the Christians described in the epistle to the Hebrews: "For by this time you ought to be teachers, you have need again for someone to teach you the elementary principles of the oracles of God, and you have come to need milk and not solid food. For every one who partakes only of milk is not accustomed to the word of righteousness, for he is a babe. But solid food is for the mature, who because of practice have their senses trained to discern good and evil" (Hebrews 5:12-14).

The restoration process begins with the individual and must be total. Restoration affects body and soul (1 Thessalonians 5:23; 2 Corinthians 5:17; Romans 6:12-14; 12:1; 1 Corinthians 6:15, 20); the understanding (Proverbs 2:2; John 6:45; Romans 12:2; Colossians 3:1, 2; 1 Peter 1:13); the will (Ezekiel 36:25-27; Matthew 7:21; Mark 3:35; Colossians 1:9-12, 21); the passions (Galatians 5:24; Colossians 3:5-17); and the conscience (Titus 1:15; Hebrews 9:14).

Every state is based upon some fundamental ideas; and the study of those ideas is the most important object of inquiry in the study of its constitution. No social system can be understood without a knowledge of its fundamental principles.

—E. C. Wines

"Society" possesses no will of its own, but reflects the people's will. The will of the people is either based on the autonomous will of men or reflects the will of the Triune God of Scripture. E.C. Wines (1806–1879) writes: "In political, as well as physical science, there are certain great principles, true or false, from which, in any given case, all the numerous details of social organization flow. Every state is based upon some fundamental ideas; and the study of those ideas is the most important object of inquiry in the study of its constitution. No social system can be understood without a knowledge of its fundamental principles. . . . The first and most essential of these fundamental principles was the unity of God" (*The Hebrew Republic*, p. 1). If "society" is to be restored, individuals must be restored to the knowledge that God is one and that His law is one, binding individual, family, church, and State. Christians must understand that the Christian life goes beyond regeneration and justification to discipleship and sanctification, being conformed "to the image of God's Son" (Romans 8:29). We are held accountable for the "whole purpose of God" (Acts 20:27).

126

The Bible, from Genesis to Revelation, must become our steady diet. If we do not know how to "handle accurately the word of truth" (2 Timothy 2:15), we cannot discern the times and offer biblical solutions to personal, family, and societal problems (cf.1 Chronicles 12:32). "If we want truth, we must go to the source of truth. Scripture equips believers to [do] all good works (2 Tim. 3:16-17), whether the arena is familial, economic, political, or jurisprudence. *We need to be aware of the intellectual and practical destruction latent in all humanistic theories of knowledge.* 'Beware lest any man spoil you through philosophy and vain deceit, after the tradition of men, after the rudiments of the world and not after Christ' (Col.2:8)" (Tommy Rogers, "An Epistemology of Dominion," in *The Journal of Christian Reconstruction,* Symposium on Social Action, ed. Gary North, Vol.VIII, No.1 [Summer, 1981], p.81). Besides a comprehensive biblical education, we must develop an educational program for dominion purposes that will cover the world (Isaiah 11:9). This means applying what we learn from the Bible to every area of human thought. We should read and study books on economics, politics, education, law, medicine, journalism, foreign policy, ecology, philosophy, agriculture, ethics, psychology, science, and every other God-created sphere of learning. God supplies His people with gifts and talents for building the Kingdom. God requires us to account for our use of those gifts and talents. He does not restore us simply to provide for our private and self-centered use of those gifts.

Christians also must be future-oriented. Decisions made today affect future generations. We cannot give up on this world. Jesus calls us to victory now! Satan was crushed under the feet of the first century Christians (Romans 16:20), not Jesus.

Why do many Christians act as though Jesus was not raised from the dead? There could be no power in a crucified Jesus who remained in a tomb. Thus, Paul wanted to know the "*power* of His resurrection" (Philippians 3:10). Paul also writes that Jesus is the "*power* of God" (1 Corinthians 1:24), the gospel is the "*power* of God for salvation" (Romans 1:16), and "all *authority* and *power* and *dominion*" belong to Jesus (Ephesians 1:21).

Christians should work to rebuild all institutions according to the blueprint laid down in Scripture. Too often we satisfy ourselves with occupying a square foot of living space in what we perceive to be the humanists' palace. Tommy Rogers writes:

> We must know our enemy, but we must have a solid base from which to evaluate our position and to assess the enemy. We must learn, first, to direct our efforts at *substance* rather than symbol. It is not of particular importance to return "prayer" to public schools, or to pass bills requiring "creationism." Why should we be satisfied with so-called "prayer" offered to an unknown god in a humanistically dominated establishment? The overriding issue is to dismantle the public schools, for the whole humanistic system seeks to avoid God (Tommy Rogers, "An Epistemology for Dominion," p.80).

We fight for crumbs when Jesus tells us to sit with Him and feast in the presence of our enemies (Psalm 23:5; cf. Matthew 15:21-28).

We now live under a *better* covenant with a *greater* measure of God's Spirit but it is supposed that our sphere of ministry has *decreased*. Israel was confined to the *land* of Canaan, but Jesus has given us the *world* and yet the impact we are to have as Christians, if we believe some of our critics, is to be minimal. But the kingdom is now: "Thy kingdom come. Thy will be done, on earth as it is in heaven" (Matthew 6:10). The kingdom comes and advances by *doing* God's will. The devil only has a foothold when Christians fail to obey. When we resist the devil, he will flee from us. Satan's counterfeit and corrupt kingdom is then supplanted by God's rightful claim to the world. Resisting the devil is never passive.

"Blessed are the meek, for they shall inherit the earth" (Matthew 5:5; cf. Psalm 37:11). Now, if the earth is ours as an inheritance, then why do we act as if the inheritance belongs to someone else? This passage does not say that the weak shall inherit the earth or the passive or the non-involved. Meekness is an ethical attribute. Meekness or being humble means to rely on God for all things. The Bible makes it clear that a double portion of a father's inheritance goes to the faithful first-born son (Deuteronomy 21:17; see 2 Kings 2:9). If he is unfaithful, he can be disinherited (Deuteronomy 21:18-21). Reuben lost his right of inheritance because of immorality (Genesis 49:3, 4); and Jacob gave Joseph a double portion because of his faithfulness and righteousness (Genesis 48:22). Jesus, as God's firstborn, receives a double portion. We, as God's adopted children and brothers of Jesus, participate in the inheritance. If the nations are given to Jesus as an inheritance, then we participate in His inheritance (see Psalm 2). It is someone who submits to a greater authority in this case, to God (cf. Matthew 11:28f.; 2 Corinthians 10:1; Galatians 5:22ff.; Colossians 3:12; 1 Peter 3:15f.; James 1:19-21). The way we will inherit the earth is by obeying God in all things, humbly submitting to Him. Moses is said to be the meekest man who ever lived (Numbers 12:3). But no one could portray him as being non-activistic.

Only the Christian has a rightful claim to the earth and all its potential. God requires His people to lay hold of that claim ethically by submitting to God's sovereign rule in all things and taking dominion over the whole redeemed world for Jesus and His glory.

Our nation was built on self-government that grew out of a Christian world view. Productivity, industry, security, and stability could not have been realized unless there was a foundation of Christian absolutes. The future will be maintained as long as the nation remains faithful to its original covenant with God.

Questions for Discussion

1. How do false spiritual/material and sacred/secular divisions work to keep Christians from involving themselves in the restoration of the Republic? (Genesis 1:26-28, 31; Matthew 5:13, 14; 15:11; 28:18-20; John 17:15; Acts 10:15; Romans 14:14, 20; Colossians 2:16-23; 1 Timothy 4:4, 5; Hebrews 2:14; 1 John 4:1-4; 2 John 7)

_____

_____

_____

_____

_____

_____

_____

_____

_____

2. How would you answer the following objections that are often raised in opposition to Christians' attempts to restore the Republic regarding political participation?

Objection 1: *The Bible is neutral about political issues so Christians have no business involving themselves in something in which the Bible shows no interest.* (Genesis 9:6, 7; 41:38-49; Exodus 18:13-27; 21-23; Deuteronomy 17:14-20; Judges 3:14; the books of Samuel, Kings, and Chronicles; 2 Chronicles 25:2; 26:4; 27:2; Daniel 2, 4, 6; Nehemiah 5:14; 1 Corinthians 6:1-11; Hebrews 13:32, 33)

_____

_____

_____

_____

_____

_____

_____

_____

Objection 2: *Religion and politics do not mix so we cannot impose biblical morality on others.* (Genesis 3:24; John 14:15; Romans 13:3, 4; Exodus 20:1-17)

_____

_____

_____

_____

_____

Objection 3: *Christians should not get involved in politics because politics is dirty.* (Genesis 1:31; Romans 13:4; Colossians 3:20-23; 1 Timothy 4:15)

_____

_____

_____

_____

_____

Objection 4: *The end of the world is upon us and Jesus is coming back soon, so why get involved in political affairs?* (Acts 1:68; 1 Thessalonians 5:2; 2 Thessalonians 3:11; Matthew 24:45, 46, 50; Luke 19:11, 13, 17-24)

_____

_____

_____

_____

_____

Objection 5. *Jesus said that His kingdom was not of this world; therefore, Christians should not get involved in "worldly" pursuits like politics.* (John 8:23; 15:19; 17:11, 14, 16; 18:28-40; 1 John 2:16; 4:5; Matthew 26:63; Luke 1:32, 33; 3:2; 23:2, 3; Revelation 1:5)

_____

_____

_____

_____

_____

3. Who was a citizen in Israel and what obligations and protections did foreigners have? (Exodus 12:38; 2 Chronicles 2:17; Numbers 13:30; 32:12; Joshua 14:6, 14; 15:13; 2 Chronicles 2:18; Exodus 12:43, 45; Leviticus 16:29; Exodus 23:12; Deuteronomy 5:14; Deuteronomy 26:11; Leviticus 22:18; Leviticus 17:8, 9; Numbers 15:14-16, 26, 29; Leviticus 25:6; Deuteronomy 16:11; 16:14; Exodus 12:19; Deuteronomy 31:10-12; cf. Joshua 8:33, 35; Leviticus 24:22; cf. Exodus 12:49; Leviticus 25:47; Leviticus 19:33, 34; Exodus 22:21; 23:9; Deuteronomy 1:16; cf. 24:16; 27:19; Jeremiah 7:6, 7; Zechariah 7:10; Malachi 3:5; Deuteronomy 24:14; Deuteronomy 10:19; Numbers 35:15; Joshua 10; Leviticus 20:2; Leviticus 24:16; Exodus 20:10; 2 Samuel 1:3-16; Leviticus 20:2; Leviticus 18:26; Leviticus 19:10; 23:22; Deuteronomy 24:19, 20; Deuteronomy 14:29; 26:12; Ruth 2:10; Jeremiah 7:57; cf. 22:3; Ezekiel 22:7, 29; Zechariah 7:10; Malachi 3:5; Matthew 25:35; cf. v. 43)

_____

_____

_____

_____

_____

_____

_____

_____

4. What does the Bible teach about *multiple* civil citizenships and compare this with our system of civil government as it was originally designed and of today? (Acts 21:39; 22:3, 24-29; Philippians 3:5)

_____

_____

_____

_____

_____

_____

_____

_____

5. What does the Bible mean when it states that our "citizenship is in heaven" (Philippians 3:20) and that Abraham, Isaac, and Jacob were "strangers and exiles on the earth" (Hebrews 11:13)?

_____

_____

_____

_____

_____

_____

_____

_____

Summary

"Biblical faith finds great power — as does its imitator, Marxism — in the conviction that history is going its way. Or rather, that since Christ is the Lord of history, it is going history's way. Final victory is not dependent upon how well its work is done; rather it is assured regardless of all contingent factors. 'Thy kingdom come, they will be done on earth as it is in heaven,' is not a pious wish, but a certainty. We do not question if we shall be able to bring such a happy state of affairs into being, but rather what our role should be in its inevitable fulfillment. Since the world's powers were 'disarmed' in Christ (Col. 2:15) their might is limited, despite the illusions of invincibility they are able to project. The eschatology of victory is a principle theme of the New Testament.

"Yet, we live in a world of phenomena as well as eschaton, and we must face the question of what good the gospel of Christ is in the here and now. Ironically, those who seek their ultimate value in the next world are the only ones able to do much good in this one. Those in love with this present world destroy it along with themselves" (Herbert Schlossberg, _Idols for Destruction: Christian Faith and Its Confrontation with American Society_, p. 333).

Answers to Questions for Discussion

1. To be "spiritual" means to be governed by the Holy Spirit. For many, spirituality means to be preoccupied with non-physical reality. Therefore to be spiritual means not to be involved with the material things of this world. Biblically, this is not the case. The devil and his demons are spiritual (non-physical) and evil: "And I saw coming out of the mouth of the dragon and out of the mouth of the beast and out of the mouth of the false prophet, three *unclean spirits* like frogs; for they are *spirits of demons*, performing signs, which go out to the kings of the whole world, to gather them together for the war of the great day of God Almighty" (Revelation 16:13, 14). There are "deceitful spirits" (1 Timothy 4:1), "unclean spirits" (Revelation 18:2), and spirits of "error" (1 John 4:6). There is even "spiritual wickedness" (Ephesians 6:12).

Spirituality is not limited to non-physical reality. Our forefathers saw coming to the new world as a very spiritual enterprise because all endeavors that extend the Kingdom of God are *spiritual things*. Christians are to transform the world through the power of the Spirit, using the spiritual law as the standard of righteousness for appraising (judging) where regeneartion and restoration are needed.

On the other hand, Jesus has a body (physical reality) and He is good: "For David, after he had served the purpose of God in his own generation, fell asleep, and was laid among his fathers, and underwent decay; *but He whom God raised did not undergo decay*" (Acts 13:36, 37). Jesus was raised with His body. He is "the Holy and Righteous One" (Acts 3:14). Spirituality is directly related to righteousness. The reason Jesus' body did not undergo decay was because He was without sin.

There is the "Holy Spirit" (e.g., Acts 13:2), a "spirit of truth" (1 John 4:6), "spiritual things" (1 Corinthians 9:11), "spiritual food" (10:3), a "spiritual body" (15:44), "spiritual sacrifices" (1 Peter 2:5), "spiritual wisdom and understanding" (Colossians 1:9), and "ministering spirits, sent out to render service for the sake of those who will inherit salvation" (Hebrews 1:14).

To be "spiritual" is to exhibit the "gifts of the Spirit" (Galatians 5:22). These "gifts" operate in the world for we are told to "walk in the spirit" (5:16). But how does a Christian know when he or she is walking "in the spirit"? We are told that the "Law is spiritual" (Romans 7:14). The Law, then, is the rule by which we measure our spirituality. Notice also that the spiritual person "appraises [judges] *all things*" (2:15).

The Bible does not support the belief that Christians should abandon the world because it is not "spiritual." Rather, Christians are to transform the world through the power of the Spirit, using the spiritual law as the standard of righteousness for appraising (judging) where regeneration and restoration are needed. Christians are to be "salt" and "light" in the world (Matthew 5:13, 14). Salt is useless unless applied to potentially decaying material; light is not needed unless there is darkness (Matthew 5:15; Luke 2:32). Without involvement in the world, neither salt nor light avail. Christians are to be in the world, but they are not to be of the world (John 17:14-16). They are not to be squeezed into the world's mold (Romans 12:2). They are not to be led astray by the "elementary principles of the world" (Colossians 2:8). They are to keep themselves "unstained by the world" (James 1:27). They are warned not to get entangled in the "defilements of the world" (2 Peter 2:20). Nowhere are they told to abandon the world (cf. Matthew 28:18-20; John 3:16).

The "world" is corrupt because people are corrupt. Where corrupt people control certain aspects of the world we can expect defilement. But the world does not have to remain in decay. When individuals are redeemed the effects of their redemption should spread to the society in which they live and conduct their affairs.

Could one properly say that a Christian operating a business according to biblical laws should allow himself and his business to be squeezed into the world's mold, stained by the world, defiled, and led astray? Certainly not! We would encourage other businessmen to follow his example of transforming and restoring all their business dealings. The world of pagan thinking and practice is to be replaced by Christian thinking and practice.

Jesus taught that all of life is spiritual. He fed those who were in need of food and healed those in need of restoration.

It is a perversion of the gospel to maintain that the world, as the domain where evil exists, is inherently corrupt. We should remember that Jesus came to this world to give His life for its redemption (John 3:16). Christians must be transformed by God's word and not be conformed to the world's principles. As Christians work in the world through the power of the Holy Spirit, the world will be transformed.

There is no inherent sinfulness in material things. Scripture says Jesus shared in "flesh and blood" (Hebrews 2:14). He who denies that Jesus Christ has come in the flesh "is the deceiver and the antichrist" (2 John 7; cf. 1 John 4:1-3). Man's body is not inherently sinful. We shall have bodies in the resurrection, as Jesus does (John 20:24-27). In the resurrection, we will be "raised imperishable" (1 Corinthians 15:52).

By denying the spirituality of God's created order, we neglect its importance and give it by default to those who deny Christ. *Worldliness* is to be avoided, not the world. The Apostle James warns us

against worldliness *wherever* it is found [James 1:27], certainly in the church, and he is emphasizing here precisely the importance of Christian involvement in *social* issues. Regrettably, we tend to read the Scriptures as though their rejection of a "worldly" life-style entails a recommendation of an "otherworldly" one.

This approach has led many Christians to abandon the "secular" realm to the trends and forces of secularism. Indeed, because of their two-realm theory, to a large degree, Christians have themselves to blame for the rapid secularization of the West. If political, industrial, artistic, and journalistic life, to mention only these areas, are branded as essentially "worldly," "secular," "profane," and part of the "natural domain of creaturely life," then is it surprising that Christians have not more effectively stemmed the tide of humanism in our culture? (Albert M. Wolters, *Creation Regained: Biblical Basics for a Reformational Worldview*, p. 54).

God created everything wholly good (Genesis 1:31). Man, through the fall, became profane, defiled by sin. Redemption restores things in Christ. Peter failed to understand the gospel's comprehensive cleansing effects. He could not believe the Gentiles were "clean": "What God has cleansed, no longer consider unholy" (Acts 10:15; cf. Matthew 15:11; Romans 14:14, 20). The fall did not nullify God's pronouncement that the created order "was very good" (Genesis 1:31). The New Testament reinforces the goodness of God's creation: "For everything created by God is good, and nothing is to be rejected, if it is received with gratitude; for it is sanctified by means of the word of God and prayer" (1 Timothy 4:4, 5).

Scripture is our guide and not the Platonic view of matter as something less than good. God "became flesh and dwelt among us" (John 1:14). Jesus worked in his earthly father's shop as a carpenter, affirming the goodness of the created order and the value of physical labor.

2. Answer 1: The Bible is filled with "politics." Here are just a few examples of political involvement found in the Bible. Noah, an agent of the civil magistrate, is given authority to execute murderers (Genesis 9:6, 7); Joseph is made ruler in Egypt (Genesis 41:38-49); Moses was the civil ruler in Israel and, because of Jethro's counsel, appointed lesser magistrates (Exodus 18:13-27); "case laws" are tabulated for the government of family, church and State (Exodus 21-23); God instructs both priests and kings to follow the law of God (Deuteronomy 17:14-20); the book of Judges is filled with examples of civil rulers (Othniel [3:9], Ehud [3:15], Shamgar [3:31], Deborah/Barak [4:4, 6], Gideon [6:11], Jephthah [11:1], and Samson [14:1]) delivering Israel from political oppression; the book of Hebrews commends these civil rulers with these words:"And what more shall I say? For time will fail me if I tell of Gideon, Barak, Samson, Jephthah, of David and Samuel and the prophets *who by faith conquered kingdoms, [and] performed acts of righteousness. . .*" (Hebrews 13:32, 33). The books of Samuel, Kings, and Chronicles tell of the rise and fall of kings and kingdoms, with individual kings singled out for their obedience to God's law (e.g., 2 Chronicles 25:2; 26:4; 27:2). Daniel serves as one of Darius' three commissioners (Daniel 6). Nehemiah was appointed "governor" in Israel (Nehemiah 5:14).

Denial of political involvement repudiates most of the Bible. Paul makes it clear that the "saints will judge the world" (1 Corinthians 6:2). The context of this verse has to do with constituting "the smallest law courts." Christians at various times in history have "judged the world." The foundation of Western legal tradition is Christian. The demise of the West results from Christians' non-involvement in every sphere of life, the civil sphere included.

Answer 2: Life's political sphere should not be used to change or reform men and women (though the fear of punishment has an effect on people who might consider a criminal act). The purpose of the law as it relates to the civil magistrate is to punish and restrain evil, to protect human life and property, and to provide justice for all people, using God's word as the standard. Only God can regenerate the heart, however. An individual cannot be made good by law-keeping. Traditionally, the law has had three uses. First, to make sinners aware of their rebellion against God and driving them to embrace Jesus Christ as Lord and Savior (Galatians 3:24). Second, to serve as a standard of obedience for those whose hearts the Spirit of God lives and rules (John 14:15). Third, to serve as the standard for the just ordering of society (Romans 13:3, 4).

The Bible exists as the State's perfect standard of justice. In fact, this truth remains primary in the establishment of justice. When the Bible speaks to *civil* affairs, *civil* government has a duty to heed its commands.

Joesph succeeded in Egypt because he faithfully kept the law of God in the most adverse circumstances. Joseph became a ruler in Egypt, directing the course of the nation.

139

How will civil government determine what is good or evil, unless God's law is consulted? Where God's law is not the standard, there can be no objective standard for man to follow. We live in an era in which the Bible is rejected as the State's authority. Killing unborn babies is legal, and the State, through a corrupt tax system, uses the tax money to support this heinous crime. Religion, and in particular, biblical law, cannot be separated from life in general and politics in particular.

Politics has to do with civil government. Politicians get elected, make laws, tax, spend, regulate, and control. Every law passed and every spending decision is based on some moral system. All morality is based on a religion....The Bible says, "Thou shalt not steal." That is the basis of laws against theft. The Bible says, "Thou shalt not bear false witness against thy neighbor." That is the basis of laws against libel and slander. Make no mistake about it. What we believe religiously will affect our political beliefs and practices (Robert L. Thoburn, *The Christian and Politics*, p. 5).

For example, the speed limit was reduced from 70 mph to 55 mph for two advertised reasons. First, to save lives. Second, to cut fuel consumption. Both reasons are value-laden and rest on moral considerations. They presuppose that human life is valuable and that society at large is valuable (if the world runs out of fuel then everyone is hurt). Laws, political laws, were instituted to enforce these moral, value-laden concerns.

Where reason or the will of the people determine what should become law, in time, laws change to reflect the heightened reason of some, or the shifting opinions of others. If we divorce religion from politics, the only thing left is irreligion, which becomes a religion of its own: man is his own God, determining good and evil for himself.

When religion or morality becomes divorced from decision making, convenience becomes the standard. Following a debate on the abortion issue, a lawyer who had participated with other debaters was shocked at the casual attitude of those who favor abortion for "social reasons": "[M]ost of the students *already* recognized that the unborn child is a human life. Nevertheless, certain social reasons are considered 'high enough' to justify ending that life. According to some of the women, examples of 'high enough' reasons include protecting pregnant teenagers from the psychological distress of bearing a child, helping poor women who aren't able to care adequately for a child, and preventing children from coming into the world 'unwanted.' Many charged that pro-life philosophies are not 'socially acceptable' because they fail to deal realistically with these problems" ("Students Defend Abortion For 'High' Social Reasons," in *The Rutherford Institute*, Vol.1, No.2, January/February 1984, p.8).

The taking of a life is justified if it benefits *society*. We are left with two options: either God's word serves as the State's standard for righteousness, or the State determines its own standard. The Governor of New York, Mario Cuomo, doesn't want to mix religion and politics:

> He maintained that as governor he was duty bound to obey, not God or his (the governor's) church, but the people, the supposed will of whom is expressed in the extant laws of the State....The majority want abortion; therefore, it's not wrong. It must be right if the *people* want it...(Steve M.Schlissel, "A Brooklyn Pastor Takes On Governor Cuomo," *The Counsel of Chalcedon*, Vol.VI, No.11, [January, 1985], p.22).

Our constitutional founders did not divorce law from morality. The Constitution is based on the premise that morality is founded on the law of God. All laws are value-laden. Someone's morality forms the foundation for all law.

He bows, not to God's law but the will of the people. Why? The people give him power to rule. The relationship between religion and politics cannot be avoided. The question is not: Do religion and politics mix? The question is: What religion will be mixed with — or form the basis for — politics? Israel was not judged because it mixed religion and politics, but because it mixed the wrong religion with politics. Today it is no different. The potential for judgment is the same.

Answer 3: The first chapter of Genesis ends with this evaluation of God's creation: "And God saw all that He had made, and behold, it was very good" (1:31). Things in themselves are not necessarily evil. The "tree of the knowledge of good and evil" was not evil. Even as Adam and Eve ate the fruit, the fruit was not evil. The Garden where they committed their sin was not evil. The decision they made was evil. What they did with God's good creation was evil. Sin, then, is what people do.

The Apostle Paul makes it clear that avoiding "things" in no way makes anyone holy: "If you have died with Christ to the elementary principles of the world, why, as if you were living in the world, do you submit yourself to decrees, such as, 'Do not handle, do not taste, do not touch!' (which all refer to things destined to perish with the using) in accordance with the commandments and teachings of men? These are matters which have, to be sure, the appearance of wisdom in self-made religion and self-abasement and severe treatment of the body, but are of no value against fleshly indulgence" (Colossians 2:20-23). In another place, the Apostle addresses a similar issue with similar statements: "For everything created by God is good, and nothing is to be rejected, if it is received with gratitude; for it is sanctified by means of the word of God and prayer" (1 Timothy 4:4, 5). While these passages do not *directly* mention civil government, they do set forth a series of principles that can be applied to politics. First, civil government is established by God and therefore it is a legitimate area of activity for Christians.

Second, the political sphere is a created entity like the family and church. "God has instituted civil government just as He has set up the church and the family. To say we want nothing to do with civil government is to say that God's institution is not important" (Robert L. Thoburn, *The Christian and Politics*, p.17). We image God. God is the

Governor over all creation; He has called us to be governors under His one government. The civil or political sphere is an area of legitimate governmental activity. It is dirty (i.e., evil) when evil men practice evil schemes. "So is business, law, labor, education, sports, and just about every other activity you can imagine. It's part of the human condition known as sin" (John Eidsmoe, *God and Caesar: Christian Faith and Political Action*, p. 56). Salt and light are necessary because of the reality of sin. Christians should be involved in politics even if it is dirty. Who else has the means to clean up politics (or any other area of human activity)? If Christians do not, who will? That's the point! Christians have stayed out of politics, making its corruption even more pronounced. The answer is not to consign politics to even more corruption by ignoring its potential as an area for redemption and restoration.

The Bible never condemns political involvement. John the Baptist does not rebuke Herod for his political position, but for his sinful actions as ruler. Jesus does not quarrel with Pontius Pilate over whether he should rule, but only reminds him *why* he rules and, implicitly, by what standard he ought to rule. Paul calls rulers God's "ministers," servants in the political sphere (Romans 13:4). Paul appeals to Caesar, the seat of Roman *political* power, in order to gain a hearing.

John Witherspoon (1723-1794), a minister in the Presbyterian church and the President of Princeton College, signed the Declaration of Independence. For him, Christianity and politics were a good mix.

The desire to retreat from political concerns is recent within our history. John Witherspoon, a minister in the Presbyterian church and the President of Princeton College, was a signer of the Declaration of Independence. The framers of the Constitution, "with no more than five exceptions (and perhaps no more than three), ...were orthodox members of one of the established Christian communions: approximately twenty-nine Anglicans, sixteen to eighteen Calvinists, two Methodists, two Lutherans, two Roman Catholics, one lapsed Quaker and sometime-Anglican, and one open Deist — Dr.[Benjamin] Franklin, who attended every kind of Christian worship, called for public prayer, and contributed to all denominations" (M.E. Bradford, *A Worthy Company*, p.viii).

Answer 4: This objection probably is the most debilitating. When Jesus' disciples asked Him at the ascension if at that time He was "restoring the kingdom to Israel," Jesus diverted their attention from final restoration to the work at hand: "It is not for you to know times and epochs which the Father has fixed by His own authority; but you shall receive power when the Holy Spirit has come upon you; and you shall be My witnesses both in Jerusalem, and in all Judea and Samaria, and even to the remotest part of the earth" (Acts 1:6-8). In effect, Jesus was saying, "Do not worry about God's timetable; it is already fixed. Busy ourself with the affairs of the kingdom."

Some of the Thessalonian Christians were "leading an undisciplined life, doing no work at all, but acting like busybodies" (2 Thessalonians 3:11). While this may have little to do with a preoccupation with "the day of the Lord" (1 Thessalonians 5:2), it reminds us that God requires us to work regardless of external circumstances. Faithfulness is evaluated in terms of kingdom work: "Who then is the faithful and sensible slave whom his master put in charge of his household to give them their food at the proper time? Blessed is that slave whom his master finds so doing when he comes" (Matthew 24:45, 46). Jesus goes on to hint at the time and circumstances of His coming: "The master of that slave will come on a day *when he does not expect him and at an hour which he does not know*" (v.50). Nowhere does Scripture intimate we should cease any aspect of kingdom work, even if we *think* Jesus' coming is near. "*The delay of the master made no difference to the true servant*: he busied himself about his Lord's business.... But the master's delay induced the false servant to a sinful course of action. *The Lord's delay brought out the true character of his servants*" (George Eldon Ladd, *The Blessed Hope*, p.106).

Jesus related a parable to His disciples when "they supposed that the kingdom of God was going to appear immediately" (Luke 19:11). In Jesus' day many of His disciples assumed the kingdom would arrive through a cataclysmic event with no effort on their part. Jesus told them through the parable to "do business until I come back" (v.13). When the master finally returns he will take an accounting. Those who made a profit on the money given by the master will "be in authority over" ten and five cities" (vv.17-19). The one who put the money "away in a handkerchief" (v.20), not being industrious enough to "put the money in the bank" to collect "interest" (v.23), loses everything (v.24). Charles Haddon Spurgeon (1834-1892), the great Baptist preacher and evangelist of the 19th century,

Charles Haddon Spurgeon (1834-1892) believed that one of the most unscriptural doctrines was the theory *that the world would grow worse and worse, and that the dispensations will wind up with general darkness, and idolatry.* He declared of such a belief: *Far hence be it driven.*

shows how pessimism robs the church of its vitality and stunts its growth. David was not a believer in the theory that the world will grow worse and worse, and that the dispensations will wind up with general darkness, and idolatry. Earth's sun is to go down amid tenfold night if some of our prophetic brethren are to be believed. Not so do we expect, but we look for a day when the dwellers in all lands shall learn righteousness, shall trust in the Saviour, shall worship thee alone, O God, *and shall glorify thy name.*" The modern notion has greatly damped the zeal of the church for missions, and the sooner it is shown to be unscriptural the better for the cause of God. It neither consorts with prophecy, honours God, nor inspires the church with ardour. Far hence be it driven (*The Treasury of David*, Vol.IV, p.102).

"Therefore, my beloved brethren, be steadfast, immovable, always abounding in the work of the Lord, knowing that your toil is not in vain in the Lord" (1 Corinthians 15:58).

Answer 5: Many Christians have not transported the first-century faith to the twentieth century. Often they are confused when they read Jesus' words, "My kingdom is not of this world" (John 18:36). Jesus did not say His kingdom does not operate in this world. He did not say His kingdom is not *over* this world. When Jesus states His "kingdom is not *of* this world," He emphasizes the origin of His kingdom's power and authority; it "does not derive its origin or its support from earthly forces. Comp.viii.23, xv.19, xvii.14, 16; I John ii.16, iv.5. At the same time Christ's kingdom is 'in the world,' even as His disciples are (xvii.11)" (B.F. Westcott, *The Gospel According to St.John*, p.260). Caiaphas, the high priest, interrogated Jesus on *religious* questions. Caiaphas wanted to know if Jesus was "the Christ, the Son of God" (Matthew 26:63). This did not concern Pilate. In fact, in order to have Pilate hear the grievances of the religious leaders, a *political* threat to the jurisdiction of Pilate and Rome had to be fabricated: "And they began to accuse Him saying, 'We found this man misleading our nation and forbidding to pay taxes to Caesar, and saying that He Himself is Christ, a King' " (Luke 23:2). Unless Jesus was portrayed as a *political* threat to the Roman Empire, they knew Pilate would not hear their case.

Pilate's question about kingship and kingdoms concerned mere political power. Jesus was questioned from Pilate's perspective. Would Jesus bring an army? How large would it be? Since He was said to be "King of the Jews" (Luke 23:3), would Jesus incite a rebellion among the Jews to usurp Pilate's position of authority? What sort of weaponry would He use? Pilate believed, as did many Jews of that day, that armed conflict alone could extend a kingdom. It was a king's duty, Pilate thought, to use the power of the military against an enemy. Since Jesus was a king, Pilate assumed He must command. This was the Roman way. The *Pax Romana* was maintained through force. Jesus' response to Pilate shows that Pilate failed to understand the nature of Jesus' kingdom.

The reader is presented with a dramatic scene, in which two types of kingships are contrasted; the kingship backed by the authority and might of imperial Rome represented by Pilate, a kingship *of this world* and upheld by this world's weapons, and the kingship of Jesus *not of this world,* in which the monarch is to reign by being lifted up on a cross ([John 18:]36). The narrative clearly presupposes that it had been intimated to Pilate that Jesus, by claiming kingship over Jewry, was in effect a political revolutionary and therefore a potential danger to Rome... (R.V.G.Tasker, *The Gospel According to John,* p.201).

In John 18:37 Pilate says, "So You are a king?" Pilate understood that Jesus did not deny kingship, for Jesus answered Pilate's tentative question: "You say correctly that I am a king. For this I have been born [Luke 1:32, 33; 2:2], and for this I have come into the world, to bear witness to the truth. Every one who is of the truth hears My voice" (John 18:37). Later, Jesus informed Pilate that his position of political authority, and, by intimation, that of all who rule (cf.Romans 13:1), was subject to God's kingly rule: Jesus is "ruler of the kings of the earth" (Revelation 1:5). When Jesus kept silent regarding Pilate's question concerning His origin (John 19:9), Pilate grew indignant: "You do not speak to me? Do you not know that I have authority to release You, and I have authority to crucify you?"(v.10). Jesus' answer settled the matter about the operation of God's kingdom. Unless the kingdom of God operated *in* and *over* this world, what Jesus next said would be false: "You would have no authority over Me, unless *it had been given you from above*..."(v.11).

Jesus' words to Pontius Pilate, *My kingdom is not of this world*, do not refer to the sphere where the kingdom operates but to the source of its power. Jesus does not say that His kingdom is not *in* this world or that His kingdom is not *over* this world. He makes it clear that the source of power for the operation of His kingdom is heavenly and that it influences the earth (Matthew 6:10; 28:18-20).

Confusion over Jesus' words develops from a false notion that the answer to man's problems is solely political. There were numerous occasions when the crowds wanted to make Him King (e.g., John 6:15). While there are political implications to Jesus' kingship, just as there are personal, familial, economic, business, ecclesiastical, and judicial implications, the kingdom of God is not brought about politically. Good laws do not make good people. Only the sovereign work of the Holy Spirit in regeneration makes people good. The State has a God-imposed jurisdiction to perform kingdom activities according to the specifics of God's word.

The people in Jesus' day saw the kingdom of God in externals only. They visualized the kingdom of God as coming, not through regeneration, but revolution. Jesus said of His followers: "Truly, truly, I say to you, you seek Me, not because you saw signs, but because you ate of the loaves, and were filled" (John 6:26). It was Jesus' message about mankind's need for salvation and about Him as the Savior, the Messiah of God, that caused the religious and political establishments of the day to seek His death.

The kingdom of God never advances through political intrigue, backed by military power. Though power-directed, its power comes from above and works on the heart of man: "I will give you a new heart and put a new spirit within you; and I will remove the heart of stone from your flesh and give you a heart of flesh. And I will put My Spirit within you and cause you to walk in My statutes, and you will be careful to observe My ordinances" (Ezekiel 36:26, 27). Self-government, wherein God subdues the heart to teachableness, leads to godly family, church, and civil governments (cf. 1 Tim. 3:1-13). Implements of war which deteriorate over time or become obsolete are only as reliable as those who manufacture and use them. Moreover, such weapons affect only externals. They can subdue a people, but they cannot regenerate those dead in their trespasses and sins (Ephesians 2:1). God's word "is living and active and sharper than any two-edged sword, and piercing as far as the division of soul and spirit, of both joints and marrow, and able to judge the thoughts and intentions of the heart" (Hebrews 4:12).

The supernatural power which energizes God's kingdom is never bound by political rhetoric: "For the kingdom of God does not consist in words, but in power" (1 Corinthians 4:20). The battle against the kingdoms of this world is waged through the awesome power inherent in God's word, energized by His Spirit: "For though we walk in the flesh, we do not war according to the flesh, for the weapons of our warfare are not of the flesh, but divinely powerful for the destruction of fortresses" (2 Corinthians 10:3, 4). As Christians, "we are destroying speculations and every lofty thing raised up against the knowledge of God, and we are taking every thought captive to the obedience of Christ" (v. 5). This is kingdom living, dominion living. The kingdom of God advances by changing the hearts and minds of those who oppose Jesus Christ and His word. The kingdoms of this world are at war with the kingdom of Jesus Christ and it is the duty of all Christians to be involved in that war until the gates of Hades can no longer stand (Matthew 16:18).

Restoration begins by realizing that we live in the midst of God's kingdom. God's pattern for godly living is established in heaven. In the Lord's Prayer we petition God, "Thy Kingdom come. Thy will be done, *on earth as it is in heaven*" (Matthew 6:10). God has not called us to forsake the earth, but rather "to impress its pattern on earth" (James B. Jordan, "Editor's Introduction," *Christianity and Civilization*, No. 1, Spring 1982, p. ix).

3. The terms 'citizen' and 'citizenship' do not occur in the Old Testament. But the *concept* of citizenship is present. Today, a citizen would be someone who participates in the civil sphere of government. He could vote, run for political office, and sit on a jury. In Israel, an individual automatically becomes a citizen by birth and circumcision. In the United States, convicted felons cannot sit on juries or vote. Citizenship, therefore, was tied to ethics because circumcision tied an individual to the requirements of the covenant law. For similar reasons, foreigners were excluded from holding political office: "You shall surely set a king over you whom the LORD your God chooses, *one from among your countrymen* you shall set as king over yourselves; *you may not put a foreigner over yourselves who is not your countryman*" (Deuteronomy 17:15). The dangers of having a foreigner as king can be seen in King Solomon's life. His marriage to foreign wives "turned his heart away after other gods; and his heart was not wholly devoted to the LORD his God, as the heart of David his father had been" (1 Kings 11:4). Solomon "loved many foreign women along with the daughter of Pharaoh: Moabite, Ammonite, Edomite, Sidonian, and Hittite women. . ." (v. 1; cf. vv. 4-13). Jesus said, "No one can serve two masters; for either he will hate the one and love the other, or he will hold to one and despise the other" (Matthew 6:24). There cannot be neutrality in political affairs, whether you are a ruler or a citizen. Either an individual is loyal to God or to foreign gods; either to himself or the State.

Our own Constitution requires that only citizens by birth are eligible to the office of President or VicePresident: "No person except a natural born citizen, or a citizen of the United States, at the time of the adoption of this

Constitution, shall be eligible to the office of President" (Article II, section 1:4). The Articles of Confederation (agreed to by Congress November 15, 1777; ratified and in force, March 1, 1781) stated that "the free inhabitants of each of these states, paupers, vagabonds and fugitives from Justice excepted, shall be entitled to all privileges and immunities of free citizens in the several states" (Article IV). Again, citizenship was based on ethical considerations and not just birth.

A *mixed multitude* came out of Egypt (Exodus 12:38) and entered the promised land. There were over 150,000 Gentiles during Solomon's reign (2 Chronicles 2:17). And even some non- Israelites had civil (e.g., Numbers 13:30; 32:12) and ecclesiastical (2 Chronicles (2:18) responsibilities. The law made provision for them all.

While some individuals and groups (e.g., Moabites and Ammonites) did not have citizenship privileges, the Bible gives all equal protection under the law. It should be remembered that a "mixed multitude" came out of Egypt (Exodus 12:38). There were over 150,000 Gentiles during Solomon's reign (2 Chronicles 2:17). A number of non-Israelites had civil (e.g., Numbers 13:30; 32:12; Joshua 14:6, 14; 15:13) and religious (2 Chronicles 2:18) responsibilities. Of course, in the case of Caleb, he had identified himself with the covenant of Israel but when it came time for a successor to Moses, Joshua was chosen.

An individual was either an Israelite (a descendant of Abraham), a proselyte (a convert from paganism to Judaism), a resident alien (a pagan who decided to reside in Israel but did not convert to Judaism), or a nonresident transient foreigner (a pagan who was passing through the land of Israel). While resident aliens and nonresident aliens could not participate in the passover meal (Exodus 12:43, 45) (unless they became proselytes and, thus, were circumcised), they had full protection under the law.

Even though aliens could not partake of the passover meal, they rested on the Day of Atonement (Leviticus 16:29) and the weekly Sabbath (Exodus 23:12; Deuteronomy 5:14). They could offer firstfruits (Deuteronomy 26:11), freewill, and burnt offerings (Leviticus 22:18). They could offer a "burnt offering or sacrifice" according to the directives laid down in the law (Leviticus 17:8, 9; Numbers 15:14-16, 26, 29). They could participate in the red heifer ceremony and undergo purification along with "the sons of Israel" (Numbers 19:10). They all had the "sabbath products of the land for food" during the sabbath year (Leviticus 25:6). Finally, they were welcome to participate in the annual Feast of Weeks (Deuteronomy 16:11) and Feast of Booths (16:14). During the Feast of Unleavened Bread, however, they were not to eat leavened bread or "that person shall be cut off from the congregation of Israel" (Exodus 12:19).

Let us look at what the Old Testament says about the obligations and protections for Israelites and aliens: First, the written law of God was the standard for both the covenant-bound Israelite and the alien: "At the end of every seven years, at the time of the year of remission of debts, at the Feast of Booths, when all Israel comes to appear before the LORD your God at the place which He will choose, you shall read this law in from of all Israel in their hearing. Assemble the people, the men and the women and children and *the alien who is in your town*, in order that they may hear and learn and fear the LORD your God, and be careful to observe all the words of this law" (Deuteronomy 31:10-12; cf. Joshua 8:33-35).

The alien could not rebel against the law of the land because he did not

152

accept the religion of the Jews: "There shall be one standard for you; it shall be for the stranger as well as the native, for I am the LORD your God" (Leviticus 24:22; cf. Exodus 12:49). Aliens were not forced to become Israelites. There was no compulsion. The alien's participation in many of the feasts and sacrifices open to him would serve as an evangelistic tool to remind him of his sin and his need of redemption through shed blood.

Second, the alien was given "equal protection under the law." Aliens could acquire property and accumulate wealth (Leviticus 25:47). They were protected from wrongdoing and treated like the "native" Israelite (Leviticus 19:33, 34). A native-born Israelite could "not wrong a stranger or oppress him" (Exodus 22:21; 23:9). If the alien was bound to keep the law of God, then the law of God was the standard for protecting him against injustice as well: "Then I charged your judges at that time, saying, 'Hear the cases between your fellow-countrymen, and judge righteously between a man and his fellow-countrymen, or the alien who is with you' " (Deuteronomy 1:16; cf. 24:16; 27:19). The prophets repeated the warning against oppression of strangers and aliens (Jeremiah 7:6, 7; Zechariah 7:10; Malachi 3:5). Aliens should not be defrauded of their wages (Deuteronomy 24:14). Love was to be shown to the alien, "for you were aliens in the land of Egypt" (Deuteronomy 10:19). The cities of refuge were open "for the alien and for the sojourner" (Numbers 35:15). Aliens were protected against their enemies (Joshua 10).

Third, they had the same civil duties as the Israelites. They were prohibited from public idolatry (Leviticus 20:2). They could, however, worship their false gods in the privacy of their households. They could not blaspheme (Leviticus 24:16), break the sabbath (Exodus 20:10), show disrespect for authorities (2 Samuel 1:3-16), offer their children in sacrifice to idols (Leviticus 20:2), or engage in sexual abomination (Leviticus 18:26).

Fourth, the poor alien could enjoy the privileges of gleaning (Leviticus 19:10; 23:22; Deuteronomy 24:19, 20) and could gain assistance from the poor tithe (Deuteronomy 14:29; 26:12). Ruth is amazed that Boaz shows her favor: "Why have I found favor in your sight that you should take notice of me, *since I am a foreigner?*" (Ruth 2:10)

Fifth, the treatment of aliens was an indication of either blessing or

153

cursing. The alien was often put in the same category as the widow and fatherless: "For if you truly amend your ways and your deeds, if you truly practice justice between a man and his neighbor; *if you do not oppress the alien*, the orphan, or the widow... then I will let you dwell in this place, in the land that I gave to your fathers forever and ever" (Jeremiah 7:57; cf. 22:3; Ezekiel 22:7, 29; Zechariah 7:10; Malachi 3:5). Jesus views the treatment of strangers as an indicator of a nation's commitment to Him: "For I was hungry, and you gave Me something to eat; I was thirsty, and you gave Me drink; *I was a stranger, and you invited Me in*" (Matthew 25:35; cf. v. 43).

Christians have a duty to participate in the political process. Since no law can be morally neutral and the Bible is the foundation of all morality, it is necessary that Christians be salt and light everywhere God has commanded us to have dominion.

Those who are so concerned about the establishment of a Christian civilization voice fears about the persecution of non-Christians in such a society. Of course, this concern cuts both ways. In a secularized State, what happens to Christians and their many religious activities when the

154

courts try to be "religiously neutral"? We've already seen some of the effects. Christian schools are required to meet state standards for teachers and educators; prayer and Bible reading are not permitted in government schools; zoning laws have prohibited Bible studies in suburban neighborhoods without special permits; the placement of religious symbols has been outlawed in many communities; and when protection of the unborn is desired, Christians are accused of "imposing their values on society" while nothing is said of the opposition when they impose their immoral values on society. As we have seen, while non-Israelites could not eat the Passover meal, they had all the protections afforded an Israelite. Non-Christians would not be forced to become Christians but they would have to obey laws that came from the Bible. This would mean that homosexuality and abortion, for example, could not be claimed as "civil rights." They would be crimes. While the law of God grants equal protection, it also requires the same obedience.

4. The Christian is a citizen of a number of locales — a city, county, state, and nation. For example, the Apostle Paul was a Roman citizen (Acts 22:27-29) of the city of Tarsus in the region of Cilicia (21:39) and a resident of Jerusalem in the district of Judea (22:3). Had Israel not been a subject nation, Paul could have exercised his tribal citizenship as a resident of Benjamin (Philippians 3:5). Paul had *multiple* civil citizenships. This array of providential circumstances proved to be very beneficial to the apostle.

The Roman view of citizenship was quite different from that of the Bible. While Roman citizenship was obtained by birth (Acts 22:28), citizenship was often given to an individual as an act of grace by the State. In some cases, citizenship was earned for services rendered to the State. Josephus, the Jewish historian for the Romans was granted citizenship. Citizenship could be bought (Acts 22:28). In each of these cases, one's exclusive loyalty was to the State. In Rome, more often than not, an alien was not granted "equal protection under the law." The Apostle Paul, not thought to be a Roman citizen, was to be "examined by scourging" (Acts 22:24), certainly not the way a Roman citizen would have been treated: "And when they stretched him out with thongs, Paul said to the centurion who was standing by, 'Is it lawful for you to scourge a man who is a Roman and uncondemned?' " (v. 25).

155

In the United States an individual has a national, state, county, and city citizenship. In some states borough governments (e.g., Pennsylvania, New Jersey, New York, Minnesota) and parish governments (e.g., Louisiana) operate. Each of the many civil authorities holds real power and influence in these locales. Their real authority and power can be used to curtail the power of another legitimate government that might abuse its authority, or an illegitimate governing power assuming rule through coercion. Through multiple civil citizenships citizens have access to the seats of power where influence can be exerted on a local level. Abolition of these many civil distinctions leads to despotism and tyranny. One way that sovereignty and power has been siphoned from the states is through federal taxing power. The sign of political sovereignty is the power to tax. This is why the taxing power in Israel, at the national and local levels, was limited while a tax of ten percent was considered tyrannical (1 Samuel 8).

In the United States, we find more and more taxing power being given to the Federal government. Money is taken from the many states, through the power to tax, and then is paid out as favors to other states. Consider how much tax is levied against American citizens: There is a federal income tax, state income taxes, excise taxes, sales taxes, local option sales taxes, property taxes, school taxes, import taxes, gasoline taxes, road taxes, and numerous hidden taxes that are tacked on nearly every commodity we purchase. The Federal government dilutes the sovereignty of the states, the states dilute the sovereignty of the counties, the counties dilute the sovereignty of the cities, and the cities dilute the sovereignty of individuals. Of course, in all taxing power, sovereignty is taken from the individual. The ability freely to choose how to spend money is a symbol of sovereignty. When money is taken from individuals through taxation, the economic choices these individuals could have made are limited.

Adolph Hitler knew the necessity of abolishing local sovereignty. He did not remove local sovereignty gradually (e.g., through increased taxing power). He was able to consolidate his power outright by eliminating the many civil distinctions within the nation:

> [H]e had abolished the separate powers of the historic states and
> made them subject to the central authority of the Reich, which was
> in his hands.... 'Popular assemblies' of the states were abolished,
> the sovereign powers of the states were transferred to the Reich, all

state governments were placed under the Reich government and the state governors put under the administration of the Reich Minister of the Interior (William L. Shirer, *The Rise and Fall of the Third Reich*, p. 200).

One of the tenets of Marxism is the "gradual abolition of the distinction between town and country, by a more equable distribution of the population over the country" (*The Communist Manifesto*, written with Friedrich Engels, 1848).

One of the basic tenets of Marxism, as Karl Marx wrote, is the *gradual abolition of the distinction between town and country, by a more equable distribution of the population over the country.* Local sovereignty is destroyed to advance the power of the State.

Our nation's earliest founders designed a decentralized civil government which also decentralized power and authority. A system of government that gave specific and direct powers to a new central government and at the same time kept in tact the individual political sovereignty of the several states was set forth in the Articles of Confederation: "Each state retains its sovereignty, freedom and independence, and every Power, Jurisdiction and right, which is not by this confederation expressly delegated to the United States, in Congress assembled" (Article II). Our forefathers feared the type of government that gave birth to Nazism and Marxism.

157

5. In the Old Testament, Abraham, Isaac, and Jacob were "strangers and aliens" in "the land of promise" (Hebrews 11:9). The promise was not realized until Israel entered the land of Canaan, soon after God "redeemed" His people from Egyptian slavery. But once the Israelites were in the land, the Canaanites became "strangers and aliens." But a little background is necessary if we are really going to understand this concept. Remember, Adam and Eve had direct access to God's presence. They had a dual citizenship. They were citizens of heaven and citizens of the earth. After all, heaven and earth met in the Garden (Genesis 2:7-9, 15-18). Even after the fall "they heard the sound of the LORD God walking in the garden in the cool of the day. . ." (Genesis 3:8). Here God comes to evaluate their work. Unfortunately, it was a time of judgment and expulsion from the gate of heaven.

After meeting with God, the instructions Adam and Eve received in blueprint form were to be used to build on the earth the pattern of heaven. Adam and Eve were not created to remain in the Garden. They were to extend the boundaries of the Garden with God's blueprint in their hands. When Adam and Eve rebelled against God, they no longer were able to enter the heavenly kingdom to meet with God. This is why God "drove the man out; and at the east of the garden of Eden He stationed the cherubim, and the flaming sword which turned every direction, to guard the way to the tree of life" (Genesis 3:24). At this point, Adam and Eve and their descendants were "strangers and aliens" while Satan and his followers were squatters in the land of promise. But this too would change.

God would once again meet with His people in the heavenly kingdom, the kingdom of God as it is progressively worked out on earth by regenerate men and women keeping and implementing the commandments of God. The tabernacle, where the ark of the covenant was placed, was guarded by cherubim. The people were reminded of this because they saw the cherubim on the curtains (Exodus 26:1) and on the ark itself (Exodus 25:18-20).The cherubim guarded the place where man met with God. These cherubim struck Nadab and Abihu "when they offered strange fire before the LORD" (Numbers 3:4; cf. 26:61): "Fire came out from the presence of the LORD and consumed them, and they died before the LORD" (Leviticus 10:2; cf. Genesis 3:24).

Even the pattern for the sanctuary came from heaven: "And let them construct a sanctuary for Me, that I may dwell among them. According to all that I am going to show you, as the pattern of the tabernacle and the pattern of all its furniture, just so you shall construct it" (Exodus 25:8, 9). It is here where God met with Moses: "And there I will meet with you, and from above the mercy seat, from between the two cherubim which are upon the ark of the testimony, I will speak to you about all that I will give you in commandment for the sons of Israel" (Exodus 25:22; cf. 24:9-18). Moses received the blueprint from heaven and then gave it to the sons of Israel. The heavenly citizenship had an effect on the earth.

The New Testament gives us a more vivid picture of this relationship between heaven and earth, between heavenly and earthly citizenships. Jesus Himself is God's tabernacle: "In the beginning was the Word, and the Word was with God, and the Word was God. . . And the Word became flesh, and dwelt [Lit., *tabernacled*] among us, and we beheld His glory, glory as of the only begotten from the Father, full of grace and truth" (John 1:1, 14). Jesus, as God's "tabernacle in human flesh," took Peter, James, and John and "brought them up to a high mountain" (Matthew 17:1).

The First Prayer in Congress, led by Rev. Duche, is a testimony to the effect that heaven has on earthly affairs. Jesus told us to pray: *Thy kingdom come. Thy will be done, on earth as it is in heaven* (Matthew 6:10).

159

Notice that they "went up to a high mountain," Jesus' garments "became white as light" (v. 2), and a "cloud overshadowed them" (v. 5). Now, compare this with Moses' meeting with God: "Now the LORD said to Moses, 'Come up to Me *on the mountain. . . .*' Then Moses went up *to the mountain,* and *the cloud covered the mountain. . .* And to the eyes of the sons of Israel the appearance *of the glory of the Lord was like a consuming fire on the mountain top*" (Exodus 24:12, 15, 17).

Now, what does this have to do with dual citizenship and the Christian's responsibility to work out his heavenly citizenship on the earth? First, God's pattern for living comes from heaven and is given in blueprint form in the Bible. Isn't this what happened when Moses received the law from the mountain?: "Then [Moses] took the book of the covenant and read it in the hearing of the people; and they said, 'All that the LORD has spoken we will do, and we will be obedient!' " (Exodus 24:7; cf. 24:3; 19:38). Second, the world is now cleansed by the blood of Christ and is open for Christians to take dominion. This was Jesus' emphasis when He told His church to "go. . . and make disciples of all the nations, baptizing them in the name of the Father and Son and the Holy Spirit, teaching them to observe all that I commanded you; and lo, I am with you always, even to the end of the age" (Matthew 28:19, 20). Third, we pray, "Thy kingdom come. Thy will be done, on earth as it is in heaven" (Matthew 6:10). In the book of Hebrews, the kingdom of God is called a "heavenly one" (11:16). The kingdom of God is on the earth, but for the Christian it is a heavenly one. So, we do not despise the world. Rather, we progressively work out our salvation with fear and trembling and extend the boundaries of our kingdom-influence.

We can make better sense of Paul's words in Philippians 3:20: "For our citizenship is in heaven, from which also we eagerly await for a Savior, the Lord Jesus Christ." This idea corresponds to Jesus informing Nicodemus that he must be "born again [Lit., *born from above*]" (John 3:5; cf. John 14:1-3). In effect, the rebel must become a citizen of heaven before he can realize the privileges that come with being a member of God's kingdom on the earth. The Christian's heavenly citizenship does not cancel his earthly citizenships and corresponding obligations, however. In fact, in order to be an effective earthly citizen, one must first be a citizen of heaven. Citizenship is redemptive and ethical. Only the redeemed who are able to think God's thoughts after Him will be effective in bringing the imprint of heaven on earth.

The Christian has an obligation to follow the law of God as it applies to all locales. God's law is the standard whereby all the above mentioned citizenships must operate. Our heavenly citizenship involves comprehensive law keeping. Jesus said, "If you love Me, you will keep My commandments" (John 14:15). Jesus does not restrict the locale of law keeping; therefore, we can conclude that the keeping of His commandments includes every citizenship without exception. When Scripture speaks about obeying the civil magistrate (Romans 13:1-7; 1 Peter 2:13-17), citizens must obey. When State laws conflict with the laws of heaven, the Christian's first obligation is to his heavenly citizenship (Acts 5:29). While the Christian lives on earth he remains responsible to various governments, but looks for the day when his heavenly citizenship will be fully realized: "For to me, to live is Christ, and to die is gain" (Philippians 1:21).

The Great Commission is for the nations, calling them to repentance and making known the salvation that God makes available in His Son Jesus Christ. Micah is exhorting the Israelites to *do justice, to love kindness, and to walk humbly with your God* (Micah 6:8).

All law has a religious foundation. Paul Robert's (1851-1923) mural entitled *Justice Lifts the Nations* makes this point very clear. Justice is standing without a blindfold pointing her sword to an open book, "The Law of God."

Lesson 6

The Foundation of Law

A revolution is occurring around the world concerning the foundation of law and its relation to the courts. In the United States, the Constitutional safeguard of checks and balances is out of balance. For the courts and the majority of citizens there is no law outside of man that is fixed and can stand the test of time and circumstances. The courts have assumed that law and its application to everyday circumstances reside in the hands of judges, independent of any objective standard of justice. The Constitution often is viewed as an outdated historical document which might have sentimental value, but very little contemporary legal value.

The courts have made revolutionary judgments by defining the nature of religion and the significance or insignificance of human life. We are witnessing the deification of the courts because we have observed the deification of man. For example, previous courts were erected to "protect" and "guard" the citizens' God-granted rights (immunity from coercion by the State). Modern courts see themselves as being able to "grant" or "create" rights, something only God can do. "In contemporary society it is coming to be assumed that the state grants rights to the American citizen. This is dangerous thinking. Government is not God, to create rights, but is God's minister to protect the rights God has given man" (John W. Whitehead, *The Second American Revolution*, p. 89). It is time we reevaluate the nature of law, the purpose of the courts, the function of judges, the responsibilities of citizens, and the proper methods for administering justice.

The fall of man has made it necessary that judgments be made in behalf of those who are wronged. The most fundamental aspect of making judgments is the requirement for an unchanging standard. The idea that law should rest on an unchanging standard has its roots in the biblical idea that God does not change: "For I, the LORD, do not change" (Malachi 3:6). It is said of Jesus: "Jesus Christ is the same yesterday and today, yes and forever" (Hebrews 13:8). Israel could count on God acting on the basis of His unchanging character. God could be appealed to on the basis of the covenant He established with Abraham, Isaac, and Jacob because He is an unchanging God: "Remember Abraham, Isaac and Israel, Thy servants to whom Thou didst swear by Thyself, and didst say to them, 'I will multiply your descendants as the stars of the heavens, and all this land of which I have spoken I will give to your descendants, and they shall inherit it forever' " (Exodus 32:13). Because God is unchanging, His covenant is unchanging and His holy law is unchanging.

But a fatal element of error inheres in this position, if it is thought that the Christian revelation, the Bible, does not come to the civil authority with a demand for obedience to its direction and precept as stringent and inescapable as it does to the individual, to the family and to the church.

—John Murray

The most striking illustration of the unchanging applicability of the law of God is the death of Jesus Christ. God views His own law as an absolute standard that must be obeyed. "There is none righteous, not even one" (Romans 3:10). God's holiness demands perfection before the law, and fallen men and women are hopeless without the perfect law-keeping of Jesus Christ. The righteous merits of Jesus Christ must be transferred to the defiled sinner. The mercy and grace of God extends even to wretched sinners, but not at the expense of the requirements of the law. Jesus took upon Himself the punishment due those who broke the law: "He was pierced through for our transgressions, He was crushed for our iniquities; the chastening for our well-being fell upon Him, and by His scourging we are healed" (Isaiah 53:5). Every demand of the law had to be kept. God did not give up the requirements of the law for the salvation of sinners. Jesus was the great law-keeper: God "made Him who *knew no sin* to be sin on our behalf, that we might become the righteousness of God in Him" (2 Corinthians 5:21).

The Christian, though free from the curse of the law, acknowledges he must obey the law. This concept of freedom *with* responsibility regarding the law was built into our young country's judicial system. Christians are saved to *keep* the law. What other way can the Christian show God that he loves Him? Jesus said, "If you love Me, you will keep My commandments" (John 14:15). Even love of our neighbor is defined in terms of the law: "Owe nothing to anyone except to love one another; for he who loves his neighbor has fulfilled the law" (Romans 13:8). But how does one know when he is loving his neighbor?: "For this, 'You shall not commit adultery, You shall not murder, You shall not steal, You shall not covet,' and if there is any other commandment, it is summed up in this saying, 'You shall love your neighbor as yourself' " (v. 9). The modern conception of love, however, defines it as *freedom from the demands of the law.*

The absolute nature of law was reflected in our courts as well. In many cases there was a conscious effort to reflect the biblical standard of law in rendering court decisions. It was assumed there was an absolute law because there was a "higher law." John W. Whitehead, a constitutional attorney, makes the following point about law being rooted in a higher law:

The fact that this principle [that God is the final lawgiver] carried over into the early life of America is apparent in the natural way the summary of biblical law, the Ten Commandments, functioned as a pattern and a guide both in court decisions and in the framing of individual pieces of legislation. Episcopalian theologian T. R. Ingram has observed that the reference point for the common law was in the Ten Commandments: "Christian men have always known that what we might call political liberty as part of all Christian liberty is a consequence of upholding the common law. . . the Ten Commandments." (*The Second American Revolution*, p. 77).

The idea of absolute law is a fading memory for our courts. Darwinian evolution has placed law in the arena with evolving man. If man has evolved then the standards primitive man once held must change along with him. When the higher law is abandoned, another law takes its place. The humanistic doctrine of evolution allows man to create for himself the law he believes will most benefit evolving man. Law then is what men or the courts say it is. Wrongs are defined in terms of what hurts *man*. There is no appeal to a law-order outside man. For example, abortion is made legal because it is convenient for the mother. For some women, having a baby is "harmful" because it restricts their freedom. These women are "wrongfully" curtailed in their desire to live as they wish. Laws are then passed to alleviate the "problem." The developing fetus is termed a "non-person" without protection from the more powerful. There is no consideration that God has defined the nature of life, or that freedom should be defined in terms of submission to the commandments of God. Nor are the necessarily destructive and suicidal long-term consequences of such legal thought and practice seriously considered.

In developing a just judicial system, an unchanging standard of law is fundamental. Such a standard would legislate impartially among rich and poor, the majority and the minority, the weak and the strong, and the small and the great. Justice would not be defined in terms of who can wield the greatest power or make the loudest noise. Justice is an immovable standard that judges between a man and his neighbor: "If a powerful and evil man, class, or group can push an innocent man out of his property, or in any way abuse him, the evil is compounded if they can command the state to help them in their theft. . . . The courts must transcend the passions of the day. It must represent a law-order which judges the entire social order, and this is possible only if the judges represent God, not the people or the state" (R. J. Rushdoony, *Institutes of Biblical Law*, p. 611). The law should be no respecter of persons. The people, as well as the courts, must act in terms of that immutable higher law, the law of God.

The first and almost the only Book deserving of universal attention is the Bible (John Quincy Adams, President of the United States, 1825-1829).

166

Questions for Discussion

1. What standard of authority should form the foundation for a nation's judicial system, and why? (Genesis 3:1-5; Exodus 18:15-16; Deuteronomy 4:2; 17:8-13; 2 Chronicles 19:5-7; Isaiah 8:19-20; 33:22)

_____

_____

_____

_____

_____

_____

_____

_____

2. What is the modern conception of law as reflected in our courts? Compare the following Scripture passages with recent court decisions. (Psalm 93:5; 111:7, 8; 119:151, 152, 160; Isaiah 40:6-8)

_____

_____

_____

_____

_____

_____

3. How does the Constitution express the idea that it rests upon a Christian foundation of law? (A copy of the Constitution, especially the Preamble, is needed to answer this question.)

_____

_____

_____

_____

_____

_____

4. Why do sinful men and women need a judicial system? (Genesis 3:11-13; 4:8, 23; 6:2; 9:6; Exodus 20:1-17)

_____

_____

_____

_____

_____

5. Must all disputes be handled in civil court rooms established by the State? (Matthew 5:23-25; 16:19; 18:15ff.; 1 Corinthians 11:2, 3; Ephesians 5:22-26; 6:1-4; Hebrews 13:17; 1 Corinthians 6:1-11)

_____

_____

_____

_____

6. What is the significance of this statement?: "You shall appoint for yourselves judges and officers _in all your towns_ which the LORD your God is giving you, according to your tribes, and they shall judge the people with _righteous judgment._" (Deuteronomy 16:18; cf. 21:1-9).

_____

_____

_____

_____

_____

7. What is the significance of the following verse: "You shall not distort justice; you shall not be partial, and you shall not take a bribe, for a bribe blinds the eyes of the wise and perverts the words of the righteous" (Deuteronomy 16:19; cf. 1:17; Exodus 23:3, 6, 8; Leviticus 19:15; James 2:1-13)

_____

_____

_____

_____

8. The source of law in a society is the god of that society. What does the command "not to plant. . . an Asherah [an idol] of any kind. . . beside the altar of the LORD your God," have to do with instituting justice? (Deuteronomy 16:21-22; 1 Kings 11:1, 2; Exodus 23:32, 33; 34:12-17; 1 Corinthians 6:14, 15; cf. Matthew 6:24)

_____

_____

_____

_____

_____

_____

_____

_____

_____

Summary

"Those who do not favor taking God's law as the ultimate standard for civil morality and public justice will be forced to substitute some other criterion of good and evil for it. The civil magistrate cannot function without some ethical guidance, without some standard of good and evil. If that standard is not to be the revealed law of God (which, we must note, was addressed specifically to perennial problems in political morality), then what will it be? In some form or expression it will have to be a law of man (or men) — the standard of self-law or autonomy. And when *autonomous* laws come to govern a commonwealth, the sword is certainly wielded *in vain*, for it represents simply the brute force of some men's will against the will of other men. 'Justice' then indeed becomes a verbal cloak for whatever serves the interests of the strongmen in society (whether their strength be that of physical might or of media manipulation). Men will either choose to be governed by God or to be ruled by tyrants" (Greg L. Bahnsen, *By this Standard*, p. 264f.)

Answers to Questions for Discussion

1. A nation's judicial system rests on law — the law of God or the law of man. There is no neutrality. When man's law prevails we can expect God's law to be invalidated (Mark 7:8, 13). Satan attacked God on the basis of His law: "Indeed, has God said, 'You shall not eat from any tree of the garden?' " (Genesis 3:1). He appealed to Adam and Eve to be a law unto themselves — to "be like God" (v. 5).

A nation's judicial system rests on law — the law of God or the law of man. There can be no neutrality. Supreme Court Justice Joseph Story remarked: *There never has been a period of history, in which the common Law did not recognize Christianity as laying at its foundation.*

God thought enough of His law to send His Son to keep it in every detail. If the Son of God was required to keep the law, should anything less be expected of the created sons of God?

Christ was tempted at every point with respect to obeying the commands of God, yet He remained sinless throughout (Heb. 4:15). Because He kept the law perfectly, Christ had no need to offer up sacrifice for His own sins (Heb. 7:26-28). Instead He offered Himself up without spot to God, a lamb without spot or blemish as the law required, in order to cleanse us of our sins (Heb. 9:14). As the Old Testament had foretold, "righteousness will be the belt around His loins" (Isa. 11:5), and the Messiah could declare, "Thy law is within my heart" (Ps. 40:7-8; Heb. 10:4-10).

We read in Galatians 4:4 that "when the fulness of the time came, God sent forth His Son, born of a woman, born under the law, that he might redeem them that were under the law." Christ was neither lawless nor above the law; He submitted to its every requirement, saying "it becomes us to fulfill all righteousness" (Matt. 3:15). He directed the healed to offer the gift commanded by Moses (Matt. 8:4), kept the borders of His garments (9:20; 14:36), paid the temple tax (21:12-17), etc. He directed His followers to do those things which conformed to the law's demand (Matt: 7:12), told the rich young ruler to keep the commandments (19:17), reinforced the Old Testament law by summarizing it into two love commandments (22:40), indicted the Pharisees for making God's commandments void through traditions of men (Mark 7:6-13), and insisted that even the most trite or insignificant matters of the law ought not to be left undone (Luke 11:12) (Greg L. Bahnsen, *By This Standard*, p. 57).

The entire human race has been found "guilty" on the basis of God's law. While the law ceases to condemn the Christian (Galatians 3:13) because of Jesus' perfect obedience and His substitutionary atonement as payment for the law's demands, all are held accountable to keep the law as a standard of right and wrong (Romans 3:31). Individuals, families, schools, churches, business establishments, civil governments, and the courts must choose the law of God as the standard for decision-making. Since the individual is not free to break the law, the courts are not free to judge on any other basis of law-order than that set forth in the Bible.

When a dispute arose among the people, Moses directed them to the law of God: "When they have a dispute, it comes to me, and I judge between a man and his neighbor, and make known the statutes of God and His laws" (Exodus 18:16). The judges appointed by Moses to share in the task of settling disputes also were required to judge according to the law of God (vv. 19-20). The people as a whole must be careful not to add to the law of God or take away from it (Deuteronomy 4:2). This indicates that

God's law must be used as it is and not mixed with the changing laws of men. Men often are tempted to adapt God's commandments to fit the times. Thus the judgment of man is deemed superior to that of God, and the commandments of God often nullified (cf. Mark 7:13). (While the law itself does not change, the application may. For example, the Bible tells us that a railing is required to be built around a roof: "When you build a new house, you shall make a parapet for your roof, that you may not bring blood-guilt on your house if anyone falls from it" [Deuteronomy 22:8]. In the ancient world, the flat roof was utilized as a patio [Joshua 2:6, 8; 2 Samuel 11:2; 18:24]. How would the law requiring a "parapet for your roof" apply today? A fence would be required for a swimming pool or an open pit [Exodus 21:33, 34]).

Oliver Wendell Holmes, a Supreme Court justice from 1902 to 1932 proclaimed: *Truth [is] the majority vote of that nation that could lick all others.*

The Levitical priests as well as the judges of Israel were bound to follow the law. The people of Israel also were instructed to heed the judges' verdict because the decision was based upon the unchanging law of God and not upon the decision of men: "According to the terms of the law which they teach you, and according to the verdict which they tell you, you shall do; you shall not turn aside from the word which they declare to you, to the right or the left" (Deuteronomy 17:11). (We can draw an interesting and important political lesson from this: We are neither to abandon God's laws for humanistic conservatism, nor for humanistic "liberalism," Marxism, fascism, national socialism, and the like.)

172

When Jehoshaphat initiated reforms, one of the first affected the judicial system: "And he appointed judges in the land in all the fortified cities of Judah, city by city. And he said to the judges, 'Consider what you are doing, for you do not judge for man but for the LORD who is with you when you render judgment. Now then let the fear of the LORD be upon you; be very careful what you do, for the LORD our God will have no part in unrighteousness, or partiality, or the taking of a bribe'" (2 Chronicles 19:5-7). Judges' decisions must not issue from political or economic pressures or calculations, or any merely human purposes, but from obedience to the Lord of heaven and earth, and to the righteous laws He has revealed to us in Scripture.

The prophets of Israel continued to warn the nation that only the law of God serves as a legal system's foundation: "To the law and to the testimony! If they do not speak according to this word, it is because they have no dawn" (Isaiah 8:20). Any attempt to repudiate the law of God as a standard for righteousness establishes man as judge, lawgiver, king, and savior; it leaves man under the rule of darkness. The Bible clearly shows that law originates in the character of God, and definitions for justice and righteousness find their meaning in Him and not in the finite, fallible, and fallen nature of the creature: "For the LORD is our judge, the LORD is our lawgiver, the LORD is our king; He will save us" (Isaiah 33:22).

2. The Bible presents law as abiding forever because it reflects God's own immutable character: "The works of His hands are truth and justice; all His precepts are sure. They are upheld forever and ever; they are performed in truth and righteousness" (Psalm 111:7, 8); "Thy testimonies are fully confirmed; holiness befits Thy house, O LORD, forevermore" (Psalm 93:5); "All Thy commandments are truth. Of old I have known from Thy testimonies, that Thou has founded them forever" (Psalm 119:151b-152); "The sum of Thy word is truth, and every one of Thy righteous ordinances is everlasting" (v. 160); "The word of our God stands forever" (Isaiah 40:8). The word of man is feeble and failing because his nature is finite and fallen: "All flesh is grass, and all its loveliness is like the flower of the field. The grass withers, the flower fades, when the breath of the LORD blows upon it; surely the people are grass. The grass withers, the flower fades, but the word of our God stands forever" (Isaiah 40:6-8).

The modern use of law makes it arbitrary, based in one case on a judge, in another, on the word of the Fuhrer. Thus man becomes the lawmaker, and the word of human authority becomes the new law. The courts, therefore, no longer are bound by any law. They have in effect become a law unto themselves.

In 1907 Supreme Court Justice Charles Evans Hughes remarked that "the Constitution is what the judges say it is." Thus, in Hughes's view, law is arbitrary and is shaped by what a majority of nine Supreme Court justices say it is. Such an attitude is not that far removed from the 1936 decree of the Third Reich Commissar of Justice: "A decision of the Fuhrer in the express form of a law or decree may not be scrutinized by a judge. In addition, the judge is bound by any other decisions of the Fuhrer, provided that they are clearly intended to declare law" (John W. Whitehead, *The Second American Revolution*, p. 20).

Satan's lie is alive and destroying our nation: "And you will be like God, knowing good and evil" (Genesis 3:5).

In 1907 Supreme Court Justice and Governor of New York Charles Evans Hughes (1862-1942) remarked that *the Constitution is what the judges say it is*. For Hughes and many judges of our day, law is based on the will of the courts and can and should change with the times.

Modern legal thought is based on at least two beliefs: first, evolution; and second, faith in the scientific method divorced from God. The evolutionary concept of law denies the existence of God's laws or any other absolutes or universally valid moral and legal principles. Believing in the truth of evolution, this view sees law as part of an evolutionary process, a process of continual change. Some believe this evolutionary process to be guided by no moral principles or universal laws. Others believe the process is producing a one-world, socialist government. In the "pragmatic" version, the "evolution" of the law is guided by nothing more than the mind of man responding to the changes of historical circumstances. In this version, the "evolutionary" process just "happens" to demand that State intervention and controls over people's personal and economic lives (the essence of Socialism) increase.

The common denominator of all evolutionary theories is the notion that Christian elements of the law must be abandoned, to be replaced by new and ever-changing laws in accordance with men's desires. In some forms of evolutionary theory, the majority of the people determine which changes must be made in the law. In others, an elite — such as judges for life — determine what changes are needed. At other times, elected representatives of the people bring about legal change. (A combination of these forces has drastically changed our nation's laws.)

In a particularly virulent variety of this evolutionary view, the Communist Party is the elite which guides the "evolution" of law. In any case, law continually changes as the will of man changes. The Soviet Union feeds on this type of legal pragmatism:

[F]or the person who has grown up in a democratic country the most difficult thing to grasp is the fact that ways and means of governing the huge superpower, and the rights and duties of its citizens, are defined not by a constitution or any other written laws but by a whole body of unwritten laws, which, although not published anywhere, are perfectly well known to all Soviet Citizens and are obeyed by them.

The present Soviet constitution states that the power belongs to the people, who exercise it through elected soviets — councils — and the government of the country is carried out by the Council of Ministers and other administrative bodies. The fact is, however,

175

that true power in the Soviet Union belongs to the apparat of the Communist party, and it is the members of that apparat who are the true leaders of the country (Konstantin M. Simis, *USSR: The Corrupt Society*, p. 23f.)

The Soviet system is based on evolutionary theory. Karl Marx understood that he needed the evolutionary theory to develop his new society: "Darwin's book is very important and serves me," he wrote, "as a basis in natural science for the class struggle in history. . ." (Karl Marx to Friedrich Engels [Jan. 16, 1861], in *Marx-Engels Selected Correspondence*, edited by Dona Torr [New York: International Publishers, 1935], p. 125. Quoted by Gary North, *The Dominion Covenant: Genesis*, p. 18).

The handmaiden of evolutionary thought is modern man's faith in the scientific method, divorced from God. By this, some men believe all problems can be solved, producing the notion that law should be made according to the scientific method. (This is known as "Legal Positivism.") The trouble is, this theory denies that man can "scientifically" have any certain or "positive" knowledge of moral principles. Since the scientific method limits itself to evidence that can be apprehended by the senses, it is limited to mere empirical evidence. And since it can deal only with physical evidence, the scientific method never can have a positive knowledge of moral principles. The consequence of this view, of course, is that God's word and law must be removed as the basis of law. This means the Christian principles upon which the Constitution, the constitutions of the many states, the Common Law, and even the Bill of Rights are established, must be abandoned, replaced by new, man-centered principles of man's own making. The nature of these "principles," of course, varies with the particular theorist or school of thought. Some theorists want economic competition largely unrestrained by biblical law. Most, however, want one variety or another of government intervention into the economic, social and educational lives of individuals and families, or some variety of socialism. Who decides? What standard will be used?

The common denominator of legal thought based on science is that "science" (man's ability to assess evidence independent of fixed moral laws) must replace biblical revelation as the foundation of law, and that arbitrary, man-made "morals" must replace God's laws. (Of course, these men were inconsistent in speaking of morality, but they had their own

176

social and economic agendas, their own religious visions of the "good" society created by the mind and work of man, that they expected "science" to establish.) Man would manipulate the economy and society to suit his desires by means of law — his law. Law would be scientifically designed by man to fulfill the desires of man (either by central planning or pragmatic "adjustments" of the law to deal with the changes in the "times"). Man must manipulate other men by means of scientific social, economic, and educational experimentation. Amending God and His laws, man the new lawgiver, will bring blessings to society via scientifically designed law.

In order to justify the killing of unborn babies, the Supreme Court Justices in 1973 invented an absolute *right to privacy* and placed it over the Constitution, and ultimately over the law of God. Justice William O. Douglas who wrote the majority opinion said: *We deal with a right to privacy older than the Bill of Rights — older than our political parties, older than our school system.*

Both of these strains of thought have combined to produce our modern system of arbitrary, humanistic law, the deliberate erosion of the Christian principles of our laws and Constitution, and the destruction of our liberties under God.

3. The Preamble to the Constitution makes reference to the establishment of justice: "WE THE PEOPLE of the United States in order to form a more perfect Union, *establish justice* . . . ." There can be no justice unless there is a standard for defining and maintaining justice. The law of God is the only unchanging law that can effectively judge varying opinions. The Preamble states its purpose: to "secure the Blessings of Liberty to ourselves and our Posterity." The purpose of our newly formulated national government was not to provide these blessings but to maintain (secure) them. Obviously, to instruct a government to secure one's blessings must mean the individual already possesses them or gets them from another source. The framers of the Constitution attempted to assure future generations that blessings are God-given (cf. The Declaration of Independence) and not endowed by a Messianic State.

The Constitution, therefore, was not a license to implement arbitrary law. Its purpose was to maintain (secure) the existing moral order of the day — embodied and protected in the constitutions, bills of rights, and laws of the various states — without giving the newly framed federal government power to overthrow the prevailing context of religion, the Christian faith: "John Witherspoon [a Presbyterian minister] and the other Christian leaders — having observed the British monarchy and hierarchy as both the head of the church and the state — did not want a connection between their church and the new federal government. They considered such an association a calamity and a curse. But at the same time, the knowledge of God as revealed in the Bible was so commonly diffused that it was probably not anticipated by colonial Americans that the Constitution might be made to operate on non-Christian principles" (John W. Whitehead, *The Second American Revolution*, p. 95).

The theological shift from theocentric Puritanism to Arminianism clouded the potential secularization inherent in the depravity of man. Puritanism understood the pervasive depravity of man while Arminianism downplayed human depravity and asserted man's self-sufficiency. In time, the seeds of Arminianism grew and bore its rotten fruit. Even so, it took carefully planned and financed test cases to overturn 300 years of Puritan influence. The New York Prayer Case of June 25, 1962 had reversed longstanding and fully legal religious practices by the states. At the time of the drafting of the First Amendment, nine of thirteen states

178

had established churches. "Neither the nine states, nor any of the others, had any expectation whatsoever, when the first amendment was ratified, that it would do more than bar *Congress* from interference in religious matters, and not a single state practice then or later was modified because of it" (R.J. Rushdoony, *The Nature of the American System*, p. 54f.)

4. The fall and resultant sinfulness of man necessitates a system whereby those who differ on the issue of a judgment may reach a just decision. The fall of man also necessitated forming a just civil government which can protect the good against the wicked deeds of evil men, and punish and restrain evildoers in accordance with God's standards of justice.

As soon as Adam and Eve sinned, accusations began. Eve blamed the serpent: "The serpent deceived me, and I ate" (Genesis 3:13). Adam blamed his wife, and ultimately God: "The woman whom Thou gavest to be with me, she gave me from the tree, and I ate" (v. 11). Murder (4:8, 23) and other acts of violence (6:2) became part of the created order. God implemented laws to deal with the violence that resulted from man's sinful desires: "Whoever sheds man's blood, by man his blood shall be shed, for in the image of God He made man" (9:6). Laws protecting life (Exodus 20:13), property (v. 15), and relationships (vv. 12, 14, 16) were made part of the system of law that Israel was bound to follow. Justice, therefore, was defined in terms of the law.

Even with the coming of Jesus Christ and the operation of the regenerating power of the Holy Spirit, judgments between Christians of differing opinions are a reality: "Greek Christians struggled with Hebrew Christians (Acts 6). The New Testament church dealt with serious conflicts at a conference in Jerusalem (Acts 15). Paul challenged Peter over his prejudice in Galatians 2, and Paul and Barnabas disagreed so seriously over John Mark that they separated (Acts 15). Tribes, brothers, cities, religious subdivisions, disciples — all had conflicts" (Lynn R. Buzzard and Laurence Eck, *Tell it to the Church: Reconciling Out of Court*, p. 22). All the above-mentioned disputes were within the Christian community, proving that Christians are not immune from conflict.

5. The State and its courts are not given unlimited authority in judicial matters. Individuals, families, independent institutions, the church, and

179

While a judge, appointed by the State, has authority to settle disputes, those involved can and should reach a settlement before the case reaches a civil court. Those trained in law can be used in such arbitration, even in ecclesiastical courts.

the State all have authority to act as courts to reconcile opposing opinions. The individual is instructed to "make friends with [his] opponent at law while [he] is with him on the way, in order that [his] opponent may not deliver [him] to the judge, and the judge to the officer, and [he] be thrown into prison" (Matthew 5:25). While the judge, appointed by the State, has authority to settle disputes, those involved can reach a settlement before the case reaches the civil court. Moreover, the innocent party is duty bound to confront an erring brother: "If therefore you are presenting your offering at the altar, and there remember that your brother has something against you, leave your offering there before the altar, and go your way; first be reconciled to your brother, and then come and present your offering" (vv. 23, 24). In another place Jesus instructs us to reprove our brother in private before we involve others in the dispute (Matthew 18:15). "It is not insignificant that the Scriptures suggest that his first step should be in private. Before others are brought into the conflict, before witnesses or the church are included, the parties should seek a reconciliation on a personal and private basis. In such initial meetings, friends or advisors may, in fact, impede reconciliation. Others who wish to rush in quickly might note the counsel of Proverbs 26:17: 'He who meddles in a quarrel not his own is like one who takes a passing dog by the ears' (RSV)" (Lynn R. Buzzard and Laurence Eck, *Tell it to the Church: Reconciling Out of Court*, p. 31).

The family is a God-established hierarchy of authority: "Now I [Paul] praise you because you remember me in everything, and hold firmly to the traditions, just as I delivered them to you. But I want you to understand that Christ is the head of every man, and man is the head of a woman, and God is the head of Christ" (1 Corinthians 11:2, 3). Since the family is ultimately under the authority of the Lord Jesus Christ, it has the authority to settle *familial* disputes. The husband, as head of the family, must make decisions based on the word of God. He cannot claim to be an independent authority, lording it over his wife and children (Ephesians 5:22-26; 6:4). Children are to be submissive to their parents, realizing that their authority comes from God: "Children, obey your parents in the Lord, for this is right. Honor your father and mother (which is the first commandment with a promise), that it may be well with you, and that you may live long on the earth" (Ephesians 6:1-3).

When disputes cannot be settled between two individuals or among family members, the church can and must operate as a legitimate judicial authority. When individual and group confrontation fails to bring about a just decision, Jesus commands us to "tell it to the church" (Matthew 18:17). The church is a gifted body of believers (1 Corinthians 12-14) who have the word of God as the final voice of authority for all matters of faith and practice (2 Timothy 3:16, 17). If the church is not equipped to handle disputes, then what institution is? Jesus states that the church's authority comes from heaven and, therefore, does not rest upon the authority of any human institution: "Truly I say to you, whatever you shall bind on earth shall have been bound in heaven; and whatever you loose on earth shall have been loosed in heaven" (Matthew 18:18). "Jesus indicates that heaven will stand by and affirm the decisions the church makes when, in faithfulness [to the word of God], it resolves disputes. This also means that the believer who might be tempted to complain about the decision or feel it was not just is without recourse [cf. Hebrews 13:17]" (Lynn Buzzard and Laurence Eck, *Tell it to the Church: Reconciling Out of Court*, p. 34). While

Paul discouraged lawsuits between believers, he established the principle that God's people are capable of handling disputes among the brethren: "Does any one of you, when he has a case against his neighbor, dare to go to law before the unrighteous, and not before the saints?" (1 Corinthians 6:1).

In some cases the individual, the family, and the church do not have authority to make judicial decisions, nor implement the proper punishment. While the church is given the authority of the "keys" (Matthew 16:19), the State has the power of the "sword" (Romans 13:4). There are certain crimes that necessitate the use of the sword (e.g., capital crimes) where the church has no jurisdiction. "We learn from Paul in Romans 13 that the civil magistrate has a right to use an iron sword; this is the sword of the *state* (not the church) which has been delegated the task of restraining evil by punishing violators of God's holy law as it touches upon matters of social concern (i.e., outward deeds). That Paul is in harmony with Christ's teaching about the state is evidenced by the obvious parallel between Romans 13:7 and Matthew 22:21. The church and state are separate realms with different functions; only the state has a warrant to use violence and the iron sword, but then it is *not* autonomous in so doing. All who use the sword must submit to God's direction" (Greg L. Bahnsen, *Theonomy in Christian Ethics*, p. 421).

6. Israel's governmental systems were decentralized. Judges and their officers, and the elders of the people were appointed to a variety of cities on the local level. They were responsible to administer justice in the locale where they were installed to power: "If a slain person is found lying in the open country in the land which the LORD your God gives you to possess, and it is not known who has struck him, then your elders and your judges shall go out and measure the distance to the cities which are around the slain one" (Deuteronomy 21:1-2). Atonement must be made for the death of a person found in an open field outside the boundaries of any particular city. The city closest to the slain body was responsible to make atonement. The city was represented by elders (representing civil affairs) and judges (representing judicial matters). While cities had numerous elders and judges, the law of God bound them to follow the same legal procedures. The law of God insured that people were being judged by "righteous judgment," no matter which judge kept court.

182

When the anchor of law is jettisoned, the many judges who preside over the cities of the United States establish themselves and their own ideas as the standard for righteousness. Often an individual who dislikes the verdict meted out in one court appeals to a higher court to find a judge who operates with a different set of judicial principles based upon a different law. Judicial decisions from state to state often differ because of the absence of any standard of righteousness. In many courts throughout our land there is a decided bias *against* the Christian religion. Law has become sociological, pragmatic, and utilitarian. The following quotation sums up the present status of law as it has reference to the many courts of our land: "[L]aw is only what most of the people think at that moment of history, and there is no higher law. It follows, of course, that the law can be changed any moment to reflect what the majority currently thinks. More accurately, law becomes what a few people in some branch of the government think will promote the present sociological and economic good. In reality the will and moral judgment of the majority are now influenced by or even overruled by the opinions of a small group of men and women [e.g., Supreme Court]. This means that fast changes can be made in the whole concept of what should and what should not be done. Values can be altered overnight and at almost unbelievable speed" (Francis Schaeffer and C. Everett Koop, *Whatever Happened to the Human Race?*, p. 25).

When the anchor of law is jettisoned, judges often act independent of any fixed standard of law. The law, then, becomes what the judges say it is. In this scene, a young law student is being examined. What standard will be used?

7. The standard for justice already has been established — the word of God. Judges are unable to judge rightly unless the standard of righteousness comes from the law of God. To operate contrary to justice is to deny the word of God:

First, the status of a person involved in, or accused of, a crime would not be taken into account when he is judged. Fallen man tends to favor the rich because they hold greater influence in the community where the judge resides. The poor are easily disadvantaged because their meager living does not afford the options often available to the affluent. On the other hand, the poor often are pitied when they commit a crime, and thus are able to use their economic condition to arouse pity and to overrule requirements of the law. God's law makes no provision for favoring the rich or pitying the poor when a crime is committed: "You shall do no injustice in judgment; you shall not be partial to the poor nor defer to the great, but you are to judge your neighbor fairly" (Leviticus 19:15).

Second, Paul says the "love of money is a root of all sorts of evil" (1 Timothy 6:10). The Bible warns the judge not to be influenced by bribes. Moreover, in choosing men for the office of judge, one requirement is that they "hate dishonest gain" (Exodus 18:21). Instead of seeing the law as the standard of judgment, money too often becomes the dispenser of justice: "By taking a bribe, the public official or judge thereby makes a thief of himself, and a thieves' domain of his office. The most deadly and dangerous thieves are those who operate within the law and especially the officers of law. . . . The requirement of Deuteronomy 16:19, 'thou shalt not respect faces,' is in Hebrew literally, 'Thou shalt not recognize faces.' The judge thus must be blind to the *persons* in the case, and must see the *issues* involved. The bribe exactly reverses this: the judge is then *blind* to the *issues* and *sees* only the *persons*" (R. J. Rushdoony, *Institutes of Biblical Law*, p. 535).

8. The Asherah was a female deity of the Canaanites (Baal was the male counterpart), usually represented by a wooden pole or a luxuriant tree that was considered to be sacred. When the Israelites entered the land they were commanded to destroy the foreign sanctuaries so the pagan religion of the Canaanites would be rejected in the minds of the people. Any attempt to mix the prevailing religion of the day with the purity of the faith delivered to Israel was prohibited. The religion of the creature and true faith delivered by the Creator have no common ground. Given enough time, the religion of man perverts the Christian faith. For example, Jesus commends the church of Ephesus because they "cannot endure evil men" and "put to the test those who call themselves apostles" (Revelation 2:2). Moreover, they "hate the deeds of the Nicolaitans" (2:6). On the other hand, Jesus rebukes the church of Thyatira because they "tolerate the woman Jezebel, who calls herself a prophetess, and she teaches and leads My bond-servants astray, so that they commit acts of immorality and eat things sacrificed to idols" (2:20). Tolerating an admixture of pagan influence eventually leads to outright apostasy.

King Jeroboam sought to mix and adulterate God's standard of righteousness by erecting an idol to compete with the altar of God. The kingdom never recovered.

When a nation's judicial system seeks to institute a law system that mixes the law of God with the laws of men, over a period of time God's law will be repudiated. The shift from a legal system based upon the law of God to a legal system based upon the wavering laws of men takes time, however. The shift is often imperceptible. When man's laws, based upon the independent reasoning of the creature, are made equal with revelation, we can be assured that the new law system is in place. Christians must know that there can be no so-called neutral system of law. When the law of God is replaced by any other system of law, that pagan system of law is an Asherah next to the altar of God.

God warns about being "bound together with unbelievers" (2 Corinthians 6:14). This is true in marriage, church government (6:15), and *civil* government. God warned the kings in Israel not to take foreign wives because they will be enticed by their gods: "Now King Solomon loved many foreign women along with the daughter of Pharaoh: Moabite, Ammonite, Edomite, Sidonian, and Hittite women, from the nations concerning which the LORD had said to the sons of Israel, 'You shall not associate with them, neither shall they asociate with you, for they will surely turn your heart away after their gods' " (1 Kings 11:1, 2; cf. Exodus 23:32, 33; 34:12-17). Religion is the basis of law. When a nation's laws change, there was a prior shift in the nation's religion.

The Reformation of the 16th century attacked the idea that there was a foundation for law outside the Bible. Man's intellect, the church, and the State were bound by the absolute authority of the Bible. This Reformation thinking was carried to the various colonies by the Pilgrims and Puritans during the 17th century. Many of the state constitutions of the 18th century reflect the *biblical* basis for law. The will of the people or the decree of the State did not serve as the foundation for justice.

There were many in the latter part of the 18th century, however, who attempted to overthrow the Christian foundation of law by establishing the people's "collective conscience" (Social Contract) as the standard for law. This resulted in the establishment of an elite law-making group which determined the nature and direction the courts would take.

Darwinian evolutionism served as the death knell to the concept of absolute law. Law no longer is rooted in the Creator, but finds its meaning in experience. The Asherah pole of autonomous reason has been erected in the courts of our day. Law, rooted in the will of man, has replaced the law of God. The will of the court is final. While the judiciary was established to *interpret* the Constitution in light of a higher law, it now has set itself *above* the law where it *makes* law independent of any fixed authority.

Unlike today, the idea of the higher law was assumed by the late eighteenth- and early nineteenth-century American judiciary. Justice was seen in terms of the higher law and its application in the everyday life of the people. As a consequence, in early America the courts were commonly referred to as *courts of justice*, not courts of law — the distinction being between God's law and man's law as applied in the courtroom. Because the Bible was the final authority, the practice of requiring witnesses to take an oath on the Bible before testifying was begun. However, with the rise of sociological law and the loss of biblical absolutes, the courts have become courts of law where man's law is the final authority. As a consequence, the courts are no longer guardians of the covenant [Constitution], but are, instead, arbitrary decision makers (John W. Whitehead, *The Second American Revolution*, p. 84f.).

The rise of sociological law, where law is an evolving standard, has a long history. Our courts are now vehicles whereby the nation is ruled by man's law rather than God's law. In effect, man has declared himself to be a god.

The Supreme Court is bound by law. Unfortunately, the law to which it is bound is its own law. Notice the banner the top of the engraving: *In God We Trust.* The law of God should overrule all judicial decisions from the lowest the highest courts in our land.

Lesson 7

The Administration of Justice

Restoration of the judicial system requires establishing a basis of law, and implementing procedures for carrying out justice. It is not enough to revamp our justice system through the establishment of more cost-effective techniques or the latest trend in sociological law. All judicial systems require a reference point. Scripture must be that reference point for the administration of justice.

Christians are often warned not to involve themselves with religious groups advocating biblical laws for society. For some reason biblical laws are not as good as laws agreed to by men. How can "biblical" laws and "Christian" judges, and reaching the world to make it "Christian" through the preaching of the gospel be harmful, as many non-Christians and Christians maintain? Has the Great Commission become less than great? Are we to suppose that secular laws, and non-Christian judges, and non-Christian lawyers are somehow better?

Non-Christian law and non-Christian lawyers brought us the greatest holocaust the world ever has seen — the pre-meditated murder of nearly 20 million unborn babies since 1973. Non-Christian economic policy based on the premise that law is arbitrary has plunged much of the world into poverty, boom and bust cycles of inflation and recession. Socialistic welfare programs are threatening the once-prosperous Christian West because biblical law has been jettisoned for law rooted in the natural order.

Of course, Christians should not petition the State to *impose* the regenerating effects of Christianity upon the citizenry through the sword. Christianity is an inside out religion. Only the Holy Spirit can regenerate the heart of a man or woman "dead in trespasses and sins" (Ephesians 2:1).

No State has the jurisdiction or power to make people Christians. Still, those biblical laws which directly address the civil magistrate should be enacted into law: protecting the unborn; the orphan, widow and stranger; maintaining just weights and measures (no fiat paper money); enforcing judicial laws regarding restitution and capital punishment; protecting the nation's borders; and establishing a tax rate that does not exceed 10 per cent for any citizen.

Judges are in no sense representatives of the people or the king, or of any will whatever, except so far as they take a place which the people or king filled before. In a higher sense, they are not representatives of the community nor of its chief magistrates, but of justice and of God. . . . They are in fact more immediately servants of God than any other men who manage the affairs of a country.
—Theodore Dwight Woolsey

Somehow, through some strange twist of logic, Christian groups which advocate looking to Scripture as the basis for the restoration of our present legal system, are being compared to Adolph Hitler. Is it because Hitler used the church and the nomenclature of Christianity to suck in the power structures of the day? Much of the church was pulled through the vortex of Nazism because of its supposed "moral" foundation. For example, with an eye to the votes of the Catholic Center Party, which he received, Hitler hoped "to improve our friendly relations with the Holy See [Roman Catholic Church]." The *New York Times* wrote, "Hitler declares Christianity will be the basis of the government's moral conception."

In reality, however, Hitler despised Jesus Christ and His law. Martin Bormann, one of the men closest to Hitler, said publicly in 1941,

"National Socialism and Christianity are irreconcilable" (Cited by William L. Shirer, *The Rise and Fall of the Third Reich*, p. 240). Hitler was a pragmatist. He knew how to get votes. His rhetoric is no different from present-day politicians who study the agendas of special interest groups and then draft their party platform to include as many views as is possible. Today, where immorality seems to be an adopted world view, many politicians support homosexuality, abortion, and pornography (under the guise of "free speech"). Hypocritical politicians will try to appeal to both ends of the political spectrum.

Hitler didn't want a "Christian" society based on "Christian" laws. Rather, he adopted a "Natural Law" ethic based on general revelation, a "neutral" ethic so prevalent in evangelical circles today. Law without God. Law that is "natural." Law that man, through the agency of the State, defines and controls.

William Demarest writes: "Hitler's National Socialist propagandists appealed to the revelation of God in reason, conscience, and the orders of Creation as justification for the Nazi state theology or cultural religion. Biblical revelation in Old and New Testaments was regarded by the Third Reich as a 'Jewish Swindle' and thus was set aside in favor of the Nazi natural theology" (*General Revelation: Historical Views and Contemporary Issues*, p.15). In Hitler's mind, biblical law was sinister.

Once Hitler convinced the people that revelation could not form the basis of civil law, the people turned to the State for direction and salvation. God no longer operated in the universe in a personal way. His law could not be heard. Once the State put God out of the way, it then could remove the individual. The individual is nothing, the nation everything. Anyone who stood against National Socialist ideals would be eliminated. The voice of the State become the voice of God. Any dissention was treason and punishable by death.

The people were made ready for statism and the holocaust was to follow. *First*, Adolf Hitler studied Otto von Bismarck's social policies, policies which reduced the Germans to statist slaves. William Shirer writes: "[Bismarck's social policy] did have a profound influence on the working class in that it gradually made them value security over political freedom and caused them to see the State, however conservative, a benefactor and a protector" (*The Rise and Fall of the Third Reich*, p.96n). Hitler took full

191

advantage of this state of mind: "I studied Bismarck's socialist legislation in its intention, struggle and success."

Christianity takes human depravity seriously and recognizes that an objective law must provide a benchmark for all governmental policy. The State is neither a savior nor a benevolent parent. Nearly 13 million Germans voted for Hitler, hoping for political salvation. He promised security. They could turn their backs on the holocaust because they were unwilling to give up the security they thought they had.

Holocaust becomes possible when people turn to the State and declare: "Do something! Educate our children. Take care of me when I'm unemployed, ill, and without food. Put controls on those greedy capitalists. Tax the rich and redistribute their 'excess' wealth to the poor. Increase the power of the State to protect us from ourselves." Sound familiar?

Second, Hitler's romantic and perverted notions about race certainly were factors in his decision of a "final solution." But what butchering events dulled the senses of the German people and those carrying out Hitler's evil extermination plans? Prior to 1933 (the year of Hitler's rise to power) abortion laws were very strict: "A pregnant woman who shall purposely cause herself to abort or shall kill her child in utero shall be subject to a penitentiary sentence...The same punishment shall be imposed on any person who, with the consent of the pregnant woman, applied or administered the means to induce the abortion or to cause the death of the child" (Section 218, German penal code, 1871). The Nazi State steadily removed the restrictions on abortion liberalized under the Weimar Republic. Mass demonstrations, with the help of doctors, were held in order to create sentiment against Germany's abortion laws.

Where does respect for human life originate? In "natural" law? Majority opinion? The opinion of judges? The State? Only a return to biblical law solves the dilemma. The law of God protects both weak and strong, rich and poor, young and old: "For the LORD your God is the God of gods and the Lord of lords, the great, the mighty, and the awesome God who does not show partiality, nor take a bribe. He executes justice for the orphan and the widow, and shows His love for the alien by giving him food and clothing. So show your love for the alien, for you were aliens in the land of Egypt" (Deuteronomy 10:17-19). Without *biblical* law there is no standard but the everchanging opinions of men.

What is left if we cannot go to the Bible for our laws? NBC presented the gripping and courageous story of Raoul Wallenberg and his attempts to save European Jews from their Nazi tormentor, Colonel Adolf Eichmann. Wallenberg's efforts may have made a difference for nearly 120,000 Hungarian Jews.

During the course of the story, when the viewer is confronted by a scene of wholesale slaughter, a Jewish teenager turns to a rabbi and confronts him with what he perceives to be an unanswerable question: "How can you still believe in God after all of this?" The rabbi does not take long to respond: "How can you still believe in man?"

This is our dilemma. If we do not believe in God for our laws then man is all that is left. Such a foundation leads either to anarchy (Beirut, Lebanon) or totalitarianism (the Soviet Union). "And if it is disagreeable in your sight to serve the Lord, choose for yourselves today who you will serve: whether the gods which your fathers served which were beyond the River, or the gods of the Amorites in whose land you are living; but as for me and my house, we will serve the Lord" (Joshua 24:15).

Socialism has high ideals but it leads to the worship of the State. Socialism is totalitarianism. Adolf Hitler's National Socialist German Workers' (Nazi) Party worked to deify the State and eradicate all opposition.

Questions for Discussion

1. What procedures should a court utilize to secure testimony concerning a criminal act?(Deuteronomy 17:6; 19:15-21; Numbers 35:30; Matthew 18:15-16; 2 Corinthians 13:1; Isaiah 5:20; 1 Timothy 5:19; Hebrews 10:28)

_____

_____

_____

_____

_____

_____

_____

_____

2. What procedure should be followed where there is only one witness to a crime?(Deuteronomy 17:8-13; 19:15-21; Joshua 7:16-26)

_____

_____

_____

_____

_____

_____

3. How are courts limited in their evaluation of what is criminal? (Hebrews 4:12, 13; Matthew 5:21; Acts 4:18-20)

_____

_____

_____

_____

_____

_____

4. What is the penalty for perjury?(Deuteronomy 19:16-21; Proverbs 19:5, 9; 25:18)

_____

_____

_____

_____

_____

5. Is imprisonment a biblical form of punishment? (Genesis 39:11-20; Jeremiah 38:6; Matthew 14:1-12; Acts 4:1-3, 13-22; 5:17-20; 26:10; Hebrews 11:36)

_____

_____

_____

_____

_____

6. How does the Bible deal with criminal offenses, and how does this contrast with today's practice?(Exodus 21:12-14, 16, 18-19, 23-25; Leviticus 6:1-7; 24:19; cf.Luke 19:8)

_____

_____

_____

_____

_____

_____

7. What is the purpose of restitution laws and other forms of punishment, such as execution for capital crimes?(Numbers 5:5-8; Deuteronomy 17:13; 19:20; Proverbs 21:11)

_____

_____

_____

_____

_____

Summary

"The Bible passages that command the trial and execution of prisoners do not connote a 'lynch mob.' Rather, they call for an orderly system of justice. Judges were instituted (Exodus 18:13-16; cf. Deuteronomy 1:16, 17; 19:15-21), along with a multi-tier judicial system with (to use modern terminology) as justice of the peace over every ten families, a local magistrate over every fifty families, a district court judge over every hundred families, a circuit court of appeals over every one thousand families, and Moses himself as the Supreme Court. The judges were commanded to be honest and not to take bribes or favor the rich (Exodus 23:1-8) — a charge they repeatedly violated, as we see from the prophets (Isaiah 1:23; Jeremiah 5:28; Micah 3:11). Nor were they to show special favoritism to the poor: 'Neither shalt thou countenance a poor man in his cause' (Exodus 23:3). Everyone was entitled to equal justice before the law — neither more not less" (John Eidsmoe, *God and Caesar: Christian Faith and Political Action*, p. 197).

The United States Supreme Court should not *legislate* but *interpret* existing law. All law is based on some religious foundation. The court therefore must choose between itself as an independent law making body or the law of God as a fixed standard of personal and civil righteousness.

Answers to Questions for Discussion

1. An individual accused of a crime is presumed to be innocent until witnesses testify to his guilt and he then is pronounced guilty by the courts. In the case of capital crimes, the testimony of one witness is not enough to convict an individual: "On the evidence of two witnesses or three witnesses, he who is to die shall be put to death; he shall not be put to death on the evidence of one witness" (Deuteronomy 17:6). The sinfulness of man necessitates protecting the accused against testimony of fallible witnesses. Two witnesses could be cross-examined separately to have their testimonies substantiated or refuted.

Moreover, this procedure protects accused individuals who are innocent from those who would seek revenge by offering false testimony. "The witnesses, by casting the first stones, accepted the onus of the responsibility; in the event of further evidence establishing the innocence of the (now deceased) accused, and thereby the false testimony of the witnesses, they would then assume the responsibility for wrongful execution, in effect murder" (Peter C. Craigie, *The Book of Deuteronomy*, p. 251).

The New Testament continues the demand for two witnesses before action can be taken, either by the church (Matthew 18:15-16; 2 Corinthians 13:1; 1 Timothy 5:19) or the State (Hebrews 10:28). While the judicial procedure for church and State are similar, both demanding two witnesses (cf. Matthew 18:15-20), their areas of jurisdiction are dissimilar. The church is given the power of the "keys," the authority to excommunicate unrepentant members (Matthew 16:19), while the State is given the power of the "sword," the authority as God's "avenger who brings wrath upon the one who practices evil" (Romans 13:4). There is one law but a variety of jurisdictions.

The procedure for securing witnesses operated in the New Testament, although by this time corruption was common. When Jesus was brought before the Jewish tribunal, *false* witnesses were called: "Now the chief priests and the whole Council kept trying to obtain false testimony against Jesus, in order that they might put Him to death; and they did not find it, even though many false witnesses came forward. But later on two came forward, and said, 'This man stated, "I am able to destroy the temple of

Annas turned Jesus over to Caiaphas, Annas' father-in-law, who in turn led Him bound to Pilate. In each "trial," they did what was "expedient" instead of what was lawful.

God and to rebuild it in three days"'" (Matthew 26:59-61; cf. Mark 14:55-65). The entire scene is contrived for the sake of expediency.

A judicial system is only as good as those who administer the law. In the case of Jesus' trial, the law did not avail, since false witnesses testified. Religious leaders took Jesus to the civil court under Pontius Pilate and used the same tactics (Matthew 27:11-26).

Both judge and jury must be just. Those before the court must be judged by God's law and not on the basis of the their stations in life (James 2:1-13). Nor should the law be twisted to favor an individual: "Woe to those who call evil good, and good evil; who substitute darkness for light and light for darkness; who substitute bitter for sweet" (Isaiah 5:20). Should prospective jury members be required to adhere to the system of justice set forth in Scripture before being permitted to sit on a jury? Should atheists, cult members, and nonChristians be permitted to sit on juries? Should judges be required to adhere to the law of God set forth in Scripture?

Truth and justice must be sought. Legal proceedings must not be merely adversarial, encouraging two lawyers to "go at it," with each doing anything necessary to gain victory for his client, with the "best" lawyer winning. George Whyte, the great colonial lawyer, law professor, and statesman, would not defend a guilty man, but would instead drop the case and *return his fees*! Lawyers certainly can defend a guilty man to insure that he receives just and impartial treatment under the law. The judge, lawyers, and "officers of the court" should seek truth and justice, admonish the jury to do likewise, and show by example that they mean what they say.

Justice's Court in the Backwoods makes it clear that all are entitled to justice.

Juries must be instructed — as under Common Law and as denied under our current humanistic legal theory and practice — to look to the *justice or injustice of the law*, as well as to the *facts* of the case. This is absolutely essential if God's law is to be honored and the jury's verdict is not to be manipulated by judges who want people to be convicted under unjust laws. Certain procedural safeguards must be honored in obtaining evidence and in presenting evidence; i.e., no confessions via "star chamber tactics" or torture (cf. Acts 22:22-29); the right to be confronted by one's accusers and to cross-examine him or her; the right to receive a trial by a jury of one's peers and be protected against hierarchy testimony; the right to a speedy trial so witnesses do not forget important eye-witness testimony, and so forth.

In our day, the law often is controlled by self-seeking men who desire power. Facts are distorted to fit the goal of the courts. Witnesses are called and testimony secured, but only selected witnesses and testimony are utilized. A modern example of such perverted justice is found in the 1973 pro-abortion decision of the Supreme Court. The Court objected to the Hippocratic Oath and specific Christian statements denouncing abortion because of their "rigidity": "The emerging teachings of Christianity were in agreement with the Pythagorean ethic. . . . This, it seems to us, is a satisfactory explanation of the Hippocratic Oath's apparent rigidity" (*Roe v. Wade*, 410 U.S. 113 at 130. Quoted by Curt Young in *The Least of These*, p. 23). The judges disliked the idea of the Hippocratic Oath and Christian prohibitions against abortion because they were dogmatic ethical assertions. Thus, they rejected these sources and chose pagan traditions to substantiate their opinion that abortion should be legalized. Often the facts are made to fit the goals of the court. Facts which fail to conform to those goals are rejected.

2. A single witness could not ignore the facts of a committed crime, so he was responsible to approach authorities with his testimony. Moreover, the single witness could not know he alone brought evidence, unless he placed his statement on record. If, in fact, there was only one witness, the case was brought before the central tribunal where the Levitical priests or judges resided: "So you shall come to the Levitical priest or the judge who is in office in those days, and you shall inquire of them, and they will

200

declare to you the verdict in the case" (Deuteronomy 17:9). Once the case reached the tribunal, highly qualified judges could mount a thorough investigation, cross-examining the lone witness and securing additional evidence to substantiate or reverse the charges: "The judges would make a diligent investigation of the case [Deuteronomy 19:18] and pass judgment on the basis of their findings. If it turned out that the witness bringing the charge was giving false testimony, then his punishment would be determined on the basis of the intention of the crime (v. 19)" (Peter C. Craigie, *The Book of Deuteronomy*, p. 270). The book of Joshua seems to indicate that a confession from the offender as well as physical evidence can be enough to convict someone of a crime (Joshua 7:16-26).

A single witness may help an individual who is being held for a crime he did not commit. Other witnesses may have testified to his guilt mistakenly. To remain silent would seal the doom of the innocent. "Deliver those who are being taken away to death, and those who are staggering to slaughter, O hold them back. If you say, 'See, we did not know this,' does He not consider it who weighs the hearts? And does He not know it who keeps your soul? And will He not render to man according to his work?" (Proverbs 24:11, 12). The Christian cannot adopt the modern adage, "I don't want to get involved."

3. The courts can only make judgments on actions. Sinful or criminal *ideas* cannot be tried by the courts. Moreover, the Bible makes a distinction between sins and crimes. Not all crimes are sins, and not all sins are crimes. Sins of the heart may not necessarily express themselves in outward actions. Strife, jealousy, envy, anger, resentment, and lust are *sins* which cannot be punished by civil authorities who have no jurisdiction over men's minds, nor can they judge the thoughts and intentions of an individual's heart (cf. Hebrews 4:12-13).

However, some sins manifest themselves outwardly and become crimes: "You have heard that the ancients were told, 'You shall not commit murder' and 'Whoever commits murder shall be liable to the court'" (Matthew 5:21). The inward expression of the heart, hate, manifested itself in an outward action, murder. Hate and murder are sins, but only murder is a crime. While the court has authority only to punish crimes, all citizens are liable before God for both heart sins and crimes.

201

The Bible makes it clear that a lone witness cannot condemn a man. Achan was found guilty on the basis of his own testimony and the physical evidence of his theft (Joshua 7:16-26).

Courts also are limited by the requirement to have witnesses. Certain criminal acts may be prevalent in a society, but the court has no authority to render a judgment without witnesses. The courts, therefore, cannot act on hearsay testimony. The purpose of a judicial system is not to eradicate all crimes or potential crimes from the nation, but to punish criminal acts. Criminals should fear the punishment that their acts will bring so they will either discontinue them or do them in private.

There are many who believe it is the State's duty, through its judicial process, to right every wrong. This concept carries human courts beyond the biblical system of justice. While some might desire such a State function, history shows us that it is impossible and dangerous. Only God can right every wrong, and His chosen means was by Christ's atoning sacrifice for those who believe on Him, and eternal punishment in Hell for those who do not turn to Jesus in repentance and faith. The State is not God. It is not given authority or power over eternity, but only the authority, power, and duty, in specified kinds of cases, to send convicted criminals to their judgment in time. Rulers of the State have neither the omniscience (all-knowledge) nor the omnipotence (all-power) — much less the perfect righteousness — required to right all wrongs. The State, therefore, must remain within divinely ordained limits of its authority when dealing with criminals.

What happens to criminals, and sinners in general, who "get away with" their criminal activities? Rushdoony writes:

Unless a man find atonement in Christ, strict retribution prevails, so that "every idle word that men shall speak, they shall give account thereof in the day of judgment" (Matt. 12:36). While Scripture gives extensive evidence of God's avenging justice in history, and the Book of Revelation affirms that fact emphatically, it should be noted that the tribunal is not history, but "the day of judgment" (*Intellectual Schizophrenia*, p. 132).

Obviously, certain sins often may escape detection. Homosexuals who practice behind closed doors are out-of-bounds for the courts. Of course, prosecution can take place if there are witnesses of their criminal behavior or there is observable physical evidence, for example, the rape of children, which can be detected by a doctor. Such behavior may not be dealt with by courts in history, but will be dealt with by God, either in history (e.g., AIDS) or eternity (Hell). The law that requires the death penalty for homosexual acts effectually drives the perversion of homosexuality underground, back to the closet, to the dark realm of shameful activity.

Herod was not interested in justice. He was only interested in the power Jesus might have: *Now Herod was very glad when he saw Jesus; for he had wanted to see Him for a long time, because he was hoping to see some sign performed by Him* (Luke 23:8).

The courts have no authority to define what is criminal apart from biblical law. Crimes, as defined by the courts, may be neither crimes nor sins, and, therefore, would be outside the court's jurisdiction. For example, courts may declare certain actions to be criminal which, in fact, are encouraged by the word of God. The disciples of Jesus were confronted with the supposed criminality of the preaching of the gospel: The authorities "commanded them [James and John] not to speak or teach at all

204

in the name of Jesus" (Acts 4:18). Obeying "God rather than men" (5:29) may be criminal in the eyes of the courts, but such "criminality" is not sinful in the eyes of God. As a matter of fact, to obey the decision of the courts would put one in opposition to God: "Whether it is right in the sight of God to give heed to you rather than to God, you be the judge; for we cannot stop speaking what we have seen and heard" (4:19-20). There are a number of places in the Bible where acts are designated by the State as criminal and the decrees of the Sate in those cases should be disobeyed (cf. Exodus 1:15-22; Joshua 2; Daniel 3 and 6).

Nor do the courts rightly have authority to enforce an unjust, anti-biblical decree of the executive (e.g., Adolf Hitler), law of the legislature (e.g., tax-funding of abortion), or ruling of higher judicial authorities (e.g., the 1973 Roe v. Wade pro-abortion/anti-life decision of the Supreme Court). It is the duty of the courts to see justice done, and this justice must be God's or it is merely the baseless, arbitrary will of man. The divinely ordained and revealed justice of God must take precedence over the ungodly will of mere men, no matter what form it takes. Courts have no legitimate authority to replace the law of God with the will of sinful man. Just as they cannot themselves define, apart from God, they also cannot autonomously accept ungodly definitions of crimes proposed by others.

4. The penalty for the perjurer is the same as it would be for the accused: "This principle means that, in cases where the defendant's life is at stake, the false witness must be executed. If restitution of $1,000 is involved, the false witness must make a payment of $1,000. The penalty of the case falls on the perjurer" (R. J. Rushdoony, Institutes of Biblical Law, p. 571). "If the witness is a false witness and he has accused his brother falsely, then you shall do to him just as he intended to do to his brother" (Deuteronomy 19:18-19).

The perjurer will certainly think twice about offering false testimony, knowing he will incur the same punishment as the accused if his lie is uncovered. This law is especially helpful in capital offenses where punishment for the crime, the death penalty, is irreversible. Moreover, a number of trivial cases often are brought to the courts to harass an individual and later they are thrown out for lack of evidence. Such cases would be reduced considerably if the accuser knew he could be liable for the same charges were his charges proved false and malicious.

5. The Bible makes no mention of imprisonment as a legitimate punishment. Individuals accused of certain crimes (e.g., capital crimes) may have to be detained in some form of holding cell, but this constituted a temporary measure during the time prior to his trial: "And they put him [a man accused of a crime] in custody so that the command of the LORD might be made clear to them" (Leviticus 24:12; cf. Numbers 15:34; 1 Kings 22:27). Since the accused would be presumed innocent until proven guilty, the holding cell would have to reflect comfortable living conditions and the time interred would have to be of short duration. This would necessitate a speedy trial.

Imprisonment was not part of the law as given to Israel. Where prisons are mentioned, we find they are part of judicial systems of nations outside Israel. Joseph was imprisoned under Egyptian rule and Jeremiah was thrown into a cistern to silence him (Genesis 39:20-23; 40:3, 5; 42:16, 19 and Jeremiah 38:6). The fact that Jeremiah was thrown into a cistern rather than prison seems to support the thesis that imprisonment as punishment was not practiced in Israel.

During the post-exilic period imprisonment is mentioned, but this is Persian law, a proclamation of King Artaxerxes (Ezra 7:26), not part of biblical law.

Even the most primitive cultural conditions necessitate a place where civil cases can be adjudicated. The *First Courthouse in Greene County* is indicative of the importance of a sound legal system.

206

The New Testament does not sanction imprisonment as punishment. John the Baptist was put in prison by Herod, had no trial, and was executed (Matthew 14:1-12). When Peter and John were arrested they were thrown "in jail until the next day" (Acts 4:3). This was done by the "priests and the captain of the temple guard, and the Sadducees" (v.1). Apparently, Peter and John endured temporary imprisonment. The council held them in "jail" while considering how they should be punished; imprisonment, however, was not the prescribed punishment (v.13-22). A similar situation occurs in Acts 5. Even under the Roman judicial system, imprisonment served a temporary purpose. Paul, waiting for trial by Caesar, remained in his own rented quarters until the time of the trial (28:30-31). However, he lived under Roman guard throughout his internment.

Imprisonment in America is of relatively recent origin. The Quakers believed that a man who had time to think about his crime would repent of it. The older designation for a jail, "penitentiary," reflects this original Quaker idea. In the solitude of his "cell" the inner light would make the offender penitent and take over his life. Charles Colson gives the following brief history of imprisonment as punishment:

Imprisonment as a primary means of criminal punishment is a relatively modern concept. It was turned to as a humane alternative to the older patterns of harsh physical penalties for nearly all crimes. Quakers introduced the concept in colonial Pennsylvania. The first American prison was established in Philadelphia when the Walnut Street Jail was converted into a series of solitary cells where offenders were kept in solitary confinement. The theory was that they would become "penitents," confessing their crimes before God and thereby gaining a spiritual rehabilitation. Hence, the name "penitentiary" — as a place for penitents. In 1790, the State of Pennsylvania enacted laws making imprisonment the ordinary punishment for crimes. There were problems with this approach from the beginning: many early "penitents" locked in their solitary cells went mad and there was little evidence that this treatment produced any rehabilitation. Even so, the idea caught on and by 1850, all states had adopted similar laws. The concept of imprisonment as a principal form of punishment has since been exported from the United States to almost all Western nations ("Is There a Better Way?A Perspective on American Prisons" [Washington, D.C.: Prison Fellowship, 1981]. Cited by John Eidsmoe, *God and Caesar: Christian Faith and Political Action*, p. 203).

Our prison system originates with humanistic beliefs which deny man's depravity as well as a biblical moral order that demands restitution, not just repentance.

While the Quaker solution to criminal behavior stemmed from noble intent, it degenerated into an unworkable system where men and women are locked up, stripped of personal identity, given a number, and made dependent upon the State for food, shelter, clothing, and education. When they leave the prison environment they take additional criminal skills and a sense of dependency that often returns them to a life of crime.

Consider the monetary costs involved. It once appeared that "crime did not pay" because a criminal, through restitution or as an indentured servant, was made to work off the money he owed. Taxpayers now pay the bill, with prisons built and prisoners fed, clothed, taught a trade, and guarded. Victims rarely are compensated for their losses, and virtually never according to the biblical standards, which require payments proportionate to the degree of injury caused by the crime.

6. Our modern penal system requires law-abiding citizens to pay for prison facilities where criminals are caged for their crimes. While a criminal should be punished, in no way should punishment treat the man as if he were not an image-bearer of God. Restitution allows a man to retain his dignity. Imprisonment defaces the image of God in the criminal by treating him as an animal. The Bible sets forth restitution as the way an individual compensates victims of his criminal actions. Restitution means restoration; restoration for the victim and restoration for the criminal as he becomes aware that labor is a calling under God. Moreover, since biblical restitution means a victim is compensated beyond his damaged or stolen property's actual value, a would-be criminal soon learns crime does not pay.

Restitution was given in the following cases: Assault (Exodus 21:18-19); bodily injury (21:26-27); liability (21:33-36); theft (22:1-4); property

208

damage (22:5-6); irresponsibility (22:7-13); and the loss or damage of borrowed items (22:14-15). "You will note that in each case cited above, the entire matter was made by restitution. Though the public sector, including judges and others, were part of the proceedings, the actual work of correction finally was settled between the offender and his victim. The result was that the victim was restored to a better position than before his loss and the lawbreaker was punished by having to make right his wrongs in a manner that cost more than his potential gain" (Roger Campbell, *Justice Through Restitution*, p.108).

Restitution is the biblical punishment for crimes. Though the public sector, including judges and others, were part of the proceedings, the actual work of correction was settled between the offender and his victim.

In many cases civil courts would not be needed if individuals would agree to the laws of restitution. Where agreement cannot be reached, the church can act as a legitimate judicial body. The State, possessing the power of the sword, at times may force the wrong-doer to make restitution. The biblical principle, in the case of an individual who was unable to make restitution was made an indentured servant: "If he owns nothing, then he should be sold for his theft" (Exodus 22:3). This requirement

209

could be met by having an individual work and deducting a portion of his pay for the demanded restitution. Article XIII, Section I of the United States Constitution supports such punishment: "Neither slavery nor involuntary servitude, *except as punishment for a crime whereof the party shall have been duly convicted*, shall exist within the United States, or any place subject to their jurisdiction."

7. While criminal acts affect individuals, families, businesses, and the moral order of a nation, ultimately they are directed against God. David realized this when he confessed his sin of adultery and murder: "Against Thee, Thee only, I have sinned, and done what is evil in Thy sight, so that Thou art justified when Thou dost speak, and blameless when Thou dost judge" (Psalm 51:4). "In modern law, the term restitution is usually replaced by 'compensation' or 'damages.' But the significant difference is this: in Biblical law, the offender is guilty before God (and hence must make restitution to God, Numbers 5:6-8), and before the offended man, to whom he makes direct restitution, whereas in modern law the offense is primarily and essentially against the state. God and man are left out of the picture in the main" (R.J.Rushdoony, *Institutes of Biblical Law*, p.274).

Laws of restitution have been abandoned largely because crimes are perceived as ultimately directed at the State. Therefore, the State makes no attempt to see that individual victims are compensated. "As the power of government increased, crimes were considered not so much as injury to the victim but as violations of the king's peace. Laws were enacted that made it a misdemeanor for a victim to settle with an offender without bringing him to court. Instead of restoring the injured party to his condition before being wronged, fines now went into the government coffers and the attention of society turned to ingenious punishments for lawbreakers [e.g., imprisonment]" (Roger Campbell, *Justice Through Restitution*, p.108). Laws of restitution remind the criminal that he ultimately is responsible to God for his actions, and his victims, created in God's image, must be compensated in the manner prescribed by God.

Restitution puts thief and victim together. This "relationship" can have a tremendous effect on both. The criminal can learn from the responsible victim and the victim can minister in Christ's name to the offender. John Eidsmoe offers the following story as evidence of how the biblical system of restitution works.

Judge William D. Bontrager describes a case in which he required a convicted criminal to split firewood for the family he had burglarized. The first day he came to split wood, his victim came and heaped vicious epithets upon him. The second and third time the victim was little more civil. The next time the weather was cold, and the victim lent the offender his jacket. The next several times the victim came out and split wood with the offender, and finally the victim invited the offender to spend Christmas with him. In this case both the offender and his victim needed healing, and God's system of justice brought healing to both (*God and Caesar: Christian Faith and Political Action*, p. 202).

Restitution and execution for capital crimes also act as deterrents to those committing the crimes and to those who have an inclination to commit crimes. This is certainly not the main reason for punishment, however; rather it is an effect of punishment: "Then all the people will hear and be afraid, and will not act presumptuously again" (Deuteronomy 17:13; cf. 19:20). When the State ignores biblical laws designed to inhibit further criminal activity, in effect, it gives the would-be criminal license to commit unlawful acts without fear of punishment.

Man, considered as a creature, must necessarily be subject to the laws of his Creator, for he is entirely a dependent being (William Blackstone, 1723-1780).

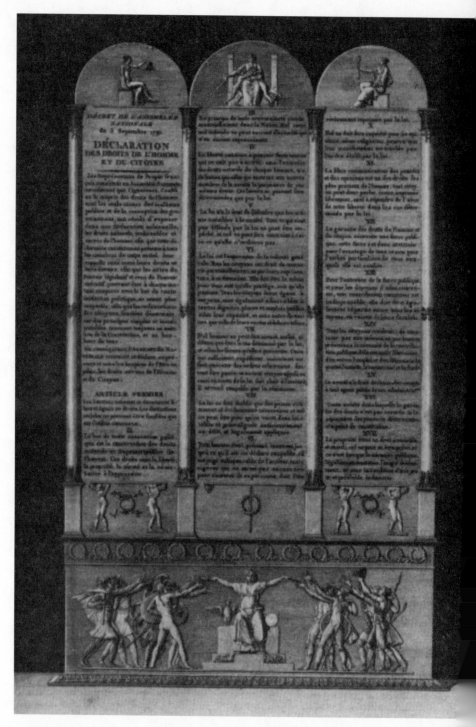

The French *Declaration of the Rights of Man* placed rights in the strong arm of the State. Rights were given by the State and could just as easily be taken away. A bloody revolution followed.

Lesson 8

Human Rights
and
Responsibilities

The study of "human rights" is featured prominently in our modern era. While it is true that talk about "rights" has been constant throughout our nation's history, at first, very little confusion arose with the discussion. State constitutions of the 18th century give ample evidence of the overwhelmingly Christian view that rights are endowed by the Creator, with a manifest connection between Christianity, moral virtue, and national liberty. Today, the human rights emphasis often seems purposely miscommunicated. There is little talk about duties, but much talk about rights, with few seeming to know what they are. A definition seems hard to come by, with the reason not always obvious to proponents of a "human rights" doctrine.

A right is a *legal immunity*, primarily from the State imposing its will on the people. For example, God had a *legal right* to the Tree of Knowledge, therefore, He could impose His will (law) on His subjects. No jurisdiction could usurp His rightful claim to the property. As Creator and Owner of all things, no creature could keep Him from making His claim. In the same way, we have no "right to" another person's property. The State has no "right to" our property. A "responsibility to" implies an *immunity from* coercive interference. When God tells the church that it has the "responsibility to preach the gospel," the church is *immune from* the jurisdiction of the State if the State makes laws prohibiting the church from fulfilling its duties.

Confusion over human rights as they relate to judicial pronouncements arises from moral and intellectual relativism. If it is assumed that no real absolute law exists, then it follows that an individual's rights must be equally relative. The reason debate over what is right (what is ethical or moral) continues is that too often no one really understands what is right. In fact, many maintain that to define what is "right" is to speak in absolute terms, which does not fit the evolving nature of ethics based on evolutionary assumptions. As long as moral relativism prevails, human rights always will be elusive. How does the West approach the leaders in the Soviet Union regarding the "right" to private property when one of the basic tenets of Marxism is the "abolition of property in land and application of all rents of land to public purposes"? There is no common ground to discuss "liberty" as a right without a *biblical* definition of liberty. The Soviet system places law in the hands of the State. "Human rights" are defined by the Soviet State. Who are we to say that "human rights" are being violated in the Soviet Union, in terms of a system without moral absolutes? Without an unchangeable law there can be nothing to criticize.

The baleful doctrine of human rights which is now turning all political societies into pandemoniums is never admitted in the kingdom of God. But the sublime doctrine of human rights in its stead binds all hearts and lives in beautiful harmony to the throne of the Prince, and to the happiness of all his subjects.

—A. A. Hodge

When a nation moves away from the absolutes of God's law we can expect an immediate substitute to fill the void. The "human rights" idea has become the alternative to biblical law; it now forms the basis and foundation for all spheres of life. Human rights has sand as its foundation because in "human rights" theory man is the determiner of what is a right. T. Robert Ingram comments:

The distortion in human rights comes from assigning lawmaking power to men as men, rather than seeing it as that by which God rules all things consummately. The difference is total. Every truly lawful right becomes twisted and its source a mysterious, unknown and impossible "state of nature" in which there was no law, and were no laws. The former implies stability, righteousness and an unchanging nature; the latter speaks of nothing but change, indetermination and fickleness (*What's Wrong With Human Rights*, p. 21f.)

The modern doctrine of human rights answers to no one but man. Man, therefore, cannot be held responsible to anyone greater than himself. Responsibility is denied because there is no one to whom responsibility must be shown. Where there is no responsibility there is no accountability. The prevailing "law" is that every man does what is right in his own eyes (Judges 17:6). Instead of working for justice (defined according to the specifics of God's Law), the disgruntled demand individual or class rights based upon their own distorted views of justice. The most powerful, those who speak the loudest and carry the most political clout, are the ones who gain the greatest number of rights, usually for themselves and at the expense of others. Human rights become a declaration of self-law. Responsibility and answerability are abandoned for self-declaration.

To be *responsible* means literally to be *answerable*. Since it is God who gives the law, it means we are answerable to Him for what we do ourselves and to our fellow men, to our neighbor. *Responsibility* is a religious, a theological idea. Without the God of Scripture, the idea of responsibility breaks down. When every man becomes his own god, then man is not responsible, because a god answers to no one and to nothing. All things answer to a god. (R. J. Rushdoony, *Law and Society*, p. 350f.)

If there are many gods (each man doing what is right in his own eyes) then there are many independent laws. Every individual is a law unto himself; therefore, he demands rights for himself or for the group of gods who join with him. Responsibility before the one true God is denied, and a struggle among the many contradictory claimants of "rights" ensues.

But this will not do, even for those who deny that God provides all that man has. Man must answer to someone. In order to make the human rights doctrine work, the State must enforce the prevailing system of human rights, or a revolution is urged to initiate a new system of rights. While we might start with civil and political rights (the rights of individual citizens to be free), we move to economic and social "rights" (the right of some to use the State to suspend various freedoms of others, to secure what some believe to be basic rights of the majority to work, health, education, economic security, and shelter). Without the particulars of God's Law, the "rights" of some can be taken away to secure the "rights" of others.

A careful study of Scripture reveals that fallen men and women really have no claim to "human rights." God's warning to Adam was that if he disobeyed the clear command not to eat of the tree of the knowledge of good and evil he would die (Genesis 2:16-17). Not even life itself is a right. Paul says God *"gives* to all life and breath and all things" (Acts 17:25). Life and everything we possess are *gifts* from God, not rights we can claim for ourselves. By understanding that all life is given by God, one can better see that to take away what God gives constitutes the height of rebellion. The modern doctrine of human rights, because it is not rooted in God's character and law, can designate some lives not worthy to be lived. Laws can be passed by some to dispose of the lives of others. Of course, all is done in the name of "my rights." Because God is the *giver* of life, it is not the duty of those in power to *grant* rights to anyone (something no institution can do) but to protect the lives that God has called into existence, whether they are healthy or "hopelessly" handicapped. This brings us back to responsibility and answerability, not "rights."

Since we are held responsible, we need *zones* of *immunity* from coercion. The State was established by God to protect those *zones* of *immunity*: freedom *of* religion, freedom *of* speech, freedom *from* fear, and freedom *from* want. The State is to "maintain the peace" so Christians can work out their "salvation with fear and trembling" (Philippians 2:12) — free from terror from the Big Brother State.

Christians are not to work for "human rights"; rather, we are to declare that every individual, family, church, and State be responsible before an all holy God to follow His Law. Those who desire their "rights" are really saying they want to be treated with justice. But no individual can understand the nature of justice until he is confronted with the realities of his own sin and the demands God makes on every one of His creatures. Justice must be defined in terms of the cross of Jesus Christ. Jesus went to the cross because the law of God was broken. In order for justice to be satisfied, Jesus had to bear the full load of the sin of His people: God "made Him who knew no sin to be sin on our behalf, that we might become the righteousness of God in Him" (2 Corinthians 5:21). Those who claim their "rights" must understand that they must be made right with God. When this happens they comprehend that God calls each of us as responsible servants for the work of the kingdom.

216

The course of the nation, therefore, depends upon God's people responsibly submitting themselves to the lordship of Jesus Christ in every area of life. Instead of criticizing the depraved institutions that have arisen because of Christian apathy and non-involvement, the people of God must be the cultural force which brings the realities of the gospel to a sin-bent world. There will be no blessings ("rights") for the people of this nation or any other nation if the Christian's sole concern is for "rights." For too long Christians have neglected their responsibilities and ignored their world for a variety of reasons. Now there is the clamor for "rights." There is talk about the "right to life," the "right to pray in public schools," the "right to a living wage," and the "right to die." The Bible makes no such declarations. All are held responsible before God to obey the demands of His law. Justice will prevail in all these areas, by His grace, when we do what God requires.

Blessed is the nation whose God is the LORD, the people whom He has chosen for His own inheritance (Psalm 33:12; cf. 144:15).

Questions for Discussion

1. What is the origin and significance of the claim to human rights? (Genesis 3:1-5; 4:1-8; 4:23; 11:1-5)

_____
_____
_____
_____
_____
_____
_____
_____

2. Why is there an emphasis on human rights today? (Judges 17:6)

_____
_____
_____
_____
_____
_____
_____

3. When the Bible uses the term "rights," what is being emphasized? (Proverbs 31:5, 8, 9; Isaiah 5:23; 1 Kings 10:9; cf. Genesis 18:19; 2 Samuel 8:15; 1 Chronicles 18:14; 2 Chronicles 9:8; Psalm 119:121)

_____
_____
_____
_____
_____
_____
_____

4. How does the Bible solve the problem of the modern-day desire for "human rights"? (Leviticus 26; Deuteronomy 8:11-20; 28; Matthew 5:3-12)

_____

_____

_____

_____

_____

_____

5. How does the phrase, all men "are endowed by their Creator with certain unalienable [inalienable] Rights, that among these are Life, Liberty and the pursuit of happiness" (Declaration of Independence, 1776), compare with the modern doctrine of human rights? Also, reflect on Romans 6:23; 2 Corinthians 3:17; Proverbs 29:18 (KJV).

_____

_____

_____

_____

_____

_____

6. What are the implications of human rights as they relate to social issues?

_____

_____

_____

_____

7. Can "freedom" and "liberty" be considered independent and absolute human rights? (Leviticus 25:10; John 8:34, 35; Romans 6:17-20)

_____

_____

_____

_____

Summary

"It is easy to understand why the human rights idea came into popularity in Christendom. It is simply that men living in Christendom enjoyed that 'blessed liberty wherewith Christ hath made us free' to such an extent and over so many centuries that they found it easy to take for granted. Liberty, instead of being recognized as the gift of Christ and the reward of Christian justice, was something that would easily be seen as an end in itself. It was easy to confuse logical origins. The common law punishes any dishonest violation of each man's person or his goods and so it is easy to understand a condition in which each may be said to enjoy the right to life, liberty and property" (T. Robert Ingram, *What's Wrong With Human Rights*, p. 49).

Thomas Jefferson of Virginia, John Adams of Massachusetts, Benjamin Franklin of Pennsylvania, Roger Sherman of Connecticut, and Robert Livingston of New York were appointed June 11, 1776 a Committee to draw up a Declaration.

Answers to Questions for Discussion

1. Satan tempted Eve with the priority of rights over obligations or responsibilities. Satan's ploy was to convince Adam and Eve that somehow God was withholding what rightfully belonged to them: "For God knows that in the day you eat from it [the tree of the knowledge of good and evil] your eyes will be opened, and you will be like God, knowing good and evil" (Genesis 3:5). Eve claimed her right to be like God by eating of the tree of the knowledge of good and evil. To claim a right is to claim something that you deserve. Since Adam and Eve were created beings nothing was theirs by nature or by right. Anything they had, they had only by God's gracious provision.

We deserve rights (immunity from judgment) when we are faithful. We deserve a removal of these rights (judgment) when we are unfaithful. Adam and Eve had a "right" to be in the Garden, and therefore were immune from judgment. But this immunity was removed when they proved to be unfaithful.

This first declaration of human rights brought the judgment of God upon all creation. Instead of obeying God and receiving God's evaluation in blessing, man usurped God's role of bestower of all gifts and claimed a superior status over God as his right. This first declaration of rights over responsibilities spread to the entire created order. Adam and Eve's offspring would now image them: "When Adam had lived one hundred and thirty years, he became the father of a son *in his own likeness, according to his image. . .*" (Genesis 5:3). Cain declared his rights over his brother by killing him (4:8). Lamech claimed his right to have two wives and threatened to kill those who opposed him (4:19, 23). His claim of such rights was a *denial* of someone else's rights

Man continued to exercise his demand for rights in building the tower of Babel, an attempt to supplant God's name and authority with man's name and authority. Corporate man desired to live independently of God. Men sought to make a name for themselves by repudiating God's name. (God's name reflects His character of independence and self-sufficiency, "I AM WHO I AM" [Exodus 3:14].): "Come, let us build for ourselves a city, and a tower whose top will reach into heaven, and let us make for ourselves a name" (Genesis 11:4). The desire for autonomous human rights is a desire to be God. It is man's attempt to live without the commandments of God. In each of the declarations for rights found in the Bible, the commandments of God are transgressed in favor of the commandments of men.

Many Christians have trapped themselves into identifying the biblical view of rights with pagan "Natural Right" theories, certainly a gross error. Such ancient thinkers and philosophers as Plato and Aristotle spoke of "Natural Right" and of that which is "right by nature." These theories, though stressing the moral *duties* of men, were radically different from, and opposed to, the scriptural teaching. First, they did not desire civil government or its rulers to be limited by God's law, nor by any set of laws above man. Instead, they wanted man to be the ruler, free to choose in view of the particular situation or set of circumstances in which he found himself or his city. These ancient philosophers viewed man's autonomous (self- sufficient, self-lawmaking) mind or reason, not God's Law revealed in Scripture, as the means to discover what is "Right by Nature." The first commandment, "You shall have no other gods before Me" (Exodus 20:3), was cast aside. Man would be the new god.

Second, they made "Nature," not God, the origin of such principles of "Natural Right" or natural justice. Third, unlike Christians who can read the Bible and agree, for example, that the Ten Commandments are true, good, and just, the ancient pagan philosophers — just like their modern counterparts — could not agree that "Nature" taught "justice" or the "right" to be. Fourth, the *content* of the "principles" or "Natural Right" or "Natural Justice" differs fundamentally from God's view of justice as told in the Bible: None would have agreed about man's duty to obey the Ten Commandments.

Fifth, such principles of "Natural Right" are not, therefore, truly absolute, but fundamentally *relativistic*. The definition of what is a right changes with the latest political theory. Sixth, these ancient pagan "principles" or "Natural Rights" — like that of modern pagan theories of "Natural Rights" — originated in the sinful, rebellious heart and mind of fallen man.

Modern theories of "Natural Rights," unlike their ancient counterparts in "Natural Right" theory, stress these "Rights," not the *duties* of man, and trace the supposed origin of "Natural Rights" in the nature of man and things to the *desires* and *passions* of man. Like their ancient pagan counterparts, modern theorists cannot agree about the *content* of such "Natural Rights." Since they claim to know of these rights, and of the content of these rights, via *reason*, obviously the claims to man's autonomous reason as an able guide in such matters are false. Modern thinkers who base "Natural Rights" or "Human Rights" on the "knowledge" man supposedly acquires via his autonomous *intuition* are on no more solid ground. There is no grace needed to sustain a theeory of "Natural Rights." Salvation is by knowledge and therefore salvation by law.

The rallying cry of the French Revolution was *Liberty, Equality, Fraternity, or Death*. For many it was death on the sharpened blade of the Guillotine.

The historical origin of modern theories of "Natural Rights" should allert us: The "Natural Rights" theory originated during the 17th-century "Enlightenment." In most respects the Enlightenment was an intellectual rebellion against God's word — the Bible — all in the name of the authority and infallibility of man's unbridled and independent *reason*.

223

2. Most people define human rights as a desire to be treated rightly (with justice) or with dignity. But what is "justice"? Justice refers to right rule, right conduct, or to each getting his due, whether good or bad. Who defines what is just? God. Man ratifies God's definition of justice by implementing laws in accordance with His definition. Man, the rebel and usurper, denies God's definition and establishes laws according to his own definition, with his own goals in mind.

Those who demand human rights are saying they are different from the animal creation (God has created man in His own image). A pursuer of human rights might deny he is created in the image of God, but no amount of denial removes the image, nor his desire to be treated rightly or with dignity. But the advocates of human rights obscure the reality of justice and dignity by denying God and His created order. If man evolved by the working of blind, irrational *chance* and impersonal matter, there can be no dignity or standard for maintaining justice. By denying God's commandments, which maintain human dignity and establish terms of justice, man's commandments have been adopted in the name of human rights, thus denying human dignity and true (biblical) justice.

The modern preoccupation with human rights is an offshoot of a Christian world view. Humanism wants the "fruit" of a Christian moral order without the "root" — Jesus Christ (cf. Isaiah 11:1, 10; Matthew 7:15-23). T. Robert Ingram makes the following point:

> It is easy to understand why the human rights idea came into popularity in Christendom. It is simply that men living in Christendom enjoyed that "blessed liberty wherewith Christ hath made us free" to such an extent and over so many centuries that they found it easy to take for granted. Liberty, instead of being recognized as the gift of Christ and the reward of Christian justice, was something that could easily be seen as an end in itself. The speeches of Patrick Henry and the widespread response they drew is typical of the day and illustrate how readily it was taken for granted that everybody knew what was meant by liberty and where it came from and how to defend it (*What's Wrong With Human Rights*, p. 49).

Thus many Christians become sucked into the humanistic preoccupation for human rights, though it is counterfeit — close to the original, but still counterfeit.

Is life so dear, or peace so sweet, as to be purchased at the price of chains and slavery? Forbid it, Almighty God! I know not what course others may take; but as for me, give me liberty or give me death! (Patrick Henry, 1736-1799)

All sorts of atrocities are committed in the name of "justice" and human rights. The high incidence of abortion and terrorism are two examples of the repudiation of true human dignity and biblical justice in the name of human rights and the exaltation of the sovereign individual as the sole determiner of what is right. The modern-day conception of

225

human rights means autonomous (self-law) rights, every man doing what is right in his own eyes (Judges 17:6). Man, in essence, becomes a law unto himself. If one person believes it is lawful (just) to steal, then he declares that right by stealing. If a civil government believes it is right (just) to imprison those who oppose State policies, prison camps soon intern all enemies of the State. If the rulers of civil government, or the majority who elect or influence them, believe it is right and just to use the law to steal from others, they proclaim "redistribution of the wealth" or some other such idea to be just. Of course, their victims cry out because their "rights" have been violated.

But what standard is used to determine injustice? Both the thief and the totalitarian State emphasize their rights, while their victims claim their own set of rights. If human rights become the criterion for justice and dignity, whose definition of "human rights" will serve? How is justice or dignity defined? The desire for human rights today results from our failure to acknowledge the dignity of man created in God's image, and our refusal to follow God's commandments to maintain that dignity. A nation cannot possibly survive by declaring that human rights are independent of God's law which defines the nature of man, and the justice he innately desires, no matter how sincere the effort.

Having said this, we must realize there is much emphasis on "human rights" today because the appeal to modern man's desire for "rights" apart from God and His law-word is a *powerful political* device. By this means men acquire power, keep their power, and increase their power over others. Communists and Marxists use the "human rights" rhetoric in non-communist countries to overthrow the existing government, acquire power, and set up communist states.

Socialists and demagogues use the "human rights" rhetoric to establish socialistic programs, welfare policies, and public (i.e., State-controlled, tax-payer-financed, and humanistic) education for all. The purpose of these programs is to keep the citizenry and especially the poor and other recipients of State "aid" dependent on the politicians and/or bureaucrats who confer such "support," thus keeping themselves in power.

3. Noah Webster's *American Dictionary of the English Language* (1828) establishes the proper definition of the word "right": "Conformity to the

will of God, or to his law, the perfect standard of truth and justice. In the literal sense, *right* is a straight line of conduct, and *wrong* a crooked one. *Right*, therefore, is rectitude or straightness, and perfect rectitude is found only in an infinite Being and his will." Human rights, therefore, becomes a misnomer and a contradiction in terms. The term *human* rights places the emphasis on man's declaration of what is right. Webster reminds us that our notion of "right" scarcely is important next to "conformity to the will of God."

The Constitution creates for us *zones of immunity* from coercion. The State (in this case the Federal Government) was established by God to protect those *zones of immunity:* freedom *of* religion, freedom *of* speech, and freedom *from* fear.

227

Frequently coupled with the concept of human rights is the word 'justice.' The Bible uses 'justice' in a variety of contexts, but most often it is tied to the words "righteousness" or "judgment" (the word "judgment" is used in the older translations of the Bible and is more accurate). The queen of Sheba notes the significance and uniqueness of Solomon's rule with these words (cf. Deuteronomy 4:1-8): "Blessed be the LORD your God who delighted in you to set you on the throne of Israel; because the LORD loved Israel forever, therefore He made you king, to do justice and righteousness" (1 Kings 10:9; cf. Genesis 18:19; 2 Samuel 8:15; 1 Chronicles 18:14; 2 Chronicles 9:8; Psalm 119:121; Proverbs 1:3; etc.). The king's duty was not to protect the "rights" of the citizens; rather, it was his obligation to judge rightly, according to the standard of justice, God's word. "To do justice and righteousness" meant to rule in terms of the unchanging standard of God's law. There is no real justice without a standard by which it is measured. God's love for Israel was expressed through His law which set a standard for maintaining justice. In the same way, the Christian who truly loves keeps God's commandments (John 14:15; Romans 13:8-10).

There is a future dimension for those who "do justice." There is *continuity*. Those who rebel against God's blueprint for a just society will be eliminated. The days of the faithful will "be prolonged" (Exodus 20:12). But the church has not been faithful. The future has been captured by those who promise an earthly kingdom without Christ. Now Christians are feeling the heat of these self-made messiahs. Christians want to resist the encroachment by these tyrannical ideologies and so have jettisoned their future pessimism and have adopted the biblical truth that the future belongs to the people of God. For Christians are "children of God, and if children, heirs also, heirs of God and fellow-heirs with Christ" (Romans 8:16, 17). The repudiation of "human rights" around the world will never go away until the gospel is preached, hearts are changed, and people apply the commandments of God to every sphere of life. A doctrine of "rights" without "ethics" — biblical ethics — will not succeed.

Some modern translations of the Bible obscure this fact by substituting the word "rights" for the more accurate word "judgment": "It is not for kings, O Lemuel, it is not for kings to drink wine, or for rulers to desire strong drink. Lest they drink and forget what is decreed, and pervert the rights (lit., *judgment*) of all the afflicted" (Proverbs 31:4, 5). Nothing was to influence the king's decision when it came to interpreting a situation in the light of the law of God ("what is decreed"). In each case, when the word "rights" is used (Proverbs 31:5, 8, 9 and Isaiah 5:23) the context makes reference to judgments based upon the word of God. The Christian character of the American colonies' and early states' laws, declarations, and constitutions makes it clear that early Americans understood "rights" in this biblical sense. The modern doctrine of human rights has no standard by which rights (justice) can be measured; it is based on ultimately unfounded claims and desires.

When biblical justice and righteousness are followed we can be assured the people's "rights" are secured. Without such a standard we see that whoever rules the prevailing system of law and order defines the terms of what is right, thus favoring one segment of society above another. The favored segment then is used as a political power base to keep the prevailing governmental system in power. The promise to protect their rights demands that they vote to continue the system which gave them their "rights."

4. People expect the blessings of God, falsely labeled as "rights," without wanting to incur the responsibilities which accompany the blessings. For example, God promised Israel economic blessings that were contingent on obedience. He also warned that a time might come when they expected the blessings of wealth (a modern "human right") without the complimentary obligations based on God's law (Deuteronomy 8:11-20; 28). This is the modern cncept of human rights.

When people speak of "human rights" they are referring to something that really does exist, but by inappropriately calling it "human rights" they suggest that it would hold even without God and His law. What really exists is the *blessing of God*. God promises that if a nation obeys His law, He will bless them with security, peace, and stability. The poor and defenseless are protected and safe, when justice prevails, that is, when Biblical law is implemented not merely by the State, but by each Christian and his family. God promises us a good and prosperous land if we hear His voice [and obey]. The people of an obedient nation shall be safe,

229

and "they shall sit every man under his vine and under his fig tree [a symbol of Eden]" (Micah 4:4). Such are the blessings of God (Deuteronomy 28:2). To call the rewards of obedience "human rights" is to assert that they rightfully belong to man apart from his obedience to the Word of God. It is to say that man has a *claim* on the blessings of God (Kevin Craig, "Social Apologetics," in *Christianity and Civilization*, Symposium on the Failure of the American Baptist Culture, ed. James B. Jordan, Vol. I, No. 1 [Spring, 1982], p. 51).

Repentance before God and obedience to the commandments of God provide the only possible solutions for those who earnestly desire what they perceive as "their rights." The desires of man — even if ordered into a "rational" structure by the autonomous reason of man — form an inadequate philosophical or practical basis for any "rights" of man. Only when man effectually desires to have faith in God and to keep His commandments, can he expect the blessings of Almighty God to be secured. "Unless the Lord build the house, they labor in vain that build it" (Psalm 127:1).

The Beatitudes of Jesus' Sermon on the Mount bring the responsibility/blessing relationship into proper perspective (Matthew 5:3-12). Blessedness is not a state of nature; rather; it is the result of hungering and thirsting for *righteousness*. To be "blessed" means to be approved. What is the standard by which blessings come? Righteousness. How is righteousness measured? The word of God.

5. The most familiar declaration of human rights is found in the Declaration of Independence: All men, it states, "are endowed by their Creator with certain unalienable [inalienable] Rights, that among these are Life, Liberty and the pursuit of happiness" (Jefferson's substitute for John Locke's "property"). The concept of rights was intimately tied to the reality of the Creator who grants those rights (blessings). No God, no rights. The Declaration made it clear that these inalienable rights are not granted by governments; rather, they are an *endowment* by the Creator of the universe. Noah Webster's definition of "endowment" in his 1828 edition of the *American Dictionary of the English Language* is significant: "That which is given or bestowed on the person or mind by the creator; gift of nature; any quality of faculty bestowed by the creator."

As Christians, we want to go farther than the Declaration. We're looking for the kingdom of God. "Life, Liberty, and the Pursuit of Happiness" (or John Locke's "property") are of little value, and are humanistic if not seen in the context of God's kingdom: "But seek first His kingdom and *His righteousness*; and all these things will be added unto you" (John 6:33). Again, God is interested in how we act. His concern is with ethics. The Christian should not be content with a secularized version of God's kingdom. Without Christ there is no kingdom.

Rights, as stated in the Declaration of Independence, must be based on moral concerns. Noah Webster makes the following point: *Conformity to the will of God, or to his law, the perfect standard of truth and justice. . . . perfect rectitude is found only in an infinite Being and his will.*

Other references to God in the Declaration of Independence make it clear that the God or Creator is none other than the God of Scripture, although weakened by decades of Arminianism and Unitarianism. (The fact that nearly all of the men who framed and signed the Declaration —

Jefferson and possibly a few others excepted — were Christians should offer sufficient evidence of the dominance of Christian intentions in the Declaration.) These references declare God to be the ruler of nature, the providential orderer and controller of history, and the "Supreme Judge of the World." Together these statements, to a certain degree, parallel Paul's description of God in Acts 17 when he addresses the Athenian philosophers. And the fact that God is presented as the Ruler of nature (creation), the Supreme Judge of the world, and the One whose Providence can aid the righteous cause of the colonists, makes it clear that the God to whom the colonists appealed is the God of Scripture, not the impotent and non-sovereign "spectator-God" of Deism.

A note of caution is in order here, however. We should not suppose that the framers of the Declaration of Independence were seeking to establish what we might call a "Christian Republic," where Jesus Christ is acknowledged as the King. Unfortunately, these men generalized rights (blessings) in terms of God as Creator but failed to acknowledge, that, because of the fall of man into sin, "Life, Liberty, and the pursuit of happiness" can only be realized through the redemptive work of Jesus Christ. Without Christ we deserve death, not life: "For the wages of sin is death, but the free gift of God is eternal life in Christ Jesus our Lord" (Romans 6:23). True liberty can only be realized where "the Spirit of the Lord" is (2 Corinthians 3:17). Finally, happiness (blessedness) results from obedience to God's revealed law: "Where there is no vision (lit., *revelation*), the people are unrestrained, but happy is he who keeps the law" (Proverbs 29:18). In this sense, the Declaration is flawed. What we do find is the desire for the fruit of Christianity with little of the root.

But the Declaration was not hostile to Christianity or the church as are many Supreme Court decisions in our day. The influence of 150 years of Puritan influence was in no way obliterated with this one document. C. Gregg Singer writes:

A Christian world and life view furnished the basis for this early political thought which guided the American people for nearly two centuries and whose crowning lay in the writing of the Constitution of 1787. This Christian theism had so permeated the colonial mind that it continued to guide even those who had come to regard the Gospel with indifference or even hostility. The currents of this orthodoxy were too strong to be easily set aside by those who in their own thinking had come to a different conception of religion and hence of government also (A *Theological Interpretation of American History*, p. 284f.)

Many historians want to maintain that the Enlightenment, the man-centered philosophy that spawned the anti-Christian, anti-church French Revolution, had a profound influence on the colonies. This is nonsense. Certainly, there was a theological shift, from theocentric Puritanism to Arminianism and to a certain degree Unitarianism, but this is hardly a shift to the Enlightenment.

Later declarations of human rights (except for those of the American states during the Revolutionary era) make no mention of God as the grantor of rights (blessings). The "inalienable rights" as an "endowment" in the Declaration of Independence were certainly not new in 1776. The declaration of rights as an endowment was a statement of what already existed in their hearts and minds and it found written expression in the earlier declarations of the colonists. Later declarations, by those nations repudiating a biblical moral order, saw the State as the grantor of rights (France is a good example). These declarations sought to create a new political ideology because the stench of a rotting humanism necessitated a new world order. Instead of turning to God in repentance, they turned to political solutions for salvation.

The Bill of Rights to the Constitution in 1791 reflects the same idea that governments have no authority to grant rights. The Christians fought for this protection against those who desired a strong central government as a possible grantor of rights. The Bill of Rights protects the states from the potential tyranny of the federal government by addressing the federal government in negative terms. We should remember that the delegates in Philadelphia were sent to *revise* the Articles of Confederation. Instead of a revision, we got a totally new document. This raised great fear among the Christians who fought for a *decentralized* government. The Bill of Rights was not drafted to demand autonomous rights for the states, but was a stand against statism — a rejection of centralized federal government's claim that it could determine what ought to be a God-given right. Nowhere do we find a demand for such rights as land reform, job security, wealth redistribution, "equal" rights, abortion rights, and "gay" rights so

233

prevalent in modern-day Declarations.

The American Declaration of Independence was, in fact, the product of a long history of Christian-influenced law and political thought. Its origins date back to the Magna Carta signed by King John in 1215 A.D. and the dominantly Christian English Common Law so highly valued by American colonial lawyers and statesmen. The Magna Carta undoubtedly was drafted by men who understood the Bible and Canon law. The parallels

between the Bible and the Magna Carta are the "self-curse" found in the [Magna Carta and the Spanish charter], the fear of monarchy and requirement that the king adhere to the law found in the Magna Carta and in Deuteronomy 17, the power of excommunication or being "cut off from the people," the land as a sanctioning agent under an oath, the requirement that law be clearly written (Deut. 27:8) and clearly explained (Deut. 1:5), limitations upon punishment (Deut 25:1-3), like punishment for perjury in criminal cases (Deut. 13:15; 19:17-21; *Magna Carta Leonesa*, articles 12-13), and the covenant as the ultimate source of authority (John Eidsmoe, *The Christian Legal Advisor*, p. 28).

Magna Carta, signed by King John in A.D. 1215, was the product of a long history of Christian influenced law and political thought.

234

The French Declaration of the Rights of Man (1789) and the more recent United Nations' Declaration of Human Rights (1948) are indicative of governments as the bestowers of rights. If governments can give rights they may just as easily revoke them. The Declaration of the Rights of Man, adopted by the French National Assembly on August 26, 1789, came on the heels of religious, political, and philosophical upheaval. In a word, the climate of pre-revolutionary France was decadent:

> For the first time since the decadent days of Rome, pornography emerged from its caves and circulated openly in a civilized nation. The Catholic Church in France was intellectually gutted; the priests lost their faith with their congregations. Strange cults appeared; sex rituals, black magic, Satanism. Perversion became not only acceptable but fashionable. Homosexuals held public balls to which heterosexuals were invited and the police guarded their carriages. Prostitutes were admired; swindlers and sharp business practices increased. Political clubs of the more radical sort proliferated (Otto J. Scott, *Robespierre: The Voice of Virtue*, p. 8).

The French Declaration attempted to establish freedom and liberty — certainly a noble desire. Its base, however, was consciously man-centered, following the humanistic philosophy of the Enlightenment made popular by Voltaire (1694-1778) and Jean-Jacques Rousseau (1712-1778). While the Declaration of the Rights of Man contained a reference to a "Supreme Being," this equaled "the sovereignty of the State" or the will of the people: "The source of all sovereignty is essentially the nation. . . ." This is a perversion of the worst kind. *The source of all sovereignty is God alone* (cf. Daniel 4:28-37; Romans 13:1). Our Constitution begins, "We, the People. . . ." Has this lead the courts and the citizenry to believe that direct sovereignty belongs to the people, independent of God? The Articles of Confederation established a decentralized political system where sovereignty was distributed among the many states.

It was natural that such a man-centered Declaration and such a perverse, man-centered philosophy should lead directly to the Reign of Terror, to massive, disgusting, abominable perversions and atrocities, and to a deliberate policy of mass murder. These policies were legitimized under the direction of the revolutionary civil government, the rapid loss of liberty in France and the export of war, revolution, and conquest to the other nations of Europe. The perverse view upon which the French Declaration was based led directly to massive violations of the very "rights of man" the Declaration was supposed to protect.

Maximilien Robespierre (1758-1794), French revolutionist who was executed by those who became consistent with the absolutes of liberty.

The American Declaration of Independence, built on a faltering Christian base, presented the rights of all citizens as at least God-given. The framers were not presumptuous enough to think they could or should list them all. The Declaration of Independence says that "among" these many rights God has bestowed are "Life, Liberty, and the pursuit of happiness." The assumption is there are more, and to list them would be to limit them. The Declaration of the Rights of Man attempts to enumerate the rights of the citizens. Thus it limits "rights" to the seventeen basic human rights listed. What happens when the State decides a certain right no longer is a right? Because the State listed them (and thus limited them), and the State determined them, power to eliminate a right becomes a tool for control and eventual tyranny.

Looking back from the vantage point of the 20th century, one would like the God of the Declaration of Independence to be more explicitly defined as the God of the Bible. Sadly, this is not the case. But there is a lesson here for all of us. Compromise in seemingly little things can bring

236

about tragic results. Our nation's courts have consistently repudiated what they define as the "nebulous" God of the Declaration. Is He the god of Islam and Mormonism or the Triune God of Scripture? When we speak of God, there is only One (Deuteronomy 6:4; Isaiah 44:6, 7).

6. The cry for human rights has far reaching ethical implications. When a demand for rights is divorced from a standard of authority, moral anarchy rules. For example, should minority rights be protected, or should the rights of the majority prevail and cancel those of the minority? The abortion issue, as presented today, is a dilemma over rights. Does the mother have a "right" over her own body and that of her developing baby? Or does the developing baby have the prevailing right to life? If the criterion for judgment is based on rights, those possessing the greatest power will insure that their rights are adopted as law. Where "rights" are based on no higher standard than the *desires* of men, politics will degenerate into a power struggle, based on deceit and force, among the various claimants of "rights." This negates any rights for the unborn baby who remains powerless and, therefore, is at the mercy of those who desire his or her demise.

But what if the issue is not rights at all? What if the issue is an unchangeable standard that judges between the majority and minority, the strong and the weak, the mother and her unborn child?:

Rights must have a reference point and a specific context or they are meaningless. The reference point determines the nature of the right exercised, defining the one who possesses it and setting limits to others who must respect it. Both the claim to and the exercise of a right, therefore, can be either valid or invalid depending upon its reference point. If the reference is the Bible, then there is an absolute base and a meaningful content to determine whether the right is indeed a right and whether the exercise of that right is proper (John W. Whitehead, *The Second American Revolution*, p. 117).

When the Bible no longer is used as the standard for making ethical decisions, then the fluctuating standards of men become the prevailing standards of the day. Definitions of right and wrong are determined from the standpoint of an individual's rights with no consideration of God's law which restricts the sinful actions of men and women. Those in the minority can only enjoy equal protection under the law when that law binds the majority as well. The unborn baby can only be protected from the power of those who look upon him/her as some*thing* less than human when there is an absolute standard determining the nature of life and the limits of personal decision making.

Proclaim liberty throughout the land, unto all the inhabitants thereof (Leviticus 25:10, KJV). True liberty is found in the redeeming work of Jesus Christ and adherence to His Law.

7. The United States of America usually are described as the bastion of freedom. Our history is filled with stories of men and women who came to these American shores to secure freedom to live lives unhindered by political or ecclesiastical oppression. That symbol of freedom is the Liberty Bell. It is inscribed with the words of Leviticus 25:10 (KJV): "Proclaim liberty throughout the land to the inhabitants thereof." When our great immigrant population arrived to these shores the Statue of

238

Liberty greeted them. The words engraved on the pedestal of Liberty extol liberty as a rare and necessary commodity.

Give me your tired, your poor, Your huddled masses yearning to breathe free, The wretched refuse of your teeming shore, Send these, the homeless, tempest-tossed, to me; I lift my lamp beside the golden door.

Liberty or freedom to live out one's life without external restraints, far from oppression, is certainly a blessed thing.

But are freedom and liberty absolute rights? Is the doctrine of freedom and liberty as independent rights found in the Bible? Can we be trapped by those who espouse and work for freedom and liberty in an absolute way? When we talk about "freedom of religion," do we mean that anyone ought to have the right to practice his or her religion without restraint? For example, do Satanists have the "right" to establish churches and offer blood sacrifices — including human sacrifices? This question and many more like it need to be answered. The Bible is our starting point, not the doctrine of freedom itself.

It is always best to begin with definitions. What do we mean by freedom and liberty? Noah Webster, in his *American Dictionary of the English Language* (1828), defines liberty this way: "Freedom from restraint, in a general sense, and applicable to the body, or to the will or mind. The body is at *liberty*, when not confined; the will or mind is at *liberty* when not checked or controlled. A man enjoys *liberty*, when no physical force operates to restrain his actions." A technical definition for "liberty" would be "the power to do as one pleases without physical or external restraint." The definition for "freedom" is similar: "The absence of necessity, coercion, or constraint in choice or action." Noah Webster's definition of freedom is telling: "A state of exemption from the power or control of another; liberty; exemption from slavery, servitude or confinement. *Freedom is personal, civil, political, and religious.*" The key issue: Who sets the boundaries? This is the heart of the debate over rights. If there are no boundaries, anarchy arises (the individual is sovereign). If there are limited boundaries, statism arises (the State is sovereign).

These definitions show that only God is absolutely free, not bound by anything or anyone. No one dictates to God what ought to be done. God is answerable to no one. When these technical definitions are taken alone and applied to finite, fallible, and fallen men and women, without biblical content, we can see that problems certainly will arise. Thieves, liars, and murderers would agree with each of the above definitions. Those who want to absolutize freedom seek to be god, living without restraint. R. J. Rushdoony defines the destructive nature of unlimited liberty devoid of law.

> [U]nlimited liberty for man is destructive of liberty itself. Can we give any man the unlimited liberty to do as he pleases? Can a man rob whenever he sees fit, kill at will, lie as he wishes, and generally be a law unto himself? If we permitted this, soon no one would have any liberty. The result would be only *anarchy*. Man's total liberty is always anarchy, and anarchy is the death of both law and liberty. Unless every man's liberty is limited by law, no liberty is possible for any man. . . . we must beware of those who talk about defending liberty when they actually want to promote anarchy. . . . There is no area where freedom is unlimited (*Law and Liberty*, p. 12f.)

Freedom of speech does not allow us to shout "fire!" in a crowded theater when there is no fire. Freedom of the press does not permit us to publish libelous statements or print copyrighted material without permission. A technical definition of liberty and freedom, therefore, will not suit our purposes. Biblical content must be given to each term.

The Bible defines freedom and liberty as being outside the realm of sin and death; therefore, only Jesus Christ, and our knowing the truth of our sin and the reality of His redemptive work, can set us free. Jesus' detractors misunderstood the nature of true freedom. They saw freedom solely in terms of political liberty. They failed to recognize that their lack of civil liberty (oppression under Egypt, Assyria, Babylon, Greece, and Rome) directly resulted from their choice of slavery to sin and God's judgment for their choice of masters (sin). Jesus answers their mistaken perceptions about freedom and liberty: "Truly, truly, I say to you, every one who commits sin is the slave of sin. And the slave does not remain in the house forever; the son does remain forever" (John 8:34, 35).

But this redemptive freedom has not freed us from the obligations to serve God with all our heart, soul, mind, and strength. "But thanks be to God that though you were slaves of sin, you became obedient from the heart to that form of teaching to which you were committed, and having

The foundation of the French Revolution was consciously man-centered, following the humanistic philosophy of the Enlightenment made popular by Voltaire (1694-1778) and Jean-Jacques Rousseau (1712-1778).

been freed from sin, you became slaves of righteousness . . . . For just as you presented your members as slaves to impurity and to lawlessness, resulting in further lawlessness, so now present your members as slaves to righteousness, resulting in sanctification. For when you were slaves of sin,

241

you were free in regard to righteousness" (Romans 6:17-20). Greg L. Bahnsen writes: "Having redeemed us from the curse of the law, Christ gives us the freedom we need: ethical ability to keep God's law in grateful love to Him — not the commonly urged type of 'freedom' which turns God's grace into licentiousness (Jude 4)" (*Theonomy in Christian Ethics*, p. 483).

We now are free and at liberty to be what God calls us to be. In this condition we are most free. As a fish is most free in water, and a train most free when confined to railroad tracks, and a bird most free in the air, men and women are most free when they are in Christ and keep His commandments.

> Obedience to the law as the means to freedom and dominion is repeatedly declared in Scripture, as in Deuteronomy 28 and Leviticus 26. Obedience, the obedience of faith, means freedom from drought (Lev. 26:4), and freedom from want (Lev. 26:5); it means peace in the land, and victory over our enemies (Lev. 26:6-8); it means fertility, and abundance (Lev. 26:9-10), and it means the tabernacling presence of God the Lord (Lev. 26:11-13) (R. J. Rushdoony, *Law and Society*, p. 206).

Freedom and liberty, if they are to remain, must find their meaning in Jesus Christ, and in His law. The nation that rejects Christ will most certainly reject the freedom and liberty that comes with knowing Him.

Redemptive liberty (ethical liberty) results in political and civil liberty. Civil liberty cannot stand on its own. This is the great mistake of those organizations and ideological movements (e.g., American Civil Liberties Union [ACLU] and Civil Libertarians) that believe true and lasting liberty is found in autonomous man. When liberty is sought ultimately through legal and political means, we can expect freedom to be defined in terms of man and his perceptions of freedom. Liberty must find its meaning in Christ and His gracious provision.

The denial of *regeneration* as the basis of true liberty leads to *revolution*. Freedom and liberty are imposed through the agency of the State or through the actions of special interest groups, each being selective in their definition of freedom. The result is the denial or loss of freedom as a direct consequence of man's seeking freedom from the wrong source.

The principles of God's word guided the decisions on which our nation built its foundations. Throughout our history, our leaders have borne eloquent testimony to this fact. Woodrow Wilson, our 28th President, wrote: *There are a good many problems before the American people today, and before me as President, but I expect to find the solution of these problems just in the proportion that I am faithful in the study of the Word of God.* Andrew Jackson, our 7th President (pictured above), wrote these words: *That book, sir, is the rock on which our republic rests.*

At an early age Samuel was instructed in the Scriptures: *Thus Samuel grew and the LORD was with him and let none of his words fail. And all of Israel from Dan even to Beersheba knew that Samuel was confirmed as a prophet of the LORD* (1 Samuel 3:19, 20).

Lesson 9

Sovereignty and Education

Who ought to educate? This is a fundamental question. Of course, the sovereign, the one who is in absolute control has the right to educate. But who is sovereign? Man or God? God is the Sovereign ruler of heaven and earth. Man is not an independent being. He is a creature who must obey God in *all* things. Students, parents, teachers, and the State have no option but to submit to God's plan for education. As the Sovereign, God sets the standards for education; He determines who may educate; He establishes the ethical nature of education; He requires that we be tested; and finally, He commands that we "graduate," that we put our education into practice.

Parents, students, teachers, and civil officials must come to grips with the sovereignty issue. Parents are responsible before God to educate their children God's way. Since God does not give educational jurisdiction to the State, educational jurisdiction remains with parents. Understanding how education shapes the views of children, and thus the direction of a nation, becomes the key to unlocking much of history. The Israelites were commanded to pass on what they had learned to their children (Deuteronomy 6:4-9) and were warned of the consequences of rejecting God's view of the world (Joshua 1:7-9). The effects of such rejection became immediately evident in family, church, and State (cf. Judges 2:6-23; 1 Samuel 2:12-17, 22-36; 8:1-22).

The Psalmist stresses how sovereignty and the future of the nation are connected. While we might not see the immediate effect of the sovereignty issue in education, future generations will reveal the results of education based on God as the sovereign: "For [God] established a testimony in Jacob, and appointed a law in Israel, which He commanded our fathers, that they should teach them to their children; that the generation to come might know, even the children yet to be born, that they may arise and tell them to their children, that they should put their confidence in God, and not forget the works of God, but keep His commandments" (Psalm 78:5-7).

In order for consistent biblical education to flourish, the God-ordained means of carrying out directives must be in place. This means parental control and supervision of education (Deuteronomy 6:6-10; Psalm 127:3-5; Proverbs 22:6; Ephesians 5:21-6:4; 2 Timothy 3:15-17). When parents abdicate this responsibility and give their children to the State for instruction and indoctrination, we can expect dominion in the name of the Triune God to be curtailed and even overruled.

The Scripture calls the members of the visible church by the name of disciples, scholars, *or* learners. . . *[T]he visible church . . . is the* school of Christ, *into which persons are admitted . . . to their* learning of Christ, *and coming to spiritual attainments, in the use of the means of teaching, discipline, and training up, established in the school.*

— Jonathan Edwards

The first thing that the despotic Babylonian ruler Nebuchadnezzar did with the captured Israelite youths was "to teach them the literature and language of the Chaldeans" (Daniel 1:4) so they would "enter the king's personal service" (v. 5).

"One of the most useful tools in the quest for power is the educational system" (Herbert Schlossberg, *Idols for Destruction*, p. 209). The implication of this statement is obvious: whoever controls the educational system establishes the religious values of the people, sets the nation's goals, and ultimately controls the future. The Reformation of the 16th century stressed the reclamation of all of life, with education an essential focal point. Education must be Christ-centered if the Reformation was to continue. Samuel Blumenfeld writes:

> Since the Protestant rebellion against Rome had arisen in part as a result of Biblical study and interpretation, it became obvious to Protestant leaders that if the Reform movement were to survive and flourish,

widespread Biblical literacy, at all levels of society, would be absolutely necessary. The Bible was to be the moral and spiritual authority in every man's life, and therefore an intimate knowledge of it was imperative if a new Protestant social order were to take root (*Is Public Education Necessary?*, p. 10).

Martin Luther (1483-1546) in Germany and John Calvin (1509-1564) in Geneva, Switzerland established schools to teach the Bible as God's word applied authoritatively to every area of life. In fact, Calvin's Academy in Geneva, founded by John Calvin in 1559, attracted students from throughout Europe. Charles Borgeaud, a historian on the Academy, writes that "Calvin had achieved his task: he had secured the future of Geneva . . . making it at once a church, a school and a fortress. It was the first stronghold of liberty in modern times." The effects of training at Geneva were far reaching: "It was not only the future of Geneva but that of other regions as well that was affected by the rise of the Geneva schools. The men who were to lead the advance of the Reformed Church in many lands were trained in Geneva classrooms, preached Geneva doctrines, and sang the Psalms to Geneva tunes" (John T. McNeill, *The History and Character of Calvinism*, p. 196).

In our own nation one of the first acts performed in the New World was the establishment of schools. The Puritan system copied that of Geneva, in design and intent. The purpose of these colonial schools was to further the gospel of Christ in all disciplines.

Regardless of the vocation for which a student was preparing, the colonial college sought to provide for him an education that was distinctly Christian. At Harvard the original goal of higher learning was "to know God and Jesus Christ which is eternal life (John 17:3), and therefore to lay Christ in the bottom as the only foundation of all sound knowledge and learning." Yale in the early 1700s stated as its primary goal that "every student shall consider the main end of his study to wit to know God in Jesus Christ and answerably to lead a Godly, sober life" (William C. Ringenberg, *The Christian College: A History of Protestant Higher Education in America*, p. 38).

The Puritan educational system trained church and civil leaders. The emphasis, however, was to train men so that future generations would not be left with "an illiterate ministry." The curriculum of Harvard, for example, emphasized the study of biblical languages, logic, divinity (theology), and skills in communica-

247

tion (public speaking and rhetoric). Churches expected their ministers to read the Scriptures in the original languages. At Princeton, even those who did not enter the gospel ministry, were expected to know their "Bible from cover to cover." Since civil government was a major concern in the colonies, courses in ethics, politics, and history also were required.

Many of the 18th century framers of the Constitution had been steeped in basic Bible doctrines. These biblical concepts founded our Constitutional political system (e.g., decentralized political power, checks and balances, a republican form of government, abhorrence of democracy, jurisdictional separation of family, church, and State, a design for stability in the rule of law, private property, the gold standard, the keeping of the Lord's Day, and the protection of Christian worship).

Courses in law and medicine also were offered, along with astronomy, physics, botany, science, and mathematics. During the colonial period, from 1636 when Harvard was established to 1769 when Dartmouth was founded, nearly all colleges were established as Christian institutions. In time, however, emphasis shifted from staunchly biblio-centric education to a "Common Sense Realism" philosophy which put reason on an equal level with special revelation. Of course, this shift did not occur overnight. Harvard moved from its original Calvinist foundation to Arminianism, then during the 18th century even beyond Arminianism to Unitarianism. "The takeover of Harvard in 1805 by the Unitarians is probably the most important intellectual event in American history — at least from the standpoint of education" (Samuel Blumenfeld, *Is Public Education Necessary?*, p. 30).

Nearly every educational institution of the early colonies has been taken over by those who denied the Bible. These schools of higher education now train millions of young people who influence every sphere of American life. Compare the educational pursuits of Harvard in 1636 with the Harvard of today:

Every child in America entering school at the age of five is mentally ill, because he comes to school with certain allegiances toward our founding fathers, our elected officials, toward his parents, toward a belief in a supernatural Being, toward the sovereignty of this nation as a separate entity. It's up to you teachers to make all of these sick children well by creating the international children of the future (Chester Pierce, Professor of Education in the faculty of Medicine and Graduate School of Education, Harvard University).

Where Christ had been considered the foundation of all knowledge, believing in "a supernatural Being" now constitutes mental illness. Dr. Pierce understands the importance of education, however; it is to mold "the international children of the *future*." Public education (Government controlled, State education) is the means by which these children will be molded.

Adolf Hitler used coercion to accomplish his goal of a Nazi future. By capturing the youth through education he could implement his vision of a new world order, a millennial reign where man would rule according to man's "enlightened" law. In *Mein Kampf* Hitler stressed "the importance of winning over and then training the youth in the service 'of a new national state' " (William Shirer, *The Rise and Fall of the Third Reich*, p. 248f.). Shirer shows how Hitler used education as a device to direct the future of the nation:

"When an opponent declares, 'I will not come over to your side,' " he said in a speech on November 6, 1933, "I calmly say, 'Your child belongs to us already . . . What are you? You will pass on. Your descendants, however, now stand in the new camp. In a short time they will know nothing else but this new community.' " And on May 1, 1937, he declared, "This new Reich will give its youth to no one, but will itself take youth and give to youth its own education and its own upbringing" (p. 249).

All German schools "were quickly Nazified." Control was taken from the parents and local authorities, and "[e]very person in the teaching profession, from kindergarten through the universities, was compelled to join the National Socialist Teachers' League which, by law, was held 'responsible for the execution of the ideological and political co-ordination of all the teachers in accordance with the National Socialist doctrine' " (p. 249). The State was to be supported "without reservation" and teachers took an oath to "be loyal and obedient to Adolf Hitler" (p. 249).

Our nation has adopted many of the ideals of Nazi Germany. The State is viewed as the only legitimate educator. Parents who do not comply with the new emphasis can be fined or imprisoned, and their children can be put in foster homes. Christian parents everywhere must take responsibility to educate their own children, either at home or by delegating that responsibility to teachers and schools who teach from a Christ-centered perspective. There is no other option. The battle for the future rests with our children. Will we turn them over to an educational system that despises the God who made them? God will hold parents accountable for the education of *His* children.

Questions for Discussion

1. In the Bible is there a separate discipline called 'education'? What is the biblical definition of education? (Leviticus 10:11; Deuteronomy 17:18; 31:9-13; 33:10; 2 Chronicles 17:7-9; Nehemiah 8:9; Psalm 18:34; 144:1; Nehemiah 4:7, 8, 11, 14-18; Exodus 31:11; 35:20-35; 1 Corinthians 12-14)

_____

_____

_____

_____

_____

_____

2. Trace the history of education through the Bible asking yourself these questions: Where does Education begin? By what standards does education operate? What was education like in Old Testament times? What was education like in New Testament times? How does this compare and contrast with education today? (Isaiah 30:20ff.; cf. 8:19; and John 3:2; Colossians 2:3; Genesis 2:20; cf. Proverbs 6:6; 26:11; 30:18, 24-31; and Genesis 2:15-17; 4:2, 17, 20-22; 5:25-27; Judges 1:11; Deuteronomy 6:4-9; Proverbs 1:8; 4:1-4; 1 Chronicles 4:14, 21; 12:32; Nehemiah 11:35; 2 Kings 18:17; 2 Samuel 8:10; Isaiah 40:19; 44:12; 2 Chronicles 24:12; Jeremiah 10:9; 2 Samuel 5:11; Exodus 28:10; 1 Kings 7:15; Judges 8:14; 2 Samuel 8:17; 20:25; 1 Kings 4:3; Jeremiah 36:4; Ezekiel 44:24, 25; Deuteronomy 31:9; 33:10; Matthew 13:55; Mark 6:3; Acts 18:3)

_____

_____

_____

_____

_____

_____

_____

_____

3. What is the goal of education? (Isaiah 48:11; Matthew 5:16; 1 Peter 4:11; 1 Corinthians 10:31; 2 Timothy 3:16, 17; Isaiah 11:9)

_____

_____

_____

_____

_____

_____

4. Can education ever be neutral? Explain. (Colossians 2:3-8; John 17:17; Ephesians 4:17, 18; 2 Corinthians 10:5; Matthew 12:30)

_____

_____

_____

_____

_____

_____

5. Who is responsible for the education of our children? (Proverbs 1:8; 4:1; 2 Timothy 1:5; 3:15; Genesis 4; Deuteronomy 6:4ff.; Daniel 1:1-7)

_____

_____

_____

_____

_____

_____

6. How is education used to control the direction of a nation? (Psalm 78; Judges 2:10, 11; Daniel 1:1-7)

_____

_____

_____

_____

_____

_____

251

7. In what way should Christians minister to the world in the area of education? (1 Kings 4:29, 30, 34; Daniel 2; Deuteronomy 4:6-8; Matthew 5:13-16; Deuteronomy 17:9, 18; 1 Chronicles 23:4; 26:29-32; 2 Chronicles 19:8-11)

_____

_____

_____

_____

_____

_____

_____

_____

_____

Summary

"It is clear, then, that education must be religious, and it is therefore understandable why Christians, desiring to protect their religious liberties, would necessarily be, at the very least, concerned about the efforts by the State to intervene in the area of Christian education programs. But for many, who perhaps do not yet fully recognize the implications of the religious character of all education, the educational crisis, no matter what else is involved, always comes back to the simple question of, 'If the State is not to ultimately regulate the education of our children, ensuring against academic child neglect, then who is?' But the State's principal concern in overseeing the education of children has never been the educational development of children but merely its own control over the educational process" (Blair Adams and Joel Stein, _Who Owns the Children: Compulsory Education and the Dilemma of Ultimate Authority_, p. 9).

Answers to Questions for Discussion

1. A separate discipline called 'education' with a separate jurisdiction does not occur in the Bible. There is probably a very good reason for this. Education was not a separate institution in Hebrew thought like family, church, and State because education is larger than any one institution. James B. Jordan comments: "There is, in fact, no such thing as a 'sphere of education'; rather, education is simply the training arm of each aspect of life" ("Tithing: Financing Christian Reconstruction," in *The Law of the Covenant: An Exposition of Exodus 21-23*, p. 213).

Parents, in family government, play a major role in education — *the* major role. The church also has educational responsibilities. In the Old Testament, the Levites were responsible for educating the people in the Law-Word of God (Leviticus 10:11; Deuteronomy 17:18; 31:9-13; 33:10; 2 Chronicles 17:7-9; Nehemiah 8:9). Such instruction obviously touched on every area of life.

A separate educational jurisdiction is not found in the Bible. Parents are responsible for the education of their children and they can delegate that responsibility to those who hold the same biblical convictions.

The State has a very minor role that is confined to military pre-paredess. The civil magistrate has the duty to defend the nation against both foreign and domestic enemies. God Himself is the Primary Instructor in this task: "He [God] trains my hands for battle, so that my arms can bend a bow of bronze" (Psalm 18:34; cf. 2 Samuel 22:35). And, "Blessed be the LORD, my Rock, Who trains my hands for war, and my fingers for battle" (Psalm 144:1). The civil magistrate receives authority from God as His "minister," as "an avenger who brings wrath upon the one who practices evil" (Romans 13:1, 4; cf. Genesis 14:14-17; Deuteronomy 20; Matthew 8:5-13; Luke 11:21, 22). The defense of the nation takes man-power, weapons, and military instruction (Nehemiah 4:7, 8, 11, 14-18; Luke 22:36, 38; cf. Luke 14:31, 32). For example, military tactics are taught at each of our military academies. This is a legitimate teaching function of the state.

Education in each of these spheres requires a proper definition. Educa-tion is simply "thinking God's thoughts after Him," and teaching others to do so, as well as obeying God's word. This definition can be extended by keeping in mind at least two general principles. First, God has given each of us certain gifts, talents, and abilities (Exodus 31:11; 35:20-35; 1 Cor-inthians 12-14; Romans 12:3-8); therefore, the task of Christian educa-tion is to *lead out* of students those gifts, talents, and abilities God has given each of us. (Education is made up of two Latin words, *e* and *duco*. When taken together they mean, "lead out of.") Those gifts, talents, and abilities differ with each student.

This view differs from John Locke's (1632-1704) view of man where the mind is *tabula rasa*, a blank tablet or "white paper," that is filled by man's many experiences. Such a view encourages a teacher to play god, making students in his own image.

The idea of leading out of a child what God has put into a child also is contrary to humanistic views of education which do not take into account man's sinfulness. "This runs directly counter to the older Protestant concept of the child as (1) a creature fearfully and wonderfully made in the image of God, and with awesome responsibilities, and yet (2) conceived in sin, that is, born with a predisposition to sin, in original sin, which radically tainted every aspect of his being" (Rousas J. Rushdoony, *Intellec-tual Schizophrenia*, p. 70).

John Locke (1632-1704) viewed the mind of man as *tabula rasa*, a blank tablet that is written on by man's many experiences. Such a view makes man God, determining for himself what is a valid experience.

Not everything that comes out of a child is good. Scripture, therefore, must be our guide. Moreover, the biblical leading-out methodology that recognizes individual differences, skills, gifts, talents, and educational background is contrary to the "democratic" view of education wherein a curriculum establishes learning on the basis of some educational common denominator. Individual differences and gifts are rarely acknowledged and cultivated in the "democratic" (humanistic) view of education.

Second, education is also *indoctrination*. "The actual process of transmission is nothing less than *indoctrination*. It is significant that, in the New Testament, the word 'doctrine' is the same noun as 'teaching' (Greek, *didaskalia*). That is, the process of true teaching is nothing more nor less than indoctrinating. Teaching is not the discovery of truth, nor sharing the truth; it is indoctrinating the truth!" (Henry M. Morris, *Education in the Real World*, p. 43).

The teacher (whether parent, minister or hired instructor) must *put into* each student what he or she *ought* to know: theology (the basis of true knowledge which is essential for the study of life), language and communication skills, a child's cultural heritage, national and world history, geography, mathematics, philosophy, physics, biology, logic, political science, economics, ethics, art and music, physical and health education, and the skills of various vocations. God's thinking must inhabit the mind of every child throughout these disciplines, for necessary execution of the dominion mandates (Genesis 1:26-28 and Matthew 28:18-20). Biblical education, therefore, is *ethical* in nature. Education is not neutral. What is put *into* a child must come *out of* Scripture. Since indoctrination is a necessary part of education, it is immoral to put our children in the educational hands of those who deny Christ and His word.

Education is a life-long process, not limited to only one phase of an individual's life. It should not be equated solely with institutional education (elementary, secondary, college, and graduate studies), which is only one aspect of one's total education. A biblical education should include the following:

(1) *A Point of Departure* — The Almighty Triune God is the Author and Sustainer of His creation and thus all things originate with Him: "Worthy art Thou, our Lord and our God, to receive glory and honor and power; for Thou didst create all things, and because of Thy will they existed, and were created" (Revelation 4:11).

(2) *A Destination Point* — Students are to be taught to learn and do all things solely to the glory of God: "Whether, then, you eat or drink or whatever you do, do all to the glory of God" (1 Corinthians 10:31).

(3) *Methods Used* — All methods used in education must be biblical and lead the student to his destination: "In all your ways acknowledge Him, and He will make your paths straight" (Proverbs 3:6).

(4) *Attitude Toward Students* — Teachers should respect individuality, God-given abilities, and especially their covenantal status before the Lord: "And, fathers, do not provoke your children to anger; but bring them up in the discipline and instruction of the Lord" (Ephesians 6:4).

(5) *Development of Students* — Teaching should be geared toward the stage of mental development the individual student has reached: grammar (particular facts), logic (analysis and a comprehensive view and under-

256

standing of the world), and rhetoric (the application of the first two stages to practical affairs, issues and activities of life): "Just as a father has compassion on his children, so the LORD has compassion on those who fear Him. For He Himself knows our frame; He is mindful that we are but dust" (Psalm 103:13, 14).

(6) *Subjects Taught* — Instruction should equip the student with tools needed for living his life in this world to the glory of God: "Make me know Thy ways, O LORD; teach me Thy paths. Lead me in Thy truth and teach me, for Thou art the God of my salvation" (Psalm 25:4, 5). (The above material is taken from Francis Nigel Lee, "Rearing, Education and School," in *Man and His Culture*, p. 45 and Dorothy Sayers, "The Lost Tools of Learning," in *The Journal of Christian Reconstruction*, Symposium on Education, Gary North, ed., Vol. IV, No. 1 [Summer, 1977], pp. 10-25).

2. Of course, education begins with God Himself. He is the Teacher (Isaiah 30:20ff.), and we should consult Him for knowledge and understanding, rather than ourselves, idols or the dead (see Isaiah 8:19). We are His students. Jesus is called "a teacher from God" (John 3:2). Even Adam and Eve, though morally perfect, did not know everything. God remained their Teacher throughout their lives. In the New Testament we are told all the treasures of wisdom and knowledge are hid in Christ (Colossians 2:3). Adam and Eve sought to be independent sources of knowledge and wisdom and brought upon themselves God's judgment.

The results of education are seen very early. We find Adam naming the created order: "And the man gave names to all the cattle, and to the birds of the sky, and to every beast of the field. . ." (Genesis 2:20). Education leads immediately to dominion. Naming is an attribute of sovereignty. In Adam's case, a delegated and limited sovereignty. By studying the animals Adam would learn much about the created order. We see this pattern reflected in Proverbs where animals are our instructors (e.g., Proverbs 6:6; 26:11; 30:19, 24-31). God taught Adam and Eve and they passed on these "language arts" to their children. Farming and agriculture (Genesis 2:15-17; 4:2), architecture (4:17), music (4:21), and metallurgy (4:22) were immediately developed. We should expect such rapid development of gifts since the descendants of Adam and Eve shared in their direct

257

knowledge from God. The working out of the curse was only in its preliminary stage.

Learning continued and included commerce. Trade and commercial cooperation took place as the nomadic lifestyle spread culture and saleable goods. In addition to city dwellers, tentmakers took their trades with them (Genesis 4:20). Education was extremely practical and was governed by families and the availability of certain skills in the marketplace. Those not willing to learn would not survive. If a marketable skill was not learned early, an individual found himself at the mercy of the elements and a competitive marketplace. The imprudent could not depend on government welfare (cf. 2 Thessalonians 3:10). Teaching children was ethical in nature. It was said, "He who does not teach his son a useful trade is bringing him up to be a thief."

Noah and his family learned much from building the ark and taught their building skills to others. Again, education is centered around the family.

Education in those earliest generations profited greatly from close proximity to Adam and Eve and the creation. Noah and his family probably knew Methuselah (Genesis 5:25-27). Only after the flood were skills very likely lost, though we find agricultural and architectural skills still present (Genesis 9:20; 11:1-9). Noah and his family learned much from building the ark and taught their building skills to others. History tells us of many advances in a number of fields. For example, by the time of the Judges, libraries had been established in Canaan. Debir was formerly called *Kiriath-Sepher*, "city of books" (Judges 1:11). "Debir was a large library city. It was where the clay tablets were stored. It was the repository for the philosophical books of the Canaanites, their geneological records, their trading records, treaties, land ownership documents, and much more. To destroy this place was to destroy their entire civilization, as can well be imagined" (James B. Jordan, *Judges: God's War Against Humanism*, p. 7). *Debir* still retains its etymological heritage with *Kiriath-Sepher*; Debir means "word."

Most education centered around the family, with a view and way of life passed from parents to children. Since children are a "gift from the Lord" (Psalm 127:3), parents are responsible for instructing their children in biblical laws and doctrines, applying them to every phase of learning. This is the biblical norm.

> From the earliest days of the human race in the Garden of Eden the family has been the most important educational agency on earth. It is so designed by God, and the Hebrews never got away from the centrality of the home in the educational experience. . . . Hebrew education technically began with Abraham and the covenant. The covenant was national and personal with profound educational implications. It was a [sovereignly imposed] contract between the Hebrews and God, but also between each individual Hebrew and God. Every person in the nation had an individual obligation to God, to his family, and to his nation (Kenneth O. Gangel and Warren S. Benson, *Christian Education: Its History and Philosophy*, pp. 21-22).

In our day the State assumes that parents are only guardians of children who really belongs to the State; therefore, education is a State responsibility. Providing a biblical education is the parent's duty, however, not the State's. Unfortunately, education has been separated into two separate realms — religious education and technical education. The home and church are responsible for religious education, while the State is responsible for *technical* education. All education is religious, however. If your children are in "Public Schools" (government schools), they are getting a "religious" education. While it is not the true religion, it is religious nevertheless.

Education continued to be the family's responsibility as the covenant family grew into a covenant nation. Even at this time in history God establishes the home as the primary educational institution: "For I have chosen [Abraham], in order that he may command his children and his household after him to keep the way of the LORD by doing righteousness and justice; in order that the LORD may bring upon Abraham what He has spoken about him" (Genesis 18:19). "It is significant that this first mention of teaching not only speaks of the father as teacher, but also reveals the importance of including moral and spiritual values in the content of the teaching. The family, therefore, is man's first and basic school" (John W. Whitehead, "Courting the Right," *Moody Monthly*, March 1984, p. 23). Even with the giving of the law, which in some ways expanded the civil magistrate's jurisdiction, education remained a family affair. There is no provision in the law for an institutional, State-directed education that would supplant the family as the primary educator. Instruction in the law of God was the starting point for all education and parents were the primary educators (Deuteronomy 6:4-9; Proverbs 1:8; 4:1-4). This is far broader than what we term "religious instruction." The law included instruction concerning all of life. Economic and governmental principles abound in the case laws of Exodus. Parents, with the help of the Priests, were responsible to give their children a civil and legal education. Instruction in the law meant an individual should be able to understand "the times, with knowledge" so the nation could be advised and directed (1 Chronicles 12:32).

Specialized education was available in Israel. Tradesmen could train young apprentices who wished to learn a craft. A list of various crafts and guilds provides an idea of how pervasive education became in Israel, even without State (Government) schools: dyers and weavers (1 Chronicles 4:21), wood and stone workers (1 Chronicles 4:14; Nehemiah 11:35), fullers (2 Kings 18:17), metal workers (2 Samuel 8:10; Isaiah 40:19; 44:12; 2 Chronicles 24:12; Jeremiah 10:9); engravers of gems (Exodus 28:9), surveyors (1 Kings 7:15), professional and private scribes (Judges 8:14; 2 Samuel 8:17; 20:25; 1 Kings 4:3; Jeremiah 36:4), etc. These were all technicians.

Jesus learned his skills as a carpenter from His father. The Greek word for "carpenter" is *tekton*, related to our English word "technician."

261

Priests, experts in the law of God, also acted as instructors. "[T]hey shall teach My people the difference between the holy and the profane, and cause them to discern between the unclean and the clean. And in a dispute they shall take their stand to judge; they shall judge it according to My ordinances. They shall also keep My laws and My statutes in all My appointed feasts, and sanctify My sabbaths" (Ezekiel 44:23, 24). Moses summarized the duties of the priests: "They shall teach Thine ordinances to Jacob, and Thy law to Israel" (Deuteronomy 33:10). The law came from God, but was entrusted to the priests for the nation: "So Moses wrote this law and gave it to the priests, the sons of Levi who carried the ark of the covenant of the LORD, and to all the elders of Israel" (Deuteronomy 31:9; cf. v. 26).

Even by the time of the New Testament apprenticeship education still operated under family oversight. Jesus was the carpenter's son and a carpenter Himself, a trade His earthly father taught Him (Matthew 13:55; Mark 6:3). The Greek word for "carpenter" is *tekton*, related to our English word "technician." Massachusetts in the late 1600s required that "masters give teaching in the liberal arts, sciences, the Christian religion and sound ethics" (Paul H. Douglas, *Apprenticeship as a Form of Education*, pp. 41-42. Quoted by Kenneth O. Gangel and Warren S. Benson in *Christian Education: Its History Philosophy*, p. 232). Notice the *ethical* dimension to education. It was not enough to teach the *technical* skills. For godly dominion to be extended, self-government had to prevail. Self-government is nothing more than keeping the commandments of God with a willing heart.

The apprenticeship pattern continued until fairly recently, and still has not died out entirely. Teachers embark on an apprenticeship program when they do "student teaching." Medical doctors spend time as interns. Trade unions work on the apprenticeship idea. During the Industrial Revolution for the first time children left home *en masse* to work for others. The skills of generations were no longer passed on and education moved more and more outside the home.

During the period of the advancing church we find the same emphasis. For example, the Apostle Paul not only had what we call a "theological" education, but a marketable skill as a tent-maker (Acts 18:3). Of course, as Christians we do not divorce theological training from other types of training. All the people should be theologically trained. The law of God provides social and political order. If the Bible is a blueprint for all of life, the reading of the law will give all the people training in economics, jurisprudence, education, politics, and foreign affairs. The law of God was not restricted to the citizens of Israel. The aliens, those who were not part of the covenant community, were also responsible to hear the law read every seven years: "Assemble the people, the men and the women and the children and the alien who is in your town, in order that they may hear and learn and fear the LORD your God, and be careful to observe all the words of this law" (Deuteronomy 31:12). Such *basic*, everyday training should not be a substitute for a comprehensive, structured education which includes all of God's world and the development of specialized skills. Paul was a Pharisee, an expert in the law, as well as a tent-maker. Tent-making gave him easy access to the entire Roman Empire.

One last point needs to be made? Who should control education? Christians or non-Christians? Who should be responsible for the education of unbelievers? Christians or non- Christians? If education is not neutral, then we must come to grips with biblical reality. Christians should be educating everyone, Christian or non-Christian. We should not be content to see a dualistic education system. Non-Christians should be flocking to Christian schools (see Deuteronomy 4:1-8). Being a "good citizen" means being an obedient citizen. Obedience comes from submitting to God's law.

Much more could be said about the history of education found in the Bible. The emphasis, however, always is on Christ, with the Bible as the touchstone of truth. The home is the primary educational facility and parents are responsible for the educational process and/or the seeking out of competent teachers who can develop a comprehensive biblical world view for their children.

3. All teaching is goal-oriented. The Christian's goal is not merely to fill students' minds with facts that have no meaning, purpose or relationship to all the other facts in the universe; Christian education develops its goals from Scripture. While tests and degrees might be a part of all education, learning with a definite purpose is certainly the main element. The most obvious goal of education is dominion in the name of and for the glory of

God. This objective needs to be made concrete, however. Giving glory to God means that in thought, word, and deed we acknowledge the Triune God as our Creator, Sustainer, Provider, Lord, King, Judge, Teacher, Redeemer, Father, and Comforter.

Learning skills as an apprentice has a long history in our nation. Teachers embark on an apprenticeship program when they do "student teaching." Medical doctors spend time as interns. Trade unions rely heavily on the apprenticeship principle.

All our good works point to Him and seek to magnify His glorious character. We either glorify Him in obedience or dishonor Him in disobedience (Leviticus 26; Deuteronomy 27 and 28). Man does not *share* God's glory (Isaiah 48:11); he *manifests* it through his good works (Matthew 5:16). "Whoever speaks, let him speak, as it were, the utterances of God; whoever serves, let him do so as by the strength which God supplies; *so that in all things God may be glorified through Jesus Christ, to whom belongs the glory and dominion forever and ever.* Amen" (1 Peter 4:11). All our obedient actions point to Him and manifest His glory: "Whether, then, you eat or drink or whatever you do, do all to the glory of God" (1 Corinthians 10:31). Thomas Watson, the great Puritan expositor, writes:

The great truth is asserted, that the end [purpose or goal] of every man's living should be to glorify God. Glorifying God has respect to all the persons in the Trinity; it respects God the Father who gave us life; God the Son, who lost his life for us; and God the Holy Ghost, who produces a new life in us; we must bring glory to the whole Trinity (*A Body of Divinity*, p. 6).

The promotion of God's glory is our object. We are to strive to act so men and women may praise the God whom we profess to serve.

How do we bring glory to God *educationally*? We must remember always that education includes all of life. The very purpose of Scripture is to give us *all* we need spiritually, materially, and educationally: "All Scripture is God-breathed and is useful for teaching, rebuking, correcting and training in righteousness, so that the man of God may be equipped for every good work" (2 Timothy 3:16, 17, NIV). Notice that this is a *comprehensive* education. Over what area of life is Jesus *not* Lord? Does Jesus' authority extend to the sciences, math, and politics? Most certainly! He is the King of kings, and Lord of lords. By beginning with Scripture, the faithful student can correctly assess all of life. This does not mean all the facts relating to mathematics, medicine, engineering, and science can be found in Scripture; but without Scripture as the starting point the facts of each of these disciplines drift without meaning. As we develop each of these disciplines, using Scripture as our point of departure for interpretation, we bring glory to God.

God is glorified when, as the prophet Isaiah writes, "the earth will be full of the knowledge of the LORD as the waters cover the sea" (Isaiah 11:9; cf. Habakkuk 2:14). What is the "knowledge of the LORD"? Do we limit glorifying God by concerning ourselves with only *some* of God's creation? R. J. Rushdoony comments:

All too many pastors and teachers assume that the goal of their work is to save souls for Jesus Christ. This is not the goal: it is the starting point of their calling. The goal is to train up those under our authority in God's word so that they are well-fitted and thoroughly equipped for all good work, to go forth and to exercise dominion in the name of the Lord and for His kingdom (Gen. 1:26-28; Joshua 1:1-9; Matt. 28:18-20). We are not saved just to be saved, but to serve the Lord. We are not the focus of salvation: the Lord's calling and kingdom are. . . . The Lord says to us all, wherever we are, 'Seek ye first the kingdom of God, and his righteousness (or justice)' Matt. 6:33, so that we are called to train up the king's men, His instruments for dominion, in order to bring every area of life and thought in captivity to Jesus Christ (*The Philosophy of the Christian Curriculum*, p. 148).

In simple terms, 'glory' reflects all that God is. The goal of education for the Christian is to teach all there is about all that God is and the world He made. This means more than the pursuit of "religious study." Every fact in the universe must be seen in the full context of God's redemptive work. We do not really "know" until we take the facts of every subject back to the Triune God. The Puritans, heirs of the Reformation heritage, understood this very well: "[T]he signal contribution of the Puritans in the seventeenth-century in England was to endow [for example] the arts and sciences with something a great deal more majestic than mere utilitarian importance: that is, with redemptive value" (Robert Nisbet, *History of the Idea of Progress*, p. 130).

All education is goal oriented. In early America, the goal of education was to teach all there is to know about God and the world He made.

Can you see why education has been taken away from Christian parents and is controlled by the State? Education means *dominion*. Through our taxes we are financing the enemy. While secularists claim *neutrality* in education, they are in fact, sovereignly and independent of God, training children for dominion in the name of Man. Would the Israelites have sent their children to the Egyptian schools? Would they have maintained that their children could get a good education in the schools of Pharaoh? How about Jesus? Do think Mary and Joseph would have considered sending Jesus to a Roman school? Secular, anti-Christian educators tell us that the purpose of education is to make "good citizens." For the Humanist, the State is the most important government. Education is a *family* blessing. Yes, the State does benefit. But making good citizens is not the goal of education. As Christians, we should stop subsidizing our own destruction by supporting a public school system that is extending dominion for the sake of Man.

4. If the Christian accepts the false idea of neutrality, he or she will be robbed of all the treasures of wisdom and knowledge which are hidden in Christ alone. For too long Christians have neutralized their faith with the myth that one must be neutral when evaluating facts. "The Christian must especially challenge the idea of neutrality. 'In spite of this claim to neutrality on the part of the non-Christian, the Reformed apologist must point out that every method, the supposedly neutral one no less than any other, presupposes either the truth or the falsity of Christian theism' " (R. J. Rushdoony, *The Word of Flux*, p. 23f.). Christians often are accused of interpreting facts with certain "religious" presuppositions (first principles of interpretation) while the non-Christian maintains he is being neutral (objective and unbiased) as he interprets facts. All people, whether Christian or non-Christian, interpret their world with religious first principles. People begin from the presupposition of God and His revealed word in Scripture, or from some other (false) god. It cannot be avoided.

Scripture declares that "all the treasures of wisdom and knowledge" are hid in Christ (Colossians 2:3). If all the treasures of wisdom and knowledge are hid in Christ, then it follows that to claim neutrality would be to cut oneself off from these treasures. This would be foolish and suicidal. It would be like a soldier leaving his ammunition behind as he went into

267

battle against an enemy. If he accepted and acted on the myth of neutrality, his enemy would defeat him with little effort. Part of the Christian armament is "the sword of the Spirit, which is the word of God" (Ephesians 6:17). How can the Christian hope to battle humanistic views of factuality if his sword remains sheathed?

Paul warns of the consequences of neutrality: "See to it that no one takes you captive through philosophy and empty deception, according to the tradition of men, according to the elementary principles of the world, rather than according to Christ" (Colossians 2:8). By claiming the false premise of neutrality, the Christian becomes bound intellectually, cut off from all the treasures of God's wisdom and knowledge. Notice that in Paul's thinking there is no middle course. Either we begin with Christ and His word, or we are taken captive through philosophy and empty deception. There is no third alternative.

All facts are created by God and, thus, are comprehensively known and interpreted by Him; therefore, facts never are neutral or independent. God "has always known everything there is to know. God has never investigated any fact to learn about it, simply because there is no fact independent of Him. . . . All created things fall within the compass of God's knowledge because nothing in the universe is outside the plan and will of God" (Robert L. Reymond, *The Justification of Knowledge*, p. 43).

To claim neutrality in education, or to claim neutrality in anything, is to claim immorality. Claiming neutrality in our educational task is an attempt to erase the antithesis between Christian and non-Christian; between the Word of God and the word of man. Jesus said, "Sanctify them in the truth; Thy word is truth" (John 17:17). To approach God's Word and His world in a neutral way (a "nobody knows as yet" attitude about truth) would be a denial of the words of Jesus. It would mean that fallen man is the ultimate judge as to what truly is. This was man's first sin: Is God's Word true ("You shall die," Genesis 2:15-17), or is the word of the devil true? ("You surely shall not die," Genesis 3:4). Here we find God's Word on trial rather than the word of the creature. When the Christian or non-Christian approaches the facts with the same type of "neutrality," he sins in the same way Adam and Eve did.

The Christian no longer is to walk as unbelievers walk, "in the futility of their mind, being darkened in their understanding . . . because of the ignorance that is in them, because of the hardness of their heart" (Ephesians 4:17, 18). The Christian has the "mind of Christ" (1 Corinthians 2:16), while the unbeliever has the futile mind of the Gentiles (Ephesians 4:17). The Christian educator and student are to bring every thought into captivity "to the obedience of Christ" (2 Corinthians 10:5). If we fail to bring into captivity all our thinking, then we remain enemies in our minds before God (cf. Colossians 1:21). By following the neutrality trap we declare that Jesus' lordship has no jurisdiction educationally, thus denying His total lordship over us. The only true and effective educational system is one that sides with Christ and His interpretation of reality. Jesus said, "He who is not with Me is against Me; and he who does not gather with Me scatters" (Matthew 12:30). He leaves no room for neutrality in any area of life.

Robert L. Dabney (1820-1898) wrote: *There can be, therefore, no true education without moral culture, and no true culture without Christianity. The very power of the teacher in the school-room is either moral or it is a degrading force.*

Those who maintain they can educate without Christ engage in deception. No matter what is taught and no matter where education takes place, someone's religious values are instilled. How can one teach mathematics (absolutes), history (providence), ethics (morality), psychology (the nature of man), and biology (creation) without implying some religious opinions? Nearly a century ago Robert L. Dabney wrote this warning:

> There can be, therefore, no true education without moral culture, and no true moral culture without Christianity. The very power of the teacher in the school-room is either moral or it is a degrading force. But he can show the child no other moral basis for it than the Bible. Hence my argument is as perfect as clear. The teacher must be Christian. But the American Commonwealth has promised to have no religious character. Then it cannot be teacher (*Discussions: Secular*, 4:222f.)

Neutrality in education, as in everything else, is a myth. We educate our children either in the things of God or the things of the devil. There is no neutral ground from which we can escape that conclusion.

5. The primary educators are parents and their designated instructors. Adam and Eve were given the command to "subdue" and "rule" the created order. This is an educational task (Genesis 1:26-28). Adam and Eve were responsible for educating their children. The whole context of family life is an educational task. Children are brought into the world, reared, and educated by their parents for the purpose of subduing the universe and advancing God's kingdom. The Bible sets fathers and mothers apart as teachers. If this seems strange, it is because we have accepted an altogether distorted view of education: "Hear, O sons, the instruction of a father, and give attention that you may gain understanding, for I give you sound teaching; do not abandon my instruction" (Proverbs 4:1, 2).

Timothy is an example of extended family education. Though his father was not a believer, this did not prevent his grandmother and mother from fulfilling the task (cf. Proverbs 1:8). "From childhood" he knew the "sacred writings" (2 Timothy 3:15). The Apostle Paul informs us that Timothy's grandmother, Lois, and his mother, Eunice, gave him a biblical education (2 Timothy 1:5).

As noted above, culture advanced with music, architecture, farming, and metalurgy, although corrupted by the lack of covenant faithfulness of Cain and his descendants (Genesis 4). The responsibility for education is broad. When we say parents are responsible for educating their children we do not mean parents must do all the educating. Certainly some parents could accomplish such a task, but not all desire (or are capable) to continue the educational process they began.

God has given gifts to men and women, and parents would be negligent and foolish not to place children under the instruction of more gifted and knowledgable individuals, when we believe our own educational abilities are limited. This does not mean, however, that parents give *control* of education to others. Parents seek out teachers. If teachers prove unsatisfactory, parents have a duty to go elsewhere. For example, parents also are responsible for the physical health of their children. When a child hurts himself, parents care for the injury. When an injury occurs that cannot adequately be cared for in the home, parents seek professional help. In education as well as health care, parents control and pay for the service.

Putting our children in the hands of those who do not hold to a full-orbed biblical Christianity denies the faith. It is not enough to say that parents will *supplement* their children's education with biblical wisdom. Every fact a child encounters will be interpreted either from a God-centered perspective or a man-centered one. God demands that everything *His* children learn (for children are an inheritance from the Lord) must be from His perspective. Increase Mather wrote:

The Lord expects that you should give the children who are baptized into His name another kind of education, that you should bring them up in the nurture and admonition of the Lord. And do you not hear the Lord expostulating the case with you and saying, you have taken my children, the children that were given unto me; the children that were solemnly engaged to renounce the pomps of Satan; but is this a light matter that you have taken these my children and initiated them in the pomps and vanities of the wicked one, contrary to your covenant? What will you say in the day of the Lord's pleading with you?" (Increase Mather, "An Arrow Against Profane and Promiscuous Dancing," *The Annals of America*, 1:273).

Does the State have jurisdiction in the area of education? The Bible offers no warrant for civil government to involve itself in the education of children. The only biblical example of the State educating is a negative one. Daniel, Hananiah, Mishael, and Azariah were *compelled* to come to Babylon and serve in the king's court (Daniel 1:1-7). Israel was a subject nation. Education was used to change the direction of the nation, to eradicate Israelite covenantalism, and establish Babylonian paganism.

It is the teaching of the Bible and of sound Political ethics that the education of children belongs to the sphere of the family and is the duty of the parents. The theory that the children of the Commonwealth are the charge of the Commonwealth is a pagan one, derived from heathen Sparta and Plato's heathen republic, and connected by regular, logical sequence with legalized prostitution and the dissolution of the conjugal tie (Robert L. Dabney, *Discussions*, 4:194).

6. Whoever owns the future educates the children. God owns the future; He wants His children educated in terms of His ownership of them and the future. Satan and his earthly followers want control of the future and the power to educate the children. Marxists, and secularists in general, understand this very well. Their god, Man, controls the future. The reason why many Christians still support public (State controlled) education is because they believe that God does not control the future. In their bankrupt theologies, Satan owns the earthly future.

We can see this worked out in Israel's concept of the future. The downfall of Israel came about when parents failed to teach future generations what they knew about "the praises of the LORD, and His strength and His wondrous works that He has done" (Psalm 78:4). As a result, following generations succumbed to the false ideology of Baalism. "And all that generation [that followed Joshua and Caleb into the land of Canaan] also were gathered to their fathers; and there arose another generation after them who did not know the LORD, nor yet the work which He had done for Israel. Then the sons of Israel did evil in the sight of the LORD, and served the Baals" (Judges 2:10, 11). All of life revolved around Baalism. For them, Baal owned the future. The nation never recovered from its abandonment of the true God. The people formalized their Baalistic allegiance by forsaking their true King (1 Samuel 8:6, 7; cf. Judges 9:1-21).

Early American settlers saw and understood the future effects of educational neglect. In 1636, six years after their arrival in the New World, the Puritans of Massachusetts Bay established Harvard College. When they established the things necessary for immediate survival — houses, places of worship, and a Civil Government — their next task became the nation's future. A full-orbed biblical education was planned and implemented: "One of the next things we longed for, and looked after was to advance *Learning* and perpetuate it to Posterity; dreading to leave an illiterate Ministry to the Churches, when our present Ministry shall lie in the Dust" (Quoted in *The Modern Age: The History of the World in Christian Perspective*, Volume II, p. 242). Christian education, therefore, is because of the future not in order to insure the future. Because the future is secured by Christ, education works — education based on the sovereign Lord of history who possesses the future.

When our forefathers established the things necessary for immediate survival — houses, places of worship, and a stable civil government — their next task became the nation's educational future.

Our founders understood the relationship between education based upon biblical absolutes and the future of the nation. At its inception, Yale College demanded the same rigorous education as Harvard: "All scholars shall live religious, godly, and blameless lives according to the rules of God's Word, diligently reading the Holy Scriptures, the fountain of light and truth; and constantly attend upon all the duties of religion, both in public and secret." The students who attended Yale would be the nation's future leaders. Their education was extensive, for the development of self-government, and covered the whole range of learning: "That none may expect to be admitted into this college unless upon examination of the president and tutors, they shall be found able extempore to read, construe, and parse Tully, Virgil, and the Greek Testament; and to write true Latin in prose and to understand the rules of prosody and common arithmetic, and shall bring sufficient testimony of his blameless and inoffensive life." In addition to language study, logic, rhetoric, geometry, geography, natural philosophy, astronomy, "other parts of mathematics," metaphysics and ethics were also included in a student's comprehensive education. "[E]very Saturday shall especially be allotted to the study of divinity, and the classes shall, during the whole term, recite the Westminster Confession of Faith received and approved by the churches in this colony" (Franklin B. Dexter, *Biographical Sketches of the Graduates of Yale College with Annals of the College History*, Vol. II, p. 2f.)

Yale College, founded in 1701, stated as its primary goal that *every student shall consider the main end of his study to wit to know God in Jesus Christ and answerably to lead a Godly, sober life.*

Beyond doubt, the Christian foundation of our nation's early educational establishment did much to build this great nation. Many, however, despised the biblical emphasis. Christian-based education was seen as a threat to those who wanted a secularized religion, based on the inherent goodness of man and the perfectibility of man and society through education. This was particularly true with the rise of Deism in the late colonial period and Unitarianism in the 1820s and 1830s. Unitarians, with their belief in the perfectibility of man, founded "public education," first in Massachusetts, in the 1830s. To these early social engineers, Christianity was the enemy. Education gradually was taken out of the hands of parents and transferred to local school boards and supported through taxation. Distinctly Christian education turned into moralistic education which has led to "values clarification," wherein a "moral decision" depends upon the situation and the individual's desires, and not any revealed absolute standard of right and wrong. Our nation now reaps the rotten fruit of this secularized education.

7. Christians must take the offensive in educational matters (as in all other pursuits). Unfortunately, our efforts are usually defensive, countering the effects of a militant humanism. For example, many Christians are attempting to get prayer back in public schools instead of establishing superior models of education where the entire curriculum is Christ-centered. We fight for the scraps from humanism's table when we should supply the entire meal. The Christ-centered school approach will raise up a generation of Christians who can evaluate all of life from a biblical perspective and thus feed the world with the knowledge needed for wisdom unto salvation. Those without Christ will come to Christians for instruction as the world came to king Solomon: "Now God gave Solomon wisdom and very great discernment and breadth of mind, like the sand that is on the seashore. And Solomon's wisdom surpassed the wisdom of all the sons of the east and all the wisdom of Egypt. . . . And men came from all peoples to hear the wisdom of Solomon, from all the kings of the earth who had heard of his wisdom" (1 Kings 4:29, 30, 34). It was Daniel who was able to instruct the king while all of Nebuchadnezzar's conjurers and magicians were without knowledge (Daniel 2).

The statutes and commandments and Israel's faithfulness to them were to be a beacon for the rest of the world: "So keep them and do them, for that is your wisdom and your understanding in the sight of the peoples who will hear all these statutes and say, 'Surely this great nation is a wise and understanding people.' For what great nation is there that has a god so near to it as is the LORD our God whenever we call on Him? Or what great nation is there that has statutes and judgments as righteous as this whole law which I am setting before you today?" (Deuteronomy 4:6-8). In the same way, the people of God today are to be a city set on a hill for all the world to see (Matthew 5:13-16). This cannot be done with a smattering of prayer each day or instruction a few hours each week at worship. The entire educational process must be Christ-centered. This means the establishment of Christian schools from first grade through the graduate level: schools of medicine, music, art, science, engineering, journalism, agriculture, economics, public policy, business, law, etc.

Jesus called His followers the light of the world. As disciples of Christ this label is ours. The world lies in darkness: only in and through God's Light can the world see light.

The church can serve the world greatly, especially in education. God's law is the standard for all institutions. Those who preach and teach should become *experts* in His law so they can be of service to those who are involved in all spheres of life. James B. Jordan writes:

42. The Levites in Israel served as advisors to the state (Dt. 17:9, 18) and they sat in on court cases to help render judgments by giving professional advice concerning the Law of God (1 Chron. 23:4; 26:29-32; 2 Chron. 19:8-11). They were the closest thing to a professional lawyer class that existed in Israel, for they were experts in the law of God.

43. Thus, the tithe should be used to maintain a corps of professional theologians and legal experts, as well as educators. The Church must ever advise the state regarding its duties before God. Rightly do the confessions of the Reformation state that the civil magistrate has the power to call Church synods to advise him. In light of this, it would be proper for a church to use part of its tithe to assist men in law school, so that they will "know the enemy better" (James B. Jordan, *The Law of the Covenant: An Exposition of Exodus 21-23*, pp. 216-17).

Those who are neither professional preachers nor professional teachers, however, have a similar obligation. Each Christian is to develop and use not only his or her talents but also his or her knowledge of the Bible as fully as possible, for the glory of God. Every Christian should strive to become a person consulted by others for his or her knowledge, character, and wisdom.

The school, because it should be exclusively Christian, should be seen as an engine of Christian dominion. We should not encourage our enemies to educate their children. First, the ungodly cannot do a good job in educating their children. The blind are leading the blind. Second, we allow them to make children "sons of perdition," sons of hell. Third, Christians must evangelize and disciple the lost. While we might be able to evangelize in "government" schools, certainly discipleship cannot take place. Fourth, by bowing to a dual education system, we acquiesce to the neutrality myth. Fifth, our nation should be thoroughly Christian. All schools should seek accreditation from Christian accrediting agencies.

For many, public education is the foundation upon which our Republic rests. This is not the case. Public education is government or State education. Parents have little control and the true foundation of Jesus Christ has been cast aside. Now, the ideals of the State are pursued.

The future of our nation is dependent upon the future of the people. Will they turn to God in repentance and faith and remove the idols from their own lives?: *And many of those who practiced magic brought their books together and began burning them in the sight of all . . .* (Acts 19:19).

Lesson 10

The Future of Government

The future of government must be considered from a variety of perspectives. It is not enough to consider only the *civil* dimensions of government. As has been pointed out, the topic of government is multifaceted. The future of government must be considered in all of its dimensions, beginning with the individual and including civil affairs. If individuals abdicate responsibilities in the areas of self-, family, business, and church governments we can expect an increase of power and the claim of absolute authority by civil government. Thus, the denial of multiple governments opens the door to the leveling of society by the State. There is no future under such a system, only a god-like State imposing its will on everyone.

Moreover, the Christian's view of the future determines how he lives and works in the present. If he believes the future to be bleak, his pessimism will be reflected in a variety of ways, usually in inactivity. The family will not be trained to consider the wider aspects of dominion as they relate to successive generations. Education will be present-oriented, with students obtaining an education merely to secure the necessary credentials for a job. While Christians might establish schooling for children in grades 1-12, very little will be done to set up colleges, universities, and graduate schools to prepare *generations* of Christians to influence their professions, nation, and world for Christ. One reason students find it difficult to apply themselves in school is their inability to work for a purpose, which in turn is largely due to many Christians' neglect of their divinely ordained duty of dominion: to create a Christian civilization.

A pessimistic view of the future, with the State embracing all other governments, fosters economic theory and practice that incites a buy-now-

and-pay-later philosophy. Why worry about debt when there may not be a future, and I may not have to repay my loan? Moreover, why consider leaving an inheritance when there will be no earthly future to inherit?

I will place no value on anything I have or may possess, except in relation to the kingdom of Christ, it shall be given away or kept, only as by giving or keeping of it I shall most promote the glory of Him to whom I owe all my hopes in time and eternity.

—David Livingstone

Christians, for too long, have believed the future should be considered only in terms of heaven or the events that lead to the second coming of Jesus Christ. Events and concerns about the time "in between" have been considered of little real importance. Because of this false idea, many Christians abdicate their responsibilities toward economics, education, science, and civil government. This conception of the future has accelerated the debilitating doctrine that the end of all things is near, leading to further inactivity on the part of God's people. God instructed His people to influence the world:

The apostle Paul had to rebuke some of the Thessalonians for ceasing to work simply because of the possibility that the Lord might return immediately (2 Thessalonians 3:10-12). Christians since then have often been notorious for embracing escapist attitudes toward work due to their eschatologies [doctrine of the last things]. Rather than aggressively moving forward to take dominion over the earth, the Church has all too often lapsed into an irresponsible passivity, approaching her commission with the attitude: "You don't polish brass on a sinking ship." Jesus, however, instructed us to take the opposite approach. In the parable of the ten minas (Luke 19:11-27), the master gave each of his servants money and told them, *"Do business with this until I come back."* In this story,

Jesus commands us to take the offensive and "do business" until He returns (Joseph McAuliffe, "Do Business Until I Return," *New Wine*, [January, 1982], p.29).

The biblical view of the future presents the truth that history is moving forward, and every Christian is responsible before God to show himself a good and faithful steward of his God-given gifts. God requires an accounting.

The pagan idea of time presents history as a series of never-ending cycles with little, if any, purpose. King Nebuchadnezzar of Babylon dreamed vividly about future purpose and development, not a series of never-ending cycles confining man to the impersonal forces of nature. The king understandably was confused about his dream because it did not fit the pagan idea of the future. After the age of iron, the age of gold should have reappeared. At the dream's conclusion, however, a new dimension was added to this pagan ruler's understanding. Time is not governed by cycles, but by God. Time is linear, with a purpose. Time is governed not by forces of nature, but by the sovereign decree of God. Nebuchadnezzar tried to adapt his pagan view with the "revealed" view. He built a golden statue, seeing himself as the one who would change the pagan cyclical history and avoid the inevitable judgment through the accomplishments of his power and authority.

The kingdom of God has purpose because God directs its every movement. History is not bound by a never-ending series of cycles, with God powerless to intervene and govern. The future, as Nebuchadnezzar came to realize, is governed by God. Earthly sovereigns who fail to recognize God's absolute sovereignty will be destroyed: "You [Nebuchadnezzar] continued looking [at the statue] until a stone was cut out without hands, and it struck the statue on its feet of iron and clay, and crushed them. Then the iron, the clay, the bronze, the silver and the gold were crushed all at the same time, and became like chaff from the summer threshing floors; and the wind carried them away so that not a trace of them was found. But the stone that struck the statue became a great mountain and filled the whole earth" (Daniel 2:34-35). The pagan idea of the future is a myth. The future belongs to God's people and Christians are not trapped in futile historical cycles.

The Christian's view of the future determines how he lives, plans, and

281

works in the present *for the future*. Even during Israel's captivity under Babylonian rule, the nation's darkest hour, the people were told to plan and build for the future: "Build houses and live in them; and plant gardens, and eat their produce. Take wives and become the fathers of sons and daughters, and take wives for your sons and give your daughters to husbands, that they may bear sons and daughters; and multiply there and do not decrease....For I know the plans that I have for you, 'declares the LORD,' plans for welfare and not for calamity to give you a future and a hope" (Jeremiah 29:5-6, 11).

God's words seemed contrary to what people saw all around them. Destruction and captivity awaited the nation, yet God commanded them to prepare for the *future*. In spite of every pessimistic view, God wanted the people's desires and hopes to be future-directed. Build for what will be. The psychological benefit of such a mind-set does much to spur the church of Jesus Christ to greater kingdom activity. A preoccupation with defeat brings defeat by default. Why would anyone wish to build for the future when there is no earthly future hope? Who would invest in a losing proposition? Why should anyone work to establish a godly home, school, business, or civil government when all such institutions seemed doomed despite our efforts?

Christians must become confident of their earthly future as well as their heavenly future. We must take God at His word as did Joshua and Caleb (Numbers 13-14). Things looked bad for Israel (13:32-33), but God's promise of victory allowed Joshua and Caleb to look beyond the apparently negative circumstances. God, on numerous occasions, promised Israel they would possess the land: "Send out for yourself men so that they may spy out the land of Canaan, *which I am going to give to the sons of Israel* ..."(13:2). Since the majority refused to believe God, they died in the wilderness, never seeing the promised land. Like Joshua and Caleb, we must trust God's sovereignty and be future-oriented: "We must become *optimists* concerning the victory that lies before Christ's people, in time and on earth. We must be even more optimistic than Joshua and Caleb, for they were only asked to spy out the land of Canaan. They were called to give their report prior to Christ's sacrifice at Calvary. Why should we be pessimistic, like that first generation of former slaves? Why should we wander in the wilderness, generation after generation? Why should we

282

despair?"(Gary North, *Unconditional Surrender*, p.214). The hope of the future is real because the Christian knows that God governs the affairs of men and nations (Psalm 22:28; 47:8; Daniel 4:35).

Too much power is given to the devil and his minions. Christians often forget that Satan is a fallen creature subject to God's judgments.

Questions for Discussion

1. How does the Christian's understanding of God as Creator, Provider, and Sustainer of all things affect his understanding of the future of governments?(Genesis 1:1; Isaiah 43:23, 24; John 1:13; Ephesians 1:11; Colossians 1:17; Hebrews 1:3)

_____

_____

_____

_____

_____

_____

2. How does an individual's perspective of the future influence his present life and how he builds for the future? (Numbers 13-14; 1 John 4:4; cf. Joshua 2:8-14)

_____

_____

_____

_____

_____

_____

3. How does sin affect the future of all governments? (Genesis 2:17; 3:17-19; Judges 2:10ff.; 4:4-10, 17-22; 5:24-31; 7:3; 9:14, 15; 17:6; 1 Samuel 2:12-36; 8:1-22)

_____

_____

_____

_____

_____

_____

4. What is the future of government for those who reject Jesus Christ as Lord, Savior, and King?(1 Samuel 8; Daniel 1-6)

_____
_____
_____
_____
_____
_____

5. What is the future of government when the righteous and productive turn rulership over to the corrupt?(Judges 9:1-21; Proverbs 28:12; Zechariah 1:18-21)

_____
_____
_____
_____
_____

6. Must the forces of evil triumph?(2 Timothy 3; Galatians 6:9)

_____
_____
_____
_____

7. What role does Satan play in the future of government? (Job 2:6; Luke 10:17-19; 11:14-26; John 14:30; 16:11; Romans 16:20; Colossians 1:13; Hebrews 2:14; James 4:7; 1 John 3:8; 5:18)

_____
_____
_____
_____
_____
_____

Summary

"*That the world should be saved!* Here is one of the most oft-quoted passages of all the Bible, and so often we miss the point. Jesus Christ came to save the *world* — not just a sinner here, a sinner there. He wants us to disciple the *nations* — not just a few individuals. The Lord Jesus will not be satisfied in the success of His mission until the whole earth is singing His praises. On the basis of God's infallible promises, the Church must pray and work for the expansion of the Kingdom, with the expectation that God will fill His Church with 'a great multitude, which no one can count, from every nation and all tribes and peoples and tongues'(Rev. 7:9).

"We must stop acting as if we are forever destined to be a sub-culture. *We are destined for dominion;* we should straighten up and start acting like it" (David Chilton, *Paradise Restored: An Eschatology of Dominion*, p. 218).

The Lord Jesus will not be satisfied in the success of His mission until the whole earth is singing His praises. The kingdom of God will be extended as the people of God remain faithful in all things.

Answers to Questions for Discussion

1. God is the Creator and Sustainer of *all* things (Genesis 1:1; John 1:3); therefore, the universe and its design are not random. Many see the universe as a clock or machine created billions of years ago, left to run according to its built-in devices ("the laws of nature"). This is the "theology" of deism: "Essentially, deism 'reduces' the number of features God is said to display. [For the deist], He is a transcendent force or energy, a Prime Mover or First Cause, a beginning to the otherwise infinite regress of past causes. But he is really not a *he*, though the Personal pronoun remains in the language used about him. Certainly, he does not *care* for this creation; he does not *love* it. He has no 'personal' relation to it at all" (James W. Sire, *The Universe Next Door: A Basic World View Catalog*, p. 49).

While many people do not consider themselves deists, they hold some basic tenets of deism. For example, they show little interest in history or the belief that God presently works to bring His purposes on earth to fruition, though our Lord commands us to pray, "Thy Kingdom come. Thy will be done, on *earth* as it is in heaven" (Matthew 6:10). God will act at the *end* of history, the deist-thinker assumes, but does not work "all things after the counsel of His will," with present concern for earthly matters (Ephesians 1:11). He concerns Himself only with the future *new* heavens and the *new* earth. The deist-thinking individual thus considers the present status of history unimportant. The consummation of all things should be the only historical event that really matters; therefore, interest in governmental affairs, because they are temporal and of this world, appear irrelevant to the Christian's purpose and unworthy of his efforts.

The Bible presents a different emphasis. The Lordship of Jesus Christ includes heavenly and earthly things, eternal and temporal matters. God providentially cares for His creation by holding all things together, including the operations of governmental systems: "And He [Jesus] is the radiance of His glory and the exact representation of His nature, and upholds *all things* by the word of His power" (Hebrews 1:3; cf. Colossians 1:17). "God did not create the world, so as afterwards to allow it to be

287

governed by chance, but...he undertakes the preservation of it, and keeps it under his power and authority.... God's government extends far and wide, so that he directs and governs everything according to his pleasure" (John Calvin, *Commentary on Isaiah*, 3:228).

The future of earthly governments is included in God's upholding of all things because all governments are controlled by God and are expected to follow His commandments. For a time they may seem to oppose His purposes and control, but continual rebellion will bring about their destruction (cf. Daniel 5).

Jezebel was a tyrant who met with a just end (2 Kings 9:35, 36). God's enemies are destined to perish. The Bible makes it clear that the enemies of God *will not make further progress; for their folly will be obvious to all* (2 Timothy 3:9).

Governments of the earth, though they impress us with their power, appear insignificant in the eyes of God: "Behold, the nations are like a drop from a bucket, and are regarded as a speck of dust on the scales; behold, He lifts up the islands like fine dust....All the nations are as nothing before Him, they are regarded by Him as less than nothing and meaningless" (Isaiah 40:15, 17). The Christian does not have to fear the designs of nations because "it is [God] who reduces rulers to nothing, who makes the judges of the earth meaningless. Scarcely have they been planted, scarcely have they been sown, scarcely has their stock taken root in the earth, but He merely blows on them, and they wither, and the storm carries them away like stubble" (vv. 23-24). Nor must the Christian fear that the design of those who would autonomously merge all nations under one *world government* will overcome the plan and providential government of God. Like its earlier prototype at the Tower of Babel, this, too, will be destroyed of its own inherent weaknesses, in the providence of God. (This is not to say that Christians should not *oppose* the ungodly schemes and plots of the rulers of the nations and the proponents of a one-world government! Far from it. Christians should be in the forefront of those opposing such wicked schemes.)

2. When Israel was taken to the borders of the promised land, twelve spies were sent to survey the land and report to the nation (Numbers 13). Before choosing twelve representatives for the task, God *promised* the land would be theirs: "Send out for yourself men so that they may spy out the land of Canaan, which *I am going to give to the sons of Israel*; you shall send a man from each of their fathers' tribes, every one a leader among them" (v. 2). No matter what the spies encountered, the *promise* of God should have had priority and overruled any desire to retreat. When the spies returned, ten brought back pessimistic (unbelieving) reports (vv. 28-29, 31-33). Two spies, Joshua and Caleb, returned with optimistic reports because they believed God and not the fears of men, nor the circumstances they encountered (v. 30). It is important to note that Caleb never denied that there were "giants in the land," but believed God was stronger than any army of giants. Why is this so?: "You are from God, little children, and have overcome them; because greater is He that is in you than he who is in the world" (1 John 4:4).

289

The nation responded to the report without faith. In effect, they called God a liar: "Then all the congregation lifted up their voices and cried, and the people wept that night" (14:1). Their refusal to believe the promise of God (cf.13:2) brought judgment upon the entire nation. Israel did not enter the promised land until forty years passed and the unbelieving generation died (14:26-38). Their pessimistic perspective of the future affected their plans for the future. The task of dominion was seen as too great for God, hence too great for man under God's providence. Instead of moving forward they chose retreat to the past: "Would that we had died in the land of Egypt! Or would that we had died in the wilderness! And why is the LORD bringing us into this land, to fall by the sword? Our wives and our little ones will become plunder; would it not be better for us to return to Egypt? 'So they said to one another,' Let us appoint a leader and return to Egypt" (14:2-4).

A pessimistic faith ruins Christian vitality. Israel lost forty years of dominion because the nation trusted the words of men and the circumstances of the world more than the word of God. When Israel entered the land forty years later, Rahab told the two unnamed spies what the inhabitants were thinking: "For we have heard how the LORD dried up the water of the Red Sea before you when you came out of Egypt, and what you did to the two kings of the Amorites who were beyond the Jordan, to Sihon and Og, whom you utterly destroyed. And when we heard it, *our hearts melted and no courage remained in any man any longer because of you*" (Joshua 2:10-11). The Canaanites looked upon the Israelites, at the time Israel was freed from Egyptian bondage over forty years before, as the giants. Forty years of constructive dominion were wasted because Israel failed to trust the God who possesses the future (and controls the present in order to fulfill His plan for the future).

3. Sin put man in ethical (moral) rebellion against God and His purposes. Man's moral rebellion affects every aspect of the created order. Man's ethical rebellion pollutes the earth, spiritually and materially. Spiritual as well as physical death are now the order of things: "For in the day that you eat from [the tree of the knowledge of good and evil] you shall surely die" (Genesis 2:17). The world as we know it manifests the effects of the fall through the created order (3:17-19). Self-government affects all

God's promises cannot fail. God told Israel that the land was *flowing with milk and honey*. The fruit they returned with showed that His promises were indeed true. The Israelites lost 40 years of dominion activity because they failed to believe that God is greater than any giant.

other governments. The pollution of family, church, and State directly results from man's single rebellion against God.

The people of God, regenerated in Christ, must not remain passive in light of the curse, but are commanded to counter the effects of the fall through becoming both salt and light. In the ancient world, salt acted to stop decay, acting as a preservative. Christians are to act as salt, countering the effects of the fall with the preserving attributes of the preaching of the gospel and the implementation of God's moral order. Light cuts

291

through darkness so paths may be seen and travelled.

In order for the Christian people to have a preservative effect on the world (or this country), they must, as Francis Schaeffer said, take charge of the cultural direction. This means that wherever a Christian finds himself he must, as God's vice-regent, control that particular area for God. To direct anything one must be in control of it. In other words, as commanded by God, the regenerate man is to subdue the earth (Genesis 1:28). To be sure, the Fall has affected this command but only in that it will take more sweat by regenerate man to accomplish God's purpose (John W. Whitehead, *The Separation Illusion*, p.173).

The steady decline of a nation and the absence of hope for the future can be traced to the spiritual condition of God's people — the rejection of the Messiahship of the Lord Jesus Christ for the messiahship of the State. The book of Judges depicts a nation's spiritual decline and the consequent effects on every aspect of culture, including civil government: A biblical education was abandoned (Judges 2:10); everyone did what was right in his own eyes (17:6); paganism was rampant (2:11-13); men abdicated their leadership responsibilities (4:4-10, 17-22; 5:24-31); cowardice prevailed (7:3); the citizens failed to act responsibly, and so turned over leadership to the "bramble men" (9:14, 15).

The outworking of sin in a culture distorts a generation's perspective of what can and should be done to return the nation to its glory. A people's abandonment of the truth that God is the sovereign Lord of history opens the way for the growth of sinful views and actions, because it leads Christians to retreat from dominion activity and surrender their culture to God's enemies. Israel's spiritual condition became so bad that they saw no hope for the future unless they forsook their true King and chose a king "like all the other nations" (1 Samuel 8:4-9). The people of Israel did not understand that the reformation of a nation must begin with the individuals who make up the nation.

The future of government is dark indeed when men lose their faith in God's plan for victory over His enemies, and in His providential control of history to bring His plan to fulfillment.

4. The rejection of Jesus Christ as Lord, Savior, and King by a nation means that nation has chosen another lord, savior, and king. God judges all nations that refuse to submit to His kingship.

Sometimes he musters up hail and mildew; sometimes he sends regiments of wild beasts; so he threatens Israel (Lev. xxvi. 22). Sometimes he sends out a party of angels to beat up the quarters of men, and make a carnage among them (2 Kings xix. 35). Sometimes he mounts his thundering battery, and shoots forth his ammunition from the clouds, as against the Philistines (1 Sam. vii. 10). Sometimes he sends the slightest creatures to shame the pride and punish the sin of man, as "lice, frogs, locusts," as upon the Egyptians (Stephen Charnock, *Discourses upon the Existence and Attributes of God*, Volume 2, p. 394).

Neutrality is not an option (Joshua 24:15), not even a possibility (cf. Matthew 7:24). By rejecting justice, mercy, and grace, the people choose injustice, tyranny, and coercion. 1 Samuel 8 shows what happens to a people, blinded by sin, who see force as a hope for the nation, and never realize that their choice will eventually be turned against them.

Several aspects of the state which rejects God are here cited: *First,* an anti-biblical military conscription will be instituted and enforced. *Second,* there will be compulsory labor battalions conscripted for state service. *Third,* the conscription will be of young men and young women, and of animals as well. *Fourth,* the state will expropriate property, both landed property and livestock. *Fifth,* because the state is now playing god-king, it will demand like God a tithe, a tenth of man's increase as its tax. *Sixth,* God will not hear a people who are complaining at paying the price for their sins (R. J. Rushdoony, *Institutes of Biblical Law*, p. 34f.)

The church of Jesus Christ must realize and convince the nation that its hope will not be realized by restoration of the political sphere alone. Certainly, politics cannot be ignored; politics, however, cannot turn the nation around, nor is politics the source of our problems. An oppressive State *results* from the rebellion of the *people:* "Then the sons of Israel did evil in the sight of the LORD, and served the Baals...And the anger of the LORD burned against Israel, and He gave them into the hands of plunderers who plundered them; and He sold them into the hands of their enemies around them, so that they could no longer stand before their enemies" (Judges 2:11, 14). The future looks bleak when a nation transfers its trust from God, who fights for His people, to man, who is but a breath: "Stop regarding man, whose breath of life is in his nostrils; for why should he be esteemed?"(Isaiah 2:22; cf. Zechariah 4:6; Isaiah 30:1-5). God's people must reassert their dominion responsibility under God by reconstructing the family, education, the media, the arts, the sciences and all other areas of thought and life.

Prior to the Reformation of the 16th century, things looked bleak. The reformers admonished the people to *stop regarding man, whose breath of life is in his nostrils; for why should he be esteemed* (Isaiah 2:22).

5. Judges 9 contrasts the rule of the nation by "worthless and reckless fellows" (v. 4) with rule by productive and godly men (vv. 8-15). Jotham's parable shows that rule by the "bramble men" results from a nation's desire for centralized power to cure all social ills. A nation prospers, say the bramble seekers, not by servanthood but by lording it over the weak:

If the bramble had never been made king, he would not have been in a position to enforce his threats. Having made him king, however, the trees must hearken to his vicious threats, for they have delivered to him the power to enforce his vengeful will.

The point of the parable is that good men do not desire to lord it over others. Good men are happy being productive for God and for their fellowmen. They realize that the road to greatness is the way of the servant, as their Lord taught (Mark 10:42-45). The only kind of men who desire political authority for its own sake are bramble men — unproductive men who seek to attain fame and fortune by taking it from others who are productive.

The political inactivity of Christians and of their sometime fellow travellers, the conservatives, in our modern society is partly explained by this parable. Christians are oriented toward serving God and man through the marketplace. Their satisfaction comes through productivity. They believe that the solution for modern social problems is faith in God and hard, productive work. Unfortunately, most modern men look to the state, to the bramble, for answers.

Those who greatly desire to be kings are usually the least qualified for the post. Far wiser government generally comes from those who only reluctantly shoulder the heavy burdens of office. The good wise trees were reluctant; the bramble was anxious to rule (James B. Jordan, *Judges: God's War Against Humanism*, p. 166).

Jotham makes it clear that the bramble offered only tyranny. The bramble is a thorny plant (Psalm 58:9) that symbolizes the curse of the ground (Genesis 3:18; Matthew 27:29). The bramble promised shade but crept along the ground, providing no possibility of shade. Any refusal to follow the will of the bramble meant destruction for the mightiest trees: "And the bramble said to the trees, 'If in truth you are anointing me as king over you, come and take refuge in my shade; but if not, may fire come out from the bramble and consume the cedars of Lebanon'"(v. 15).

The future of government, therefore, resides in the hands of the godly. Bemoaning the "fact" of the nation's future collapse simply indicts the redeemed community: "When the righteous triumph, there is glory, but when the wicked rise, men hide themselves" (Proverbs 28:12). A declining nation can be turned around if the godly remain productive in their dominion tasks and take leadership positions as they have opportunity. Christians must never fail to realize, however, that the solution to modern social problems is faith in God and hard, productive work. The prophet Zechariah, in chapter 1, verses 18-21, points out that long-term dominion does not come solely from political power (represented by the four horns), but by diligent service for God and His kingdom (represented by the four craftsmen). Politics must not be seen as the ultimate solution to our problems as the bramble men believe. Rather, the area of civil government is but one area among many that must be transformed by the regenerating power of Jesus Christ and obedience to His commandments.

Gideon's sons were killed by Abimelech. Abimelech sought to remove all governmental competition to consolidate power in himself. He and his supporters are called *worthless and reckless fellows* (Judges 9:4).

6. The Apostle Paul informs Timothy "that in the last days difficult times will come" (2 Timothy 3:1). The ungodly will manifest a variety of characteristics which evidence their opposition to God's purposes: "For men will be lovers of self, lovers of money, boastful, arrogant, evildoers, disobedient to parents, ungrateful, unholy, etc."(vv.2-5). Timothy is told to "avoid such men as these" (v.5). Questions remain, however. When are the last days? Will the ungodly dominate culture? When Christians see these characteristics surfacing, how should they respond?

When are the last days? A distinction must be made between the "last days" (2 Timothy 3:1; Hebrews 1:1-2) and "the end of the age" (Matthew 13:39). The phrase the "last days" is contrasted with the days before Jesus came to earth: "God, after He spoke long ago to the fathers in the prophets in many portions and in many ways [in the former days], *in these last days* has spoken to us in His Son, whom He appointed heir of all things, through whom also He made the world" (Hebrews 1:1-2). The writer to the Hebrew Christians made it clear that he and they were living in the last days.

Peter sees the fulfillment of Joel's prophecy as being applicable to the people who heard his message at the feast of Pentecost: "And it shall be in the last days, 'God says,' I will pour forth of My Spirit upon all mankind" (Acts 2:17). Jesus makes the same declaration when He states: "And whoever shall speak a word against the Son of Man, it shall be forgiven him; but whoever shall speak against the Holy Spirit, it shall not be forgiven him, either *in this age*, or *in the age to come*" (Matthew 12:32). Finally, Paul makes this striking assertion: "Now these things happened to them [the Israelites who wandered in the wilderness] as an example, and they were written for our instruction, *upon whom the end of the ages have come*" (1 Corinthians 10:11).

Will the ungodly dominate culture? A cursory reading of 2 Timothy 3 would seem, at first reading, to indicate that the ungodly will prevail, and godly influence decline. Further study shows that the Apostle Paul offers a different conclusion. Paul compares the progress of the ungodly in Timothy's day with that of Jannes and Jambres, the Egyptian sorcerer-priests who opposed Moses (cf.Exodus 7:11): "But they will not make further progress; for their folly will be obvious to all, as also that of those two came to be" (2 Timothy 3:9). While it is true there is an *attempt* by the ungodly to dominate culture, the fact is, "they will not make further progress"; their fling with ungodliness is only temporary (cf. Romans 1:18-32). The Christian can remain optimistic even if ungodly actions increase. In time, if Christians remain faithful in influencing their world with the gospel, actions of the ungodly will be eliminated.

The enemies of God will meet the same end as the sorcerer high priests who sought to challenge God through Aaron and Moses. Their serpent-staffs were consumed by the serpent-staff of Aaron.

298

Paul, however, does not allow the Christian to remain passive as the ungodly self-destruct. Timothy has followed Paul's "teaching, conduct, purpose, faith, patience, love, perseverance, persecutions, [and] sufferings" (2 Timothy 3:10-11) and he calls on us to do the same (vv. 16-17). While the ungodly expend their spiritual capital in present-oriented living, and, therefore, have nothing saved for the future, the Christian is to develop future-oriented spiritual capital to replace the bankrupt culture of humanism with a Christ-centered society. Notice that the characteristics of the ungodly are all self-directed and short-lived, summarized by this phrase: "lovers of pleasure rather than lovers of God" (v. 4). Sin has its pleasure for a short period of time: "He who loves pleasure will become a poor man; he who loves wine and oil will not become rich" (Proverbs 21:17). The love of pleasure is no investment in the future.

The characteristics of the godly are future directed, foregoing the lure of present pleasures for the benefit of future productivity. Teaching, conduct, purpose, faith, patience, love and perseverance take time and energy from the present, but result in future reward. For example, the farmer could consume all of his harvested grain in a year's time and have none to plant for the following year. By consuming just enough grain to feed his family and storing reserves for a potential poor crop along with some for planting, he guarantees his family security and a dominion status for the future. While the present-oriented consumer furiously looks for a way to feed his family, the future-oriented farmer spends his free time exercising godly dominion in his culture. Moreover, persecutions and sufferings should not deter the future-oriented Christian because "out of them all the Lord" delivers us (2 Timothy 3:11). In the same way, the future-oriented farmer can overcome the effects of a bad harvest because his store allows him to live until the next harvest. The effects of a bad harvest for the present-oriented consumer is disastrous. With no reserves, he possesses no hope for the future.

If the Christian looks only at present happenings he loses his hope of becoming a cultural influence, since he perceives the statement, "evil men and impostors will proceed from bad to worse, deceiving and being deceived" (2 Timothy 3:13) as something permanent. But we also must remember the previous words of Paul: "But they will not make further progress; for their folly will be obvious to all" (v. 9). In the short-term, it

The mouth of hell awaits all of God's enemies. In time, if Christians remain faithful in influencing their world with the gospel, actions of the ungodly will be eliminated.

appears that the ungodly will prevail. Christians, however, must begin to think long-term; while the ungodly burn themselves out, the godly steadily influence their world: "You, however, *continue* in the things you have learned and become convinced of" (v.14). In time the effects of dominion will be seen: "And let us not lose heart in doing good, for in due time we shall reap if we do not grow weary" (Galatians 6:9).

7. Satan has power, but it is limited by God. Even in the Old Testament, Satan's influence was restricted. Before Satan could afflict Job he had to seek God's permission: "Behold, all that he [Job] has is in your power, only do not put forth your hand on him" (Job 1:12; cf.2:6). Through it all God received glory and Job was restored (42:10-17). During Jesus' ministry on earth, the disciples had authority and power over demons because Satan's power was grounded. When the seventy disciples returned from their mission they remarked that "even the demons are subject to us" (Luke 10:17). How could this be?: "And He said to them, 'I was watching Satan fall from heaven like lightning. Behold, I have given you authority to tread upon serpents and scorpions, and over all the power of the enemy, and nothing shall injure you'" (vv. 17-18). Jesus tells the Pharisees that His casting out demons is the sign that the kingdom of God has come, displacing the enemy territory of Satan: "But if I cast out demons by the finger of God, then the kingdom of God has come upon you. When a strong man [Satan] fully armed guards his own household, his possessions are undisturbed; but when someone stronger than he attacks him and overpowers him, he takes away from him all his armor on which he had relied, and distributes his plunder [Satan's kingdom]" (11:10-22).

When Jesus prepared to go to the cross, He spoke of the effect Satan will have on His work: "I will not speak much more with you, for the ruler of the world is coming, and he has nothing in Me" (John 14:30). All the powers of death could not deter Jesus from the task that would energize the church so even the gates of Hell could not stand against her power: "Upon this rock [the sure testimony that Jesus is the Christ, the Son of the living God] I will build My church; and the gates of Hades shall not overpower it" (Matthew 16:18). The Christian is able to spoil the works of the devil because Satan has limited power over believers. He cannot "touch" a Christian (1 John 5:18); his works have been destroyed (1 John 3:8); he must flee when resisted (James 4:7); and he has been rendered powerless over believers (Hebrews 2:14).

The above scriptural evidence is useless if Christians assume Satan is now in control and his controlling influence will continue. Of course, where Christians do nothing we can expect Satan's kingdom to advance. The world lies in the power of the evil one (1 John 5:19) as long as Christians refuse to plant and water the seeds of the gospel in the world. Satan's power over the world is temporary, lasting only until the nations are discipled (cf. Matthew 28:18-20). Christians have no excuse, because God has "disarmed the rulers and authorities [and] made a public display of them, having triumphed over them through Him [Jesus]"(Colossians 2:15).

Christ's crucifixion brought the false powers to light. Jesus has exposed the powers of darkness (cf. Luke 1:79; 1 Corinthians 4:5, 6; Colossians 1:13). They are, in fact, powerless over the kingdom of Jesus Christ. The kingdom of God, when compared to the kingdom of Satan, presents a radical contrast. Satan's mask of deception has been torn from him. Christ's resurrection proved that what appeared as a triumph for Satan and his followers, actually was folly. The gates of Satan's kingdom are vulnerable and will be carried away by the advancing church of Jesus Christ (cf. Judges 16:1-3). This will be made possible under the power of God's Holy Spirit working through obedient, dominion-oriented Christians (Matthew 16:18). Victory for the people of God is certain: not because of their own strength, but because of the strength of the One whom they serve, even Jesus Christ, unto whom all power in heaven and earth has been given, and who is with His people always, even unto the end of the age (Matthew 28:18-20). The Christian's hope resides in the resurrected Jesus Christ who sits at the right hand of His Father. Present-day Christians must know the present-day power of that resurrection and act upon it (cf. Philippians 3:10; Romans 6:5).

The power of Jesus' resurrection is ours as we work to turn a wilderness into a garden.

Books for Further Reading and Study

The purpose of the *God and Government* textbook series is to give Christians an overview of what the Bible says about government, particularly civil government. *God and Government: The Restoration of the Republic*, the third volume in the three-volume *God and Government* series, was not designed to answer all the questions raised regarding authority, education, human rights, citizenship, leadership, the judicial system, and the restoration of the republic. In order to take the student further in his or her study, a list of books and newsletters has been provided covering a variety of topics relating to this study. A number of these books are out of print. I have included a list of out-of-print book services that can assist you in locating them for your library.

I. Authority

Davis, John Jefferson. *Foundations of Evangelical Theology*. Grand Rapids, MI: Baker Book House, 1984. A very readable treatment of the importance of theology and its application to the Christian experience. The nature of biblical authority is discussed from many angles. The chapter on "Reason: A Kingdom-Extending Tool" is especially helpful: "Reason is neither an autonomous master nor a useless appendage, but a servant of the resurrected and reigning Christ in the extension of his kingdom" (p. 130).

Elwell, Walter L., ed. *Evangelical Dictionary of Theology*. Grand Rapids, MI: Baker Book House, 1984. Covers the fields of systematic theology, historical theology, biblical theology, philosophical theology, and theological ethics. Related to this volume of *God and Government*, there are articles on "Authority in the Bible," "Authority in the Church," and "Authority of the Bible." In addition, "Conscience," "Reason," and "Tradition" are treated in some detail.

Friesen, Gary. *Decision Making and the Will of God*. Portland, OR: Multnomah Press, 1980. While this book does not approach the topic of authority directly, the issue of authority is found on nearly every page. The importance of this work is that it takes the Bible seriously without adding the familiar competitors to biblical authority like feelings and circumstances.

Hughes, Philip Edgcumbe. *Christian Ethics in Secular Society*. Grand Rapids, MI: Baker Book House, 1983. Ethics is theological in nature. Non-Christian ethics is man-centered while Christian ethics, rooted in Scripture, is God-centered. There is a full treatment of "Conscience" and its role as a reliable basis for authority.

Marston, George W. *The Voice of Authority.* Nutley, NJ: Presbyterian and Reformed, 1960. A full discussion of authority. "He contends, and rightly so, that every man finds his Voice of Authority either in God or in man. And he upholds unswervingly God as the Voice of Authority and rejects uncompromisingly man as the Voice of Authority."

Rushdoony, Rousas John. *By What Standard?* Tyler, TX: Thoburn Press, (1958) 1983. What is the basis of all thinking? Rushdoony answers this question by postulating that God is the only valid principle of interpretation, not only of theology, but of philosophy, science, and indeed all knowledge. All other supposed authorities, human reason included, must come under the jurisdiction of Scripture.

_____. *Infallibility. An Inescapable Concept.* Vallecito, CA: Ross House Books, 1978. The concept of authority is never in dispute. Authority ultimately resides in man, the group, the State or God; it is an "inescapable concept." The one claiming ultimate authority also claims infallibility. Rushdoony directs us to the self-contained God of Scripture as the only infallible, independent, and infinite authority.

_____. *The One and the Many.* Nutley, NJ: The Craig Press, 1971. In order to steer a proper course between anarchy and totalitarianism, an authority outside the will of the individual and the collective will of the State must be established. Rushdoony directs us to Scripture and its doctrine of the Trinity as the answer to the problem of the one and the many.

_____. *The Word of Flux.* Fairfax, VA: Thoburn Press, 1975. When man jettisons God as the starting point in determining what can be known, man's word is without stability and becomes a "word of flux." In such a condition, man is unable to come to grips with the true nature and use of authority.

Van Til, Cornelius. *A Christian Theory of Knowledge.* Phillipsburg, NJ: Presbyterian and Reformed, 1969. The author believes that "human autonomy is the root of all forms of non-Christian thought." Scripture is the only foundation of knowledge.

_____. *The Defense of the Faith* Phillipsburg, NJ: Presbyterian and Reformed, (1955) 1967. For too long Christians have attempted to steer a middle course between absolute biblical authority and autonomous reason. Somehow, it is believed, the natural man is able to evaluate the facts without dependence upon God's Special revelation and thus is able to know God and the created universe. Van Til maintains that all men must start with God if true knowledge is to be found.

Van Til, Henry R. *The Calvinistic Concept of Culture.* Grand Rapids, MI: Baker Book House, 1959. The transformation of culture is a reality only when it has something by which it can be transformed. A fixed authority is needed. For Van Til, Scripture "constitutes the final reference point for man's thinking, willing, acting, loving, hating, for his culture."

305

II. Education

Adams, Blair and Joel Stein. *Who Owns the Children? Compulsory Education and the Dilemma of Ultimate Authority.* Austin, TX: Truth Forum, (1984) 1989. While most parents are concerned with the quality of education, most educators understand that the battle is for the control of education. This book is a detailed analysis of the control factor in education. The authors go even further by establishing that Christians are engaged in a religious war with the Messianic State. This book should be on everyone's reading list.

Adams, Jay. *Back to the Blackboard. Design for a Biblical Christian School.* Phillipsburg, NJ: Presbyterian and Reformed, 1982. The author not only wants Christians to break away from the theoretical and philosophical basis of secular education, he also wants Christians to rethink the purpose and methods of education.

Blumenfeld, Samuel. *Is Public Education Necessary?* Boise, ID: The Paradigm Company, (1981) 1984. Those who are convinced of the merits of public education need to read this book. "This book tells, for the first time, the story of how and why Americans gave up educational freedom so early in their history for the imagined benefits of state-controlled education."

_____. *NEA: Trojan Horse in American Education.* Boise, ID: The Paradigm Company, 1984. The NEA (National Educational Association), which represents nearly 2 million teachers, has become a potent political force that is threatening our freedom. The NEA proposes educational legislation and lobbies state and federal legislatures. The effects have been devastating: the closing of non-public, church related schools that compete against the non-competitive public school systems. The history and detailed agenda of the NEA is masterfully presented by the author.

Byrne, H. W. *A Christian Approach to Education.* Milford, MI: Mott Media, 1977. A comprehensive guide to Christian education covering the basics of a theistic world view, a Christian philosophy of education, and the content of education. A great reference tool for those contemplating starting a Christian school.

Cummings, David B., ed. *The Basis for a Christian School: A Resource Book With Answers for the Christian Parent.* Phillipsburg, NJ: Presbyterian and Reformed, 1982. This work lays the foundation for parents contemplating sending their children to a Christian school. The approach is positive and not just a reaction to a faltering public school system.

_____, ed. *The Purpose of a Christ-Centered Education.* Phillipsburg, NJ: Presbyterian and Reformed, 1979. Secular education places the child at the center of learning. The glory of God and His Word are ruled out. What role, then, do parents, child, and teacher play in the educational process as they seek to bring glory to God? This book addresses these questions.

DeJong, Norman. *Education in the Truth*. Phillipsburg, NJ: Presbyterian Reformed, 1974. Develops a comprehensive philosophy of education; it is "a distinctive, cogently stated, biblically-based philosophy to serve as a guide for practice in Christian schools."

_____. *Philosophy of Education: A Christian Approach*. Phillipsburg, NJ: Presbyterian and Reformed, 1977. "An attempt merely to approach some of the perennial, nagging questions of pedagogy that the serious student of education is certain to encounter."

DeMar, Gary. *Surviving College Successfully: A Complete Manual for the Rigors of Academic Combat*. Brentwood, TN: Wolgemuth & Hyatt, 1988. Don't let the title fool you. This book is for anyone who wants to do better in school and deal with the many anti-Christian philosophies that confront us on a daily basis. While Part I deals extensively with world views, Part II is a comprehensive guide to the best advice in enhancing study skills. Includes chapters on How to Study, Memory Mechanics, How to Read, How to Write and Research, and Taking Exams.

Grover, Alan N. *Ohio's Trojan Horse*. Greenville, SC: Bob Jones University Press, 1977. The author deals with statist control of Christian education, using the Ohio "Minimum Standards" as an example of how Christian schools can be defined out of existence. He presents the legal, theological, educational, philosophical, constitutional, and doctrinal perspectives.

Kienel, Paul A., ed. *The Philosophy of Christian School Education*. Whittier, CA: Association of Christian Schools International, 1978. This book is designed to serve as a textbook in teacher and administrative training programs in Christian colleges and graduate schools. Parents, teachers, and teachers-to-be will find it very valuable.

Morris, Henry M. *Education for the Real World*. San Diego, CA: Creation-Life Publishers, 1977. An attempt to place education in its true biblical perspective. The author deals with competing educational theory.

North, Gary, ed. *Journal of Christian Reconstruction*, Symposium on Education. Vallecito, CA: A Chalcedon Ministry Publication, 1977. A series of essays presenting the non-option of state-controlled public education for Christians. The article by Dorothy Sayers, "The Lost Tools of Learning," is especially helpful.

Pride, Mary. *The New Big Book of Home Learning: The Basic Guide to Everything Educational for You and Your Children*. Westchester, IL: Crossway Books, 1988. A comprehensive guide for the home school movement. Nearly 400 pages of learning tools, teaching theories, mail order programs, educational suppliers, and games.

_____. *The Next Big Book of Home Learning: Everything Enriching for You and Your Children* (Westchester, IL: Crossway Books, 1987. In the same tradition of Mary Pride's *Big Book of Home Learning*.

307

_____. *Schoolproof: How to Help Your Family Beat the System and Learn to Love Learning — the Easy, Natural Way.* The task of home education can be formidable. There is more than the technique. Schoolproofing means learning how to educate, so you can recognize good and bad education. It means knowing your options.

Reed, Sally D. *NEA: Propaganda Front of the Radical Left.* Alexandria, VA: National Council for Better Education, 1983. Exposes the radical agenda of the NEA — pro-Marxist, pro-Socialist, and anti-Christian.

Rushdoony, Rousas John. *Intellectual Schizophrenia.* Nutley, NJ: Presbyterian and Reformed, 1959. Schools as such are not the problem. The presuppositions that form educational goals and methods must be exposed for what they are, religious axioms. The public, government-controlled schools have maintained an impossible religious "neutrality."

_____. *The Philosophy of the Christian Curriculum.* Rushdoony calls for all Christian educators to break from the entire humanistic mentality regarding education. A curriculum is not neutral; even it must be reconstructed according to Scripture.

_____. *The Messianic Character of American Education.* Nutley, NJ: The Craig Press, 1963. The classic work on the real purpose of humanistic, public education; its intention is to save man and all his institutions. Further, it "is a study of the philosophies of education in the United States from Horace Mann to the present (1963)."

Schlafly, Phyllis, ed. *Child Abuse in the Classroom.* Westchester, IL: Crossway Books, 1985, 2nd ed. Excerpts from the Official Transcript of Proceedings before the United States Department of Education in the matter of Proposed Regulations to implement the protection of pupil rights regarding the psychological testing of students.

Whitehead, John W. and Wendell R. Bird. *Home Education and Constitutional Liberties.* Westchester, IL: Crossway Books, 1984. Home education is on the rise and many state governments and the National Educational Association (NEA) want it eliminated. A historical, constitutional, and legal analysis of the issue.

III. Human Rights

Clark, Stephen B. *Man and Woman in Christ.* Ann Arbor, MI: Servant Books, 1980. Examines the roles of men and women in the light of Scripture and the social sciences. The author presents the very clear statement that in relation to God, we have no rights."

Craig, Kevin. "Social Apologetics" in *Christianity and Civilization*, The Failure of the American Baptist Culture, ed. James B. Jordan. Mr. Craig analyzes the mistaken view of human rights that many Christians hold. He concludes that the doctrine of human rights is the desire for human autonomy.

Ingram, T. Robert. *What's Wrong With Human Rights*. Houston, TX: St. Thomas Press, 1978. The modern conception of human rights has been substituted as an alternative to Biblical Law. The author shows that rights cannot stand on their own. The blessings of life, liberty, and property prevail when God is acknowledged as King and Redeemer and His Law is put forth as the standard for righteousness.

Montgomery, John W. *Human Rights and Human Dignity*. Grand Rapids, MI: Zondervan House, 1986. A comprehensive study of human rights, touching on the biblical, philosophical, and historical dimensions. There is a tremendous amount of thought-provoking material here.

IV. Citizenship

Draper, James T. and Forrest E. Watson. *If the Foundations Be Destroyed*. Nashville, TN: Oliver-Nelson Books, 1984. A very readable history of the United States showing that our nation has a rich biblical heritage. There are those who are calling for the State to expunge every vestige of Christian values from our nation. As Christians we must stop the slide toward paganism. The authors give us the history of the decline along with suggestions for renewal.

Eidsmoe, John. *God and Caesar: Christian Faith and Political Action*. Westchester, IL: Crossway Books, 1984. Covers a wide range of topics relating to the political sphere. It goes beyond its title, however, by dealing with issues that have been long neglected by Christians. In most cases, the author gives specific answers to hard questions. There is much biblical insight here.

Henry, Carl F. H. *Aspects of Christian Social Ethics*. Grand Rapids, MI: Baker Book House, (1964) 1980. A call for Christians to get involved in the political process. This work originally was published in 1964, long before most Christians saw that they had a responsibility to address social ethics.

Hughes, Philip Edgcumbe. *Christian Ethics in Secular Society*. Grand Rapids, MI: Baker Book House, 1983. Shows the distinction between secular ethics and Christian ethics in a wide range of subjects. Especially helpful is the chapter dealing with "The Christian and the State."

Monsma, Stephen V. *Pursuing Justice in a Sinful World*. Grand Rapids, MI: Eerdmans, 1984. Written by a political science instructor who served eight years in the Michigan legislature. While the book has a number of deficiencies, it has a very valuable discussion of political involvement and a treatment of multiple, delegated, and limited authorities.

Murray, John. "The Christian World Order," in *Collected Writings*, Vol. 1. Edinburgh: The Banner of Truth Trust, 1976, pp. 356-366. Presents a very powerful statement of the Christian's responsibility to work so "the whole of life will be brought into willing captivity to the obedience of Christ" (p. 356). The author also develops the responsibilities of the "three divine institutions" — family, church, and state.

North, Gary, ed. *Tactics of Christian Resistance*, Christianity and Civilization, No. 3, Tyler, TX: Geneva Divinity School Press, 1983. Offers specific guidelines for Christians in the face of Statist encroachment. Avoids the sensational methodology of "romantic revolutionaries."

_____, ed. *The Theology of Christian Resistance*, Christianity and Civilization, No. 2. Tyler, TX: Geneva Divinity School Press, 1983. The companion volume to *Tactics of Christian Resistance* that establishes the theological framework where legitimate (biblical) resistance ought to take place.

Thoburn, Robert L. *The Christian and Politics*. Tyler, TX: Thoburn Press, 1984. Answers some of the common arguments as to why Christians should not involve themselves in politics; develops a biblical view of civil government, economics, education, welfare, and tax policy; and explains how Christians can be involved in politics. The author served in the Virginia House of Delegates from 1978-1980.

V. The Judicial System

Bahnsen, Greg L. *Theonomy in Christian Ethics*. Phillipsburg, NJ: Presbyterian and Reformed, (1977) 1984. For too long the church has neglected the Law of God by relegating it to the "Old Testament dispensations." This has had a devastating effect upon the church and the world. The author supports the thesis that God's Law is valid for today.

_____. *By this Standard*. Tyler, TX: Institute for Christian Economics, 1985. A very readable statement of the continuing validity of God's Law for today. A good introduction to Bahnsen's larger work, *Theonomy in Christian Ethics*. Indispensible reading.

Campbell, Roger. *Justice Through Restitution*. Milford, MI: Mott Media, 1977. How should criminals pay for their crimes? Should they be incarcerated; or should they be made to pay restitution? Biblical restitution is presented as an alternative to imprisonment.

North, Gary. *The Sinai Strategy: Economics and the Ten Commandments.* Tyler TX: Institute for Christian Economics, 1986. This is the first treatment of the economic implications of the Ten Commandments. This work makes it clear that a neutral law order is impossible. "It was Western man's confidence in validity of the Ten Commandments which alone created free market institutions in world history."

Rushdoony, Rousas John. *The Institutes of Biblical Law.* Nutley, NJ: The Craig Press, 1973. A full exposition of the Ten Commandments and the first serious work on the application of biblical law to all of law. This book ought to be in every Christian's library.

Whitehead, John W. *The Second American Revolution.* Westchester, IL: Crossway Books, 1985. An evaluation of our legal system and the work of the courts. Whitehead builds his case that there must be a *foundation* for law and that foundation must rest upon the sovereign character of God.

Wright, Christopher J.H. *An Eye For An Eye.* Downers Grove, IL: InterVarsity Press, 1983. "Wright ... first examines a theological, social and economic framework for Old Testament ethics. Then in relation to contemporary issues he explores a variety of Old Testament themes — economics and the land, politics and the world of nations, righteousness and justice, society and culture, the way of the individual." While there is much helpful information here, nevertheless, the author rejects the Old Testament as a standard for civil ethics.

VI. God and the Nations

Green, Ashbel. "Obedience to the Laws of God, the Sure and Indispensable Defence of Nations." (Made available through American Vision, P.O. Box 720515, Atlanta, Georgia 30328). A discourse delivered in the Second Presbyterian Church, Philadelphia, Pennsylvania, May 9, 1798, on the day appointed by the President of the United States, to be observed as a season for solemn humiliation, fasting, and prayer.

Hodge, A. A. *Evangelical Theology.* Carlisle, PA: Banner of Truth Trust, (1890) 1976. A popular series of lectures dealing with the fundamental doctrines of the Christian faith. "The Kingly Office of Christ," "The Kingdom of Christ," and "The Law of the Kingdom" are marvelous expositions of the Lordship of Jesus Christ over every area of life, including the nations of the world.

North, Gary. *Moses and Pharaoh: Dominion Religion Versus Power Religion.* Tyler, TX: Institute for Christian Economics, 1985. "What Bible commentators have failed to understand is that the conflict between Moses and Pharaoh was at heart a conflict between the two major religions in man's history, *dominion religion* and *power religion*, with the third major religion — *escapist religion* — represented by the Hebrew slaves. What they have also failed to point out is that *there is an implicit alliance between the power religion and the escapist religion.* The alliance still exists."

311

Smith, Gary Scott, ed. *God and Politics: Four Views on the Reformation of Civil Government.* Phillipsburg, NJ: Presbyterian and Reformed, 1989. The chapter on National Confession is especially helpful. Dr. William Edgar affirms that Jesus Christ is the true Lord and Sovereign over the nations.

Symington, William. *Messiah the Prince, or The Mediatorial Dominion of Jesus Christ.* Edmonton, Alberta, Canada: Still Water Revival books, (1884) 1990. Symington asserts that Jesus Christ is mediatorial king of the nations. This means that the State and all of society come under the specifically redemptive rule of Christ. This concept is defended at length in *Messiah the Prince.*

VII. Restoration

Chilton, David. *Paradise Restored: A Biblical Theology of Dominion.* Tyler, TX: Reconstruction Press, 1985. Using eschatology, the doctrine of the "Last Things," as the focal point of this book, the author develops the encouraging news that "God wants us to have dominion over the earth, just as He originally commanded Adam and Eve." This fascinating book will help you with interpreting the Bible, especially with prophecy.

DeMar, Gary and Peter Leithart. *The Reduction of Christianity: A Biblical Response to Dave Hunt.* Ft. Worth, TX: Dominion Press, 1988. A great deal of controversy has been stirred up over the issue of Christian activism and the possibility of reform. This comprehensive book shows both the biblical and historical traditions of implementing a comprehensive biblical world view. Includes an evaluation of the New Age Movement and contemporary millennial views that have been used to stagnate the work of the church.

North, Gary. *Backward, Christian Soldiers?* Tyler, TX: Institute for Christian Economics, 1984. Christians have once again understood the implications of the "dominion covenant" of Genesis 1:28. This book is about victory. It is an action manual for Christian reconstruction.

Buzzard, Lynn R. and Lawrence Eck. *Tell It to the Church.* Elgin, IL: David C. Cook, 1982. Every year Christians sue other Christians, spending millions of dollars and violating 1 Corinthians 6. This is a very practical handbook on how to reconcile differences out of court.

Eidsmoe, John. *The Christian Legal Advisor.* Milford, MI: Mott Media, 1984. The first comprehensive legal guide for pastors, churches, Christian schools, and Christians in general. He discusses the nature of law, the background and meaning of the First Amendment and other constitutional protections, and practical legal problems involving churches and the ministry.

Jordan, James B. *The Law of the Covenant: An Exposition of Exodus 21-23*. Tyler, TX: Institute for Christian Economics, 1984. This pioneering work seeks to explain and apply the "case laws" of Exodus. The author explores for the meaning of the text and then asks, "What relevance might this law have for the Christian faith today?" A valuable work.

_____. *Sabbath Breaking and the Death Penalty: A Theological Investigation*. Tyler, TX: Geneva Ministries, 1986. A detailed look at the Old Testament death penalty for sabbath breaking. Jordan argues that it was only certain kinds of sabbath blasphemy that brought the death penalty, and that in the New Covenant this law is no longer in force. A careful study of a particularly thorny problem in Christian ethics and legal theory.

Kaiser, Walter. *Toward Old Testament Ethics*. Grand Rapids, MI: Zondervan/Academie Books, 1983. The author seeks to sort out the complexities of Old Testament law and its relation to moral behavior. The author takes the biblical text seriously and does not try to editorialize away any difficulties.

Laney, J. Carl. *A Guide to Church Discipline*. Minneapolis, MN: Bethany, 1986. The Bible states that judgment begins "with the household of God" (1 Peter 4:17) and that the church is to serve as a court to handle disputes among brothers and sisters in Christ (1 Corinthians 6:1-6). This is a very fine study of church discipline. Why is church discipline necessary? What sins require church discipline? What steps are to be taken in disciplining a church member or leader?

North, Gary, ed. *Christianity and Civilization*, The Theology of Christian Resistance and the Tactics of Christian Resistance, Volumes 2 and 3. Tyler, TX: Geneva Divinity School Press, 1983. These two volumes comprise over 800 pages of a well-thought-out theology of resistance and the tactics that Christians should take in this increasingly secular world.

North, Gary, ed. *The Journal of Christian Reconstruction*. Symposium on Social Action. Vol. VIII, No. 1. Vallecito, CA: Chalcedon, 1981. A series of essays emphasizing the application of the gospel to every area of life.

Rushdoony, Rousas John. *Salvation and Godly Rule*. Vallecito, CA: Ross House Books, 1983. "Too often, Jesus Christ is regarded by the church as simply a super-salesman of life and fire insurance rather than as Lord and Savior. Salvation means health and victory among other things, and salvation delivers us from sin and death, with all the defeat and failure thereof, into life and righteousness or justice, with victory and joy as its accompaniments."

313

Schaeffer, Franky. *Bad News For Modern Man*. Westchester, IL: Crossway Books, 1984. The choices before us are the Bible or some brand of socialism or secularism. Much of the church has fallen for a bankrupt socialism. Franky Schaeffer brings us to our senses with a biting expose of modern-day evangelicalism.

Walton, Russ. *Biblical Solutions to Contemporary Problems: A Handbook*. Brentwood, TN: Wolgemuth & Hyatt, (1984) 1988. An expanded edition of the author's *Biblical Principles Concerning Issues of Importance to Godly Christians*. With the work of restoration under way, Christians are looking for answers, biblical answers, to life's tough questions. This information-packed book is the needed ammunition to counter the effects of a creeping secularism.

Whitehead, John W. *The Stealing of America*. Westchester IL: Crossway Books, 1983. Are there parallels between the decadence and anti-life attitudes of America and those of pre-Nazi Germany? The author's conclusion is a resounding "Yes!" This book shows in striking detail what those parallels are. Mr. Whitehead, however, does not leave us wondering what the solutions are.

Bibliography

Alexander, James, W. *Thoughts on Family Worship*. Harrisonburg, VA: Sprinkle Publications, [1847] 1981.

Bavinck, J.H. *An Introduction to the Science of Missions*. Nutley, NJ: Presbyterian and Reformed, 1960.

Calvin, John. *Commentary on Isaiah*, Vol. 3. Grand Rapids, MI: Baker Book House [1554] 1979.

————. *Institutes of the Christian Religion*. John T. McNeill, ed. Philadelphia, PA Westminster Press, 1960.

Charnock, Stephen. *Discourses Upon the Existence and Attributes of God*. Vol. 2. Grand Rapids, MI: Baker Book House, (1853) 1979.

Chilton, David. *Productive Christians in an Age of Guilt-Manipulators*. 3rd rev. ed. Tyler, TX: Institute for Christian Economics, 1985.

Craigie, Peter C. *The Book of Deuteronomy*. Grand Rapids, MI: Eerdmans, 1976.

Dabney, Robert L. *Discussions: Secular*. Harrisonburg, VA: Sprinkle Publications, (1897) 1979.

Davis, John Jefferson. *Evangelical Ethics: Issues Facing the Church Today*. Phillipsburg, NJ Presbyterian and Reformed, 1985.

Demarest, Bruce A. *General Revelation*. Grand Rapids, MI: Zondervan House, 1982.

Dexter, Franklin B. "Biographical Sketches of the Graduates of Yale College with Annals of the College History," in *The Annals of America*, Vol. 2. Chicago, IL Encyclopedia Britannica, 1968.

Draper, James T. and Forrest E. Watson. *If the Foundations Be Destroyed*. Nashville, TN: Thomas Nelson, 1984.

Gangel, Kenneth O. and Warren S. Benson. *Christian Education: Its History and Philosophy*. Chicago, IL: Moody Press 1983.

Grunlan, Stanley. "Biblical Authority and Cultural Relativity," in *Christian Perspectives on Sociology*. Stephen A. Grunlan and Milton Reimer, eds. Grand Rapids, MI. Zondervan, 1982.

Jordan, James B. *Judges: God's War Against Humanism*. Tyler, TX: Geneva Ministries, 1985.

Johnson, Paul. *Modern Times: The World from the Twenties to the Eighties*. New York, NY. Harper & Row, 1983.

Kuehnelt-Leddihn, Erik. *Leftism: From de Sade and Marx to Hitler and Marcuse.* New Rochelle, NY: Arlington House, 1974.

McNeill John T. *The History and Character of Calvinism.* New York: Oxford University Press, 1954.

Marshner, Connaught. "Right and Wrong and America's Survival," in *Future 21: Directions for America in the 21st Century.* Paul Weyrich and Connaught Marshner, eds. Greenwich, CT: Devin-Adair, 1984.

Mather, Increase. "An Arrow Against Profain and Promiscuous Dancing," in *The Annals of America,* Vol. 2. Chicago, IL: Encyclopedia Britannica, 1968.

Murray, John. *The Epistle to the Romans.* One volume edition. Grand Rapids, MI: Eerdmans, 1968.

Nisbet, Robert A. *History of the Idea of Progress.* New York, NY: Basic Books, 1980.

_____. *The Social Bond: An Introduction to the Study of Society,* New York, NY: Alfred A. Knopf, 1970.

North, Gary. *Unconditional Surrender,* Tyler, TX: Institute for Christian Economics, 1983.

Packer, J.I. "Authority," in *The New Bible Dictionary,* J.D. Douglas, ed. Grand Rapids, MI: Eerdmans, 1965.

Peck, Jesse T. *The History of the Great Republic Considered From a Christian Stand-Point.* New York: Broughton and Wyman, 1968.

Pinnock, Clark H. *Biblical Revelation: The Foundation of Christian Theology.* Chicago, IL: Moody Press, 1971.

Reymond, Robert L. *The Justification of Knowledge.* Phillipsburg, NJ: Presbyterian and Reformed, 1976.

Ringenberg, William C. *The Christian College: A History of Protestant Higher Education in America.* Grand Rapids, MI: Eerdmans, 1985.

Rushdoony, R.J. *The Nature of the American System.* Fairfax, VA: Thoburn Press, [1965] 1978.

_____. *Revolt Against Maturity.* Fairfax, VA: Thoburn Press, 1975.

Rutherford, Samuel. *Lex, Rex, or The Law and the Prince.* Harrisonburg, VA: Sprinkle Publications, [1644] 1980.

Schaeffer, Francis A. and C. Everett Koop. *Whatever Happened to the Human Race?* Old Tappan, NJ: Fleming H. Revell, 1979.

Schaeffer, Franky. *A Time for Anger.* Westchester, IL: Crossway Books, 1982.

317

Schlossberg, Herbert. *Idols for Destruction*. Nashville, TN: Thomas Nelson Publishers, 1983.

Scott, Otto J. *Robespierre: The Voice of Virtue*. Vallecito, CA: Ross House Books, 1974.

Shirer, William. *The Rise and Fall of the Third Reich*. New York: Simon and Schuster, 1960.

Simis, Konstantin M. *USSR: The Corrupt Society*. New York: Simon and Schuster, 1982.

Singer, Gregg L. *A Theological Interpretation of American History*, 2nd ed. Phillipsburg, NJ: Presbyterian and Reformed, 1981.

Sire, James W. *The Universe Next Door*. Downers Grove, IL: InterVarsity Press, 1977.

Stott, John R.W. *God's New Society: The Message of Ephesians*. Downers Grove, IL: InterVarsity Press, 1979.

Taylor, E.L. Hebden. *The Christian Philosophy of Law, Politics and the State*. Nutley, NJ: The Craig Press, 1966.

Ward, Ronald A. *Commentary on 1 and 2 Thessalonians*. Waco, TX: Word Books, 1973.

Watson, Thomas. *A Body of Divinity*. London, England: Banner of Truth Trust, [1692] 1965.

Whitehead, John W. *The New Tyranny*. Ft. Lauderdale, FL: Coral Ridge Presbyterian Church, 1982.

_____. *The Separation Illusion*. Milford, MI: Mott Media, 1977.

Young, Curt. *The Least of These*. Chicago, IL: Moody Press 1983.

Picture Credits

Cover

Bishop Hugh Latimer preaching before the boy King Edward VI at Paul's Cross, 1548. Banner of Truth Trust, Edinburgh.

Introduction

Lesson 1

321

Lesson 6

Lesson 7

Lesson 8

Lesson 9

Lesson 10

Answers to Questions for Discussion

Lesson _____   Question _____

_____

_____

_____

_____

_____

_____

_____

_____

_____

_____

_____

_____

_____

_____

_____

_____

_____

_____

_____

_____

_____

_____

_____

_____

_____

_____

_____

_____

_____

_____

_____

Answers to Questions for Discussion

Lesson _____ Question _____

_____

_____

_____

_____

_____

_____

_____

_____

_____

_____

_____

_____

_____

_____

_____

_____

_____

_____

_____

_____

_____

_____

_____

_____

_____

_____

_____

_____

_____

_____

_____

Answers to Questions for Discussion

Lesson _____ Question _____

_____
_____
_____
_____
_____
_____
_____
_____
_____
_____
_____
_____
_____
_____
_____
_____
_____
_____
_____
_____
_____
_____
_____
_____
_____
_____
_____
_____
_____
_____
_____
_____

Answers to Questions for Discussion

Lesson _____ Question _____

Answers to Questions for Discussion

Lesson _____   Question _____

_____

_____

_____

_____

_____

_____

_____

_____

_____

_____

_____

_____

_____

_____

_____

_____

_____

_____

_____

_____

_____

_____

_____

_____

_____

_____

_____

_____

_____

_____

_____

_____

Answers to Questions for Discussion

Lesson _____ Question _____

_____

_____

_____

_____

_____

_____

_____

_____

_____

_____

_____

_____

_____

_____

_____

_____

_____

_____

_____

_____

_____

_____

_____

_____

_____

_____

_____

Equip Yourself with
the Best in
Biblical Worldview Literature

THIS BOOK IS JUST ONE OF THE MANY SUPERB CHRISTIAN educational products available from American Vision. The following pages contain American Vision products that complement *Ruler of the Nations*.

America's Christian History:
The Untold Story
Audio cassette

This award-winning audio drama combines professional narration with music and sound effects to bring alive the original words of America's founders....................................$6.95

America's Christian History:
The Untold Story
Christian America Series

From the founding of the colonies to the declaration of the Supreme Court, America's heritage is built upon the principles of the Christian religion. In this book, Gary DeMar provides solid proof that Christianity gave this country its life and its character..........$12.95

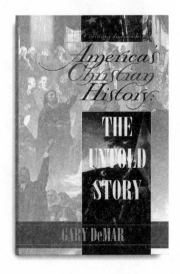

The United States: A Christian Nation

In this concise, fact-driven account David Brewer, Associate Justice of the Supreme Court, thoroughly excavates the landscape of American history. Every pebble of evidence he turns up cries out: America is a Christian nation! Brewer's landmark work studies declarations of the court, the recognition of Sunday, Chaplains, colonial charters, civil liberty, charity, and much more. $8.95

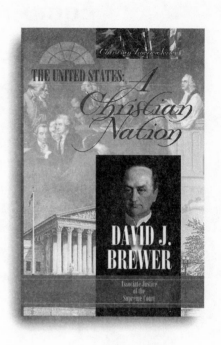

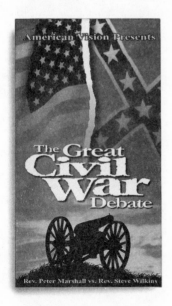

The Great Civil War Debate

On February 27th, 1998, Rev. Peter Marshall and Rev. Steve Wilkins met to debate the true victor of the Civil War. Who was right in the War Between the States: the Union or the Confederacy? You decide after watching this historic video. This special videotape includes original film footage, photos, and portraits from Civil War times. Don't miss the debate that even C-Span aired!........................$29.95

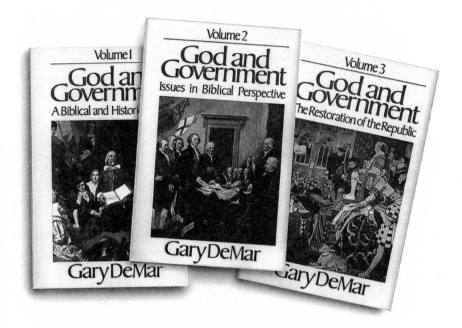

God and Government
Three-volume series

A three-volume set that defines the different spheres of government: self, family, church, and civil. Each volume is filled with historical facts and biblical truths. Historical pictures as well as helpful question-and-answer sections make this series a fascinating study.

Volume 1: *God and Government: A Biblical and Historical Study*

.... $12.95

Volume 2: *God and Government: Issues in Biblical Perspective*

.... $12.95

Volume 3: *God and Government: The Restoration of the Republic*

.... $12.95

Three-volume set $32.95

A New World in View

Volume 1 of *To Pledge Allegiance*

First in the multi-volume *To Pledge Allegiance* American History textbook series. This book lays a firm foundation, opening in classical Greece and Rome, and closing with French exploration of the New World. Full-color illustrations make history come alive. The unique timeline graphic keeps the reader aware of his place in history. Colorful sidebars are entertaining and provide further insights into the understanding of history. A must for family study, homeschool students, and Christian schools.
............................$16.95

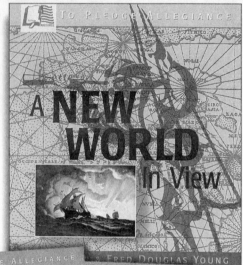

Teaching Guide	$2.65
Tests..	$2.65
Test Answers...	$2.65
Complete set	$7.95

Reformation to Colonization
Volume 2 of *To Pledge Allegiance*

Politically-correct textbooks choose to neglect the Reformation and its profound influence on the founding of America, but not *Reformation to Colonization*! This second volume in the *To Pledge Allegiance* textbook series picks up where *A New World in View* ends. With 320 full-color pages (almost twice the size of volume 1), it presents the story of America's founding and early years up through the Great Awakening.
.............................$22.95

Tests...	$2.65
Teaching Guide (includes Test Answers)	$5.30
Complete set	$7.95

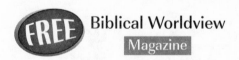 **Biblical Worldview**
Magazine

A purchase of any of American Vision's products gives you a free one-year's subscription to our monthly magazine, *Biblical Worldview*. This incredibly informative magazine covers current issues from a biblical perspective, presenting God's solutions to society's problems. Each month you will enjoy challenging articles and will gain access to many hard-to-find books in addition to the best books Christianity has to offer. *Biblical Worldview* also keeps you up-to-date with monthly book reviews and information on the ministry of American Vision...$24 value for FREE

About American Vision

AMERICAN VISION IS A CHRISTIAN EDUCATIONAL ORGANIZATION which is filling a unique place in today's Christian community. The purpose of American Vision is to help Christians understand their lives and their world in light of Scripture. American Vision publishes books and magazines, arranges seminars and debates, and produces a wide range of other materials to proclaim Christ's authority over all of life.

To place an order or to receive information, please contact:

AMERICAN VISION
P.O. Box 220
POWDER SPRINGS, GA 30127

Toll free (Orders Only Please): 800-628-9460
Business Offices: 770-222-7266
Fax: 770-222-7269

Email: avpress@mindspring.com
Web Sites: www.americanvision.org
www.prophecybooks.com